The Philosophy of Leadership

Christopher Hodgkinson

St. Martin's Press · New York

Printed in Great Britain
First published in the United States of America in 1983

ISBN 0—312—60672—9

Library of Congress Cataloging in Publication Data

Hodgkinson, Christopher.
   The philosophy of leadership.
   Includes bibliographical references and index.
     1. Leadership—Philosophy.   2. Administration.
3. Social values.   I. Title.
HM141.H55 1983   303.3'4   83—10943
ISBN 0—312—60672—9

Contents

Preface

The questions to which this book seeks answers are essentially practical; how can man-the-administrator cope? How ought he to cope? How to get through the day?

But the answers lie beyond practice. They are only to be won by virtue of heightened consciousness and deepened reflection. The book seeks to relate the world of Praxis to the world of Right. To this end it is cartography rather than homilectics — an instrument or aid to navigation in a world which is clearly as vicious as it is spasmodically virtuous.

The central problem is this: what does it mean to be an administrator, a man-of-action, in the last part of the twentieth century? And, further, what can it mean? What ought it to mean? In short, a philosophy of leadership.

Acknowledgements

In writing this book I have become indebted to writers and authorities, past and present; theoreticians and practitioners; students and colleagues; leaders and led; not to mention all manner of administrators and philosophers. To them all I would express my inadequate gratitude. There are also those to whom I am especially grateful. Foremost amongst these is the late Sir Geoffrey Vickers VC who corresponded with me throughout the time I was preparing the work. He was not merely a constant source of intellectual and moral stimulation but also, I believe, an embodiment of those Stoic and Guardian virtues discussed in some of these pages. I am also indebted, in quite the converse way, to those exponents of the other side of the dialectic of virtue and vice. To all the Alexanders and Tyrants of Syracuse wherever they may be, All Hail!

I wish to thank the Social Science and Humanities Research Council of Canada for a grant which supported part of this work and permitted some valuable international travel and contacts. I also thank my wife, Madge, for her constant support and critique and my secretary, Mrs Marion Marcus, for her highly skilled and painstaking production of type-script and drafts.

The kind permission of the following owners of copyright is also gratefully acknowledged: to Messrs Routledge and Kegan Paul and the University of Massachussetts Press for the exerpts from Simone Weil on pp. 61, 73; to the New American Library and the Vedanta Society of Southern

California for the extract on pp. 148-9; to Maurice Temple Smith for the categories of Dr Edward de Bono cited on pp. 191-3; and to Messrs Harper and Row for the passages on pp. 147, 148.

Finally I would repeat that no listing of the creditors in an enterprise such as is comprised in the following pages can ever be complete. To all who should have been, but were not, singled out by name my apologies and my thanks. Where they have led I have tried to follow.

Christopher Hodgkinson
Cambridge

1

Why Philosophize?

Why do philosophy? This is a basic question for practitioner and theorist alike. Especially when the word may be tainted in its connotations, smacking of the abstruse, the over-intellectual, the diametric opposite to the active milieu of organizations and the practicalities and constraints of the real world. Why contaminate the sober realities of honest administrative labour with academic gymnastics? To be sure there are executives who take a more sophisticated and less jaundiced view of philosophy than this, but even they might rest content with acknowledging that philosophy gets done, and that the intuitive or spontaneous or commonsensical ways in which it gets done and is fitted into the interstices of administrative life are sufficient. To go beyond these habitual ways of philosophizing and to respond to a demand for a more conscious approach would require incentives, or motives, or pay-offs of some sort, or at the very least, good reasons.

The practitioner will want to know what he stands to gain, especially as he is already a very busy man. Of course, the more he is a manager and the less he is an administrator, in our sense of these terms, the less need for his consideration of philosophy. The distinction between administration and management which will be maintained throughout this book can be understood in broad terms as paralleling the distinc-tion between policy making and policy implementation, between the judgemental and the active sides of organiza-tional life (Hodgkinson, 1978:4-6, and chapter 2 below).

'Administration' refers then to the more thinking, qualitative, humane and strategic aspects of the comprehensive executive function, while 'management' refers to the more doing, quantitative, material and technical aspects. Still, even though he acknowledges this sort of distinction and though he tends the one way or the other by practice or proclivity the executive can rightly ask, what is there in philosophy for him?

For the theorist, and for the student of organizations and administration, the question may take a different but more critical form. He might question whether there exists a body of knowledge in this field which would permit of any synthetic or philosophical treatment.

These two sorts of questions — whether philosophy is possible and whether it has any pay-off — both deserve response. In the sections below we shall explore these questions and seek to make the case for a philosophy of administration, but, for the moment, let us assert by way of anticipation that the chief postulated gain for the practitioner is power and for the theoretician, comprehension: power and comprehension.

The basic canon of this book can be stated in the form of a proposition. *Administration is philosophy-in-action.* As it stands, this statement is obscure. Its main terms are undefined. Inasmuch as these terms 'philosophy', 'administration', 'action' constitute the subject matter of all that follows, it is perhaps premature to seek precision. Nevertheless, some preliminary understandings are both desirable and necessary.

'Administration' is to be understood as referring to that most pervasive of human activities, the organization of men and means about purposes or ends. The means may be technological and superlatively complex (NASA, NORAD, neurosurgery); the ends may be diverse, subtle, obscure and infinite (from the photographing of Saturn's rings to the gratification of Lady Macbeth); but always, co-operative human organization will be necessary and its arrangement and functioning is the subject matter of administration. Organization is the canvas of the administrative art. And life within organizations, increasingly large and complex and ramifying in our day, is the administrative analogue of paint. The administrative art-form is ancient. Since time immemorial men have organized themselves about purposes. What is new is the explosion of scale, size, complexity and technology of human organization and the growth of knowledge of managerial technique, including the bureaucratic form itself. Our society is more organized now than it ever has been and this means that administration is more ubiquitous, more prepotent, more all-pervasive. And along with the potency comes prestige, power and the infinite possibilities of corruption. For in all this evolution the essential executive functions have remained unchanged.

And the essential administrative dilemma has remained unchanged. This is a double problem of reconciliation, and often a double-bind. On the one hand the administrator must reconcile the nomothetic and idiographic conflicts *within* his organization; that is to say, he must resolve the continuous tension between the human concerns of individual organization members and the overriding organizational purposes. On the other hand he must reconcile his organizational activity with all the constraining, competing and conflicting pressures of the environment within which his organization has its being. This last relationship is symbiotic; organizational birth and death are the constituents of cultural change, and the environment is not merely physical and geographic but ecological in every sense: political, social, economic, historic, even intellectual and *zeitgeistlich*.

So it can be said that administration is a complex and pervasive human process in which the executive role is Janus-like, looking outwards towards the environment and inwards towards the domestic order. Its basic tendency is to seek homeostasis and then growth, and its basic function to negotiate purposes across constraints. This it does within an overall context of human values. Values impinge upon and are intertwined in every phase of administrative process and this, of itself, guarantees conflict. The nature of this conflict will be described in the next chapter, but for the moment it can be noted that the basic lines of tension are between individual and organization in the one direction and between organization and environment in the other. These tensions, their humane bases and the pervasion of values ensure that administration is a difficult art and one which can be at once the noblest, the oldest and the basest of the professions.

PHILOSOPHY AND ADMINISTRATION

In the basic proposition that administration is philosophy-in-action, the major terms, 'administration' and 'philosophy', each represent semantic compounds which demand considerable elucidation before sensible progress can be made in their discussion. Of the two, philosophy is the more ancient, the more evocative and the more elusive. It is also the more contentious and to this day academic philosophers lock horns about its meaning. A debate which is still lively after thousands of years is unlikely to find its closure in these pages but it is possible and legitimate, nevertheless, to distinguish between four important senses or meanings of the term: the academic, the dualistic, the classical and the practical interpretations.

THE ACADEMIC SENSE

The academic interpretation refers to philosophy as a discipline of study and to its technical division into the parts of ontology, axiology and epistemology. These parts have variable significance for administration. The first, ontology or metaphysics, deals with the nature of reality or being. It shares a frontier with religion and theology and, although it would be unjustifiable to discount this body of knowledge altogether, perhaps it is fair to say that, in the late twentieth century it suffers from some academic desuetude and, moreover, does not seem to bear in any way directly upon administration. This is not to deny, of course, that indirectly and at any number of removes an executive's behaviour pattern may be significantly determined by his belief system, and this in turn by his conscious or unconscious ontological assumptions. It is these assumptions, in fact, which often determine the level and scope of an executive's commitment, not to mention his actual and perceived integrity. Of crucial concern, also, is a typically ontological question which we must raise and examine later: does man differ from the animals in kind or in degree? In other words, is there an ontological discontinuity between animal and man? (Schumacher, 1977:16-25) The answer to such a question *will* make an organizational difference.

The second division, axiology, or the study of value, with its subdivisions of ethics and aesthetics, enters rather more directly into administrative and organizational behaviour. Indeed it could be argued that the very substance of the administrative art-form is value. Much will be said about this later but, in general, the emergence of values, their realizations through co-operative action, the resolution of their conflict in administrative process, their debate and containment within the organizational political arena — all this is a daily or hourly part of executive experience. But again formal, technical philosophy is somewhat removed, as indeed is its prerogative, from the heat of the combat. Its intercourse with the field of administrative studies tends to be jejune (Waldo, 1980:99-117). Nevertheless, whatever academic philosophy can do by way of expounding on the nature and sources of ethics, or by way of synthesis of the findings of social and behavioural science concerning the nature of values, is of relevance to administration. It is only curious that so little has so far been done and that so little communication exists between the two realms.

Epistemology, the remaining division, is also of interest and relevance to administrators. It asks such questions as 'How do you know?' and 'What is true?' Its subdivision of logic bears upon most aspects of managerial and administrative process. Indeed, one could go so far as to say that logic and rationality constitute a metavalue of administration and organization (Hodgkinson, 1978:108ff); that is, a value assumption so uncontested that it goes without examination and enters unconsciously into all valuation processes. In other words, no one sets out to manage illogically or irrationally, any more than they would set out to manage inefficiently or ineffectively. Which is not to say that all of these negative things are not constantly done.

Logic is the executive's basic tool. It enters into his work through the weighing and assessing of argument, through the continuous monitoring for fallacy in presentations, projects and plans. The executive's whole armoury of critical faculties and skills is constantly called into play. And academics would be worth their weight in executive gold could they but guarantee by their instruction the honing, sharpening and strengthening of the logical faculty. Yet logic is but a subdivision of epistemology, and more recently interest and argument has been growing in theoretical circles about the general nature of organizational perception (Greenfield, 1980, 1979; Giddens, 1977; Feyerabend, 1975). What is organizational reality and how is it best understood? To what extent is it amenable to law and prediction? What are its deep inconsistencies? The answers to such questions bear importantly on executive behaviour and style.

THE DUALISTIC SENSE

This understanding of philosophy would divide the domain into two parts: logic and value. The former deals with matters of fact, structures, coherence and consistency, causal chains and explanatory systems and sequences. The latter with all matters of value from the ethical and moral, through the valuational, to all the complexities of motivation. It would thus embrace all the infra- and supra-rational elements revealed by or known from depth analysis of the human psyche. Together these two fields of knowledge encompass all organizational behaviour. It is this general understanding of philosophy which is mainly adhered to in this book and the conviction underlying it is that the successful practitioner of the art of administration must have as much understanding as possible of both fields of thought. Philosophy-in-action here means the translation of values into a world of mixed value and fact.

THE CLASSICAL SENSE

Etymologically the word 'philosophy' translates as 'love of wisdom'. With the passage of history and the establishment of philosophy in academic institutions, with all that that implies by way of patronage, perquisites and protection, it may be that the connotation of wisdom, at least in practical affairs, has leached away. And this loss of meaning is compounded by the democratic ethos. Who dares claim flatly to be wiser than his fellows, though he yet may argue his course of action over theirs? Any elitist pretensions, especially by way of philosophy, are suspect or offensive or both under a vulgarian orthodoxy. (See, too, Sir Karl Popper's denunciation of Plato in *The Open Society and its Enemies*, 1966.)

Still, the lure of wisdom itself persists though it be sought under other names and disguises, such as sophistication or know-how or common sense. Executives are not averse to wisdom; they are, or should be, wisdom seekers, and if that objective could be gained through the study of philosophy they would not be antagonistic (only, perhaps, somewhat surprised). Socrates is supposed to have said, by way of justification for such study, that the unexamined life is not worth living. Certainly we can extend this to, 'The unexamined value is not worth holding' and, perhaps, to 'Unexamined administration is not worth doing'.

Any such reasoning presumes that there is a benefit — a practical or significant benefit — to engaging in activities which are reflective, analytic, synthetic and intellectual. Wisdom, it seems, must be worked for. It does not normally come gratis. But neither need it come by way of the Academy.

On the other hand, the principle is acknowledged to some extent in certain schools of elite administrative preparation, and finds a form, for example in the Oxford PPE curriculum (philosophy, politics and economics), in the French École Normale d'Administration and the Japanese Matsushita School of Government and Management. The Germanic tendency to regard jurisprudence as the appropriate avenue of training for high level administrators is also not inconsistent with this underlying ideal.

Philosophy-in-action in this sense would mean quite simply practical wisdom or wise administration.

THE PRACTICAL SENSE

Finally, there is the ordinary sense of 'philosophy' as formulation of policy. A great deal has been said and written about the arts of policy and indeed of policy science (Tribe, 1972) but one thing at least is certain, there is no policy-making *tabula rasa*. Policy makers come to the table prejudiced and predisposed. The myth of impartiality is akin to that of scientific objectivity. Any decision implies a value component and any decision maker represents a value complex. When policy is being formed, what happens is that a factual context is *re*presented with more or less logical consistency and empirical accuracy to the policymakers — the administrators. Included within this representation, explicitly or tacitly, is a projection, an extension of projected states of affairs. This representation or reconstruction is then subjugated to value considerations. This occurs, for example, when executives determine, through dialogue and dialectic, the purposes, aims, objectives and goals of their organization. In short, they determine an organizational value complex. This then becomes the mundane, ordinary philosophy which is daily translated into realities and events in the workaday world by means of management and organizational action. Work is done and, as Bertrand Russell would have said, there is an alteration in the distribution of matter at or near the surface of the earth. Philosophy-in-action here means the formulation and implementation of policy.

In this way, then, and in the preceding ways, philosophy is seen to be integral to administration and supports the definition of administration as philosophy-in-action. But still the question is left open, why *do* philosophy? Can it not take care of itself?

WHY

Given that philosophy is so central to administrative process and behaviour, it is somewhat curious that the writings on philosophy of administration are so slender. Perhaps an explanation can be derived from certain dominant influences on contemporary thought. Logical positivism, and the positivistic attitude generally, have certainly been influential in focusing modern energies in a materialistic direction (Barrett, 1979: 49). Idea-based and reality-based developments such as computer technology, cybernetics, rational—legal bureaucracy, general systems theory and positivistic ideology as a whole (Simon, 1965) have all possibly contributed to anaesthesia of the philosophical impulse and associated humanistic sensitivities. Of course, even in our hyperrationalized and technologized era the flame has not been entirely extinguished. Ordway Tead, for example, writing at the onset of the contemporary period, gave as his justification for doing philosophy:

> If we would seek clear purposes we require a philosophy, or rather the search is part of the philosophizing. And this is true also of long-range corporate objectives, of the selective gratification of personal needs, of finding the adequate scope for individual creativity, of interrelating a single corporate organization into a national (and presently an international) economy.
>
> At bottom our professional life is meaningless unless each one works through to a philosophy which sees human dignity and significance as the essential criteria. (Dimock, 1958:xi)

And Dimock, expressing his own philosophy of administration, writes within the same time frame, as follows:

> We have swung so far in the direction of science, however, that it would be healthy for us now to realize that administration is essentially one of the humanities. Administration is, or at least ought to be, wedded to subjects such as philosophy, literature, history, and art, and not merely to engineering, finance, and

structure. That this need is already though belatedly being appreciated is evidenced by the decisions of large corporations, such as the Bell System, which recently have joined forces with the educational facilities of large educational institutions, such as those of the University of Pennsylvania. There mature executives are given executive development courses revolving around literature, the arts, and philosophy. And why not? Administration is administrators. Administrators become increasingly human and philosophical, capable of planning ongoing programs which meet human needs and aspirations, when they are unified by areas of knowledge and skill which stress man's humanity and his philosophical insights. (Dimock, 1958:5)

The validity of this quotation still holds after the lapse of several decades. That the principle involved and the responses it evokes still operate are evident from the work of the schools mentioned above (see p. 7). They are evidenced, too, in the closing lines of Barnard's classic work on administration, 'I believe that the expansion of cooperation and the development of the individual are mutually dependent realities, and that a due proportion or balance between them is a necessary condition of human welfare. Because it is subjective with respect both to a society as a whole and to the individual, what this proportion is I believe science cannot say. It is a question for philosophy and religion.' (Barnard, 1972:296)

In other words, the art of administration finds its true ground in the humanities. Dimock rightly stated the case. Administration is administrators. It is also an applied art, an interdisciplinary nexus through which all of the established disciplines may flow and to which all science can ultimately contribute, but its essence is the manipulation of men by men about goals. This is the purposive behaviour of *men*, not merely very complex animals or machines. It is because of this that administrators must learn to do philosophy for themselves and not leave it to be done by others by default. And there are stronger reasons yet, as well as counter-arguments. Perhaps the latter should be considered first.

WHY NOT

Not all authorities would agree to the above position. The positivists in particular and the behaviourists generally, with Simon as a prototypical exponent, would be content to regard administrative process as being a negotiation of means-ends chains wherein ends are given or derived from elsewhere and it is the function of the executive merely to satisfice such means-ends consummation according to metavaluational criteria of efficiency and effectiveness (Simon, 1965:62-6; Skinner, 1971). The organization is a bus and the administrator its driver. What need for philosophy in such an arrangement? Such writers are impressed by what is known in the literature as the politics-administration dichotomy (Thomas, 1978:6-12; Waldo, 1979:22), and what we have referred to above as the administration-management distinction (see chapter 2). A case in point is provided by the extremely successful administrator Albert Speer (Singer and Wooton, 1975:79-104) who directed much of Hitler's war production economy. After an extensive period of imprisonment Speer eventually was moved to declare philosophical and ethical misgivings about his administrative career, but none of these was evident during his active, positivistic phase. Indeed, at that time he might well have considered any such reflections as a debilitating and counter-productive intrusion into the practical affairs of administration and, furthermore, a career deterrent, not to mention a potential threat to the war effort. Similarly, practitioners and theorists who lean towards the managerial side of the administration-management or politics-administration distinction might be inclined to argue, since they are primarily engaged with matters of fact, tactics, quantity, accounting and materiel, that philosophical reflection would be a distraction. It could only detract from efficiency and effectiveness and would be luxurious and non-cost-beneficial if not downright demoralizing and effete (all this perhaps upon the principle that a centipede cannot indulge in too much self-analysis if it is to continue walking). Moreover, it is perhaps neither unkind nor untrue to suggest

that there is a sort of anti-intellectualism which easily attaches
to the pragmatic spirit of men of action so that they are
quickly seduced into distrust of philosophy. A distrust or
suspicion or even contempt which often goes to harden the
administration-management distinction to the point of false
dichotomy.

The rebuttal to these objections is that they are falsely
grounded and rooted in a misconception of administrative
process. Later we shall show that the positivist practitioner
and the theoretician alike commit either the militaristic
fallacy or the fallacy of immaculate perception (Kaplan,
1966:131) or both. They assume that values can somehow
be compartmentalized and divorced from fact, whereas the
truth is that fact and value are always inextricably intertwined. But ends cannot be divorced from means without
damage to the synthetic philosophical fabric and the apparent
ease with which this distinction can be made pragmatically
may lead to dangerous philosophical delusions, as well as
pragmatic dysfunctions in the so-called real world. In the next
chapter it will also be shown that the politics-administration
or administration-management distinction is properly construed as a continuum rather than a dichotomy. At no point
along this continuum can values or affect be entirely eliminated, although attenuation can occur in certain circumstances
and in a certain sense to the point of near-elimination. As
that point of seduction is approached one enters, it is true,
into a region which entertains possibilities for a relatively
value-free management science but the focus of this book
lies towards the other end of the continuum, that is, upon
administration rather than management, and upon administration defined as philosophy-in-action. In this region he who
does not hesitate is lost, and not conversely.

To put it otherwise, philosophy is a component part, the
central part, of administrative behaviour and it will be done
anyway, whether the administrator is self-conscious about
it or not. The problem then becomes to ensure that it be
done better rather than be done badly. This book seeks to
deal with this problem and rests upon an article of faith: this
is the belief that there is benefit, virtue and merit in raising

the level of administrative consciousness about the philosophical infrastructure and implications of the executive
role. Because so much of modern life is conducted in, or
governed by, organizations the import of this assertion
ramifies far beyond the executive suite and the administrator's office. In the post-industrial society we are all dependent
on the quality of administration for the quality of our lives.

From this standpoint even the purer extremes of management would tend to benefit from an exposure of their logic
and values and from general philosophical analysis and
scrutiny. Organizational reality is in large measure a construct, an open construct, of socio-phenomenological forces
which, to the extent that they are understood, contribute to
the organization member's control of himself and his environment, and the enhancement of his moral autonomy and
responsibility. In so far as administrators are a special class
of organization members their philosophical sophistication
should tend to enhance their power over and comprehension
of organizational events. In short, philosophy is power in so
far as it is knowledge and understanding of human nature.
And 'power' is the first term in the administrator's lexicon.

To recapitulate, the main counter-argument against
administrative philosophy is that intellectual activity may
prove detrimental, once means are discriminated from ends,
to managerial efficiency and effectiveness in the pragmatic
conduct of organizational affairs. But this charge rests upon
a false understanding of administrative process and a falser
understanding of the logic of value. Our task is to rectify
these misunderstandings and so contribute to administrative
logic, to the larger ends of power and comprehension, autonomy and enhanced quality of life.

PHILOSOPHY AS POWER AND COMPREHENSION

The most persuasive reason for doing philosophy in the field
of executive action is that administrators possess power.
They make decisions about other men. They affect the
quality of human life first in the workplace and thence and

thereafter in every place. Moreover our society is becoming increasingly an organizational society wherein our lives are affected and governed by the actions of increasingly large, complex organizations, the present archetype and matrix of which is the modern nation state with its advanced bureaucratic and technical apparatus. Weber foresaw this development early in the century (Bendix, 1962:423-57) and Drucker and others have sought to direct our attention to this social phenomenon from the time of World War II (Burnham, 1941; Ellul, 1954; Drucker, 1978:262, 263; Whyte, 1956; Scott and Hart, 1979:50-5). Administration may be men, as Dimock maintained, but it is men with power, and that power has ramified enormously. Philosophy of administration can therefore be conceived as the attempt to rationally comprehend and civilize power in organizational affairs.

It can of course be argued that there is nothing new in the domain of power, either in organizations with their internal hierarchies or in society at large with its hierarchical class structure based ultimately upon the distribution of power. It is an essential element of organizational logic that individual desires be suppressed where necessary through subordination to the co-operative endeavour. Power is a condition of any administration. Plato, not the first philosopher of administration, wrote of this in *The Laws* and *The Republic*. All of this is true but it ignores the enlarged capacity for good and evil attendant upon the advent of contemporary bureaucracy and technology. The scope for individual alienation within and without organizations has been multiplied in porportion to the growth in complexity of structures and the distancing of individual role from organizational purpose. It is this potential for psychological distancing which is distinctively modern. The excess and overload of information provided by technological media merely enhance modern man's discernment of his own impotence and incapacity to modify organizational action. The scope for organizational malevolence, witting or unwitting, has expanded to the point where a central administrative question has become value-philosophical and can be stated simply as, how can men administer each other so as to minimize the evil done by organizations?

We are now well into what Sir Geoffrey Vickers calls the post-liberal and Peter Drucker the post-industrial era (Vickers, 1972:182; Drucker, 1942). It might also be classified as post-Christian in that the once unifying ideologies and coherent value-orientations represented in the West by the politico-religious orthodoxies of liberal capitalism and Judeo-Christian values have weakened to the point of dissolution. If anything approaching a homogeneous or monolithic order remains it is likely to be in the nature of narcissistic or hedonistic materialism (Lasch, 1979) but more likely yet in the form, or lack of form, of heterogeneous pluralism. Certainly in administrative practice, in the leadership of organizations, the tempering and moderating influence of systematic philosophical or religious systems would seem to be on the wane. In their place, perhaps, the secular ideologies of capitalism and welfare collectivism may serve to inform those administrators who adhere to their tenets.

But concomitant with this philosophical deterioration there are the discernible facts of change: massive growth of large-scale, often transnational, corporations in the private sector, complex and proliferating bureaucracies in the public sector; oligopolies, cartels, regulated capitalism; universal technological commitment; an organizational society; a sort, in effect, of neo-feudalism.

Our society is neo-feudal because the dominant relationship for the individual within that society is his primary organizational affiliation. From this there springs not merely his economic sustenance and support but his very identity. The new fiefdoms are those of the great institutions, the new liege lords the managerial and executive elite. In this society a man without a corporation may be an outcast or a pariah, for legitimated identity within the scheme of things flows from that organizational role to which he can lay claim. That role establishes a network of organizational relationships which further establish and determine his identity as well as his meaning and purpose in life, any of which can assume more importance than mere economic life-support, especially when the latter is in any event guaranteed by the master-organization of the nation state.

This is not to say that individualism is extinct, that the entrepreneur, the artist, the radical, the inventor, and the isolate have vanished from our midst. On the contrary, they may even prosper under the blanket security of the new feudalism. But they may have to do so in the interstices, in the spaces and the slack left within and between the socio-organizational structures, and less so or not at all within organizations themselves.

Neo-feudalism has been reinforced by the growing power of nation states and the bureaucracies which subserve them. Max Weber has proven to be more credible in his prophecies than Karl Marx. And accompanying the growth of bureaucracy, to an endemic degree in the public and private sectors of developed countries, there has been, of course, a concomitant growth of bureaupathologies and all the sorts and varieties of bureaucratic ailments and dysfunctions from alienation to monetary inflation. And still the growth is inexorable.

Nevertheless, though the outward and visible facts of the emergent order are increasingly apparent, there has been, at the same time, no clearly emergent consensus about the values which ought to guide administrative behaviour. Thomas (1978) has shown, for example, that even within the British school of administrative thought, a school which has traditionally incorporated ethics along with its management science, a coherent philosophy has failed to emerge. On the contrary, modern developments such as systems theory techniques, operations research, group dynamics and personnel psychology have had the effect of emphasizing the quasi-scientific aspect of administrative thought, to the detriment of ethical and philosophical considerations. Means have overshadowed ends and there has been a sort of anaesthesia of the administrative sense of value (Waldo, 1980:16). The effect ramifies to society and the social symptoms of loss of meaning and anomie become noticeable and widespread.

Technology and modern organization are committed to the metavalues of efficiency and effectiveness but while they raise productivity they leach away meaning. Philosophy is the countervailing force. By analysis and synthesis, by description and prescription, through questioning and scrutiny and overriding devotion to truth it seeks meaning: the restoration of old meanings; the establishment of new ones. The function of administrative philosophy is to engage in this work at the level of organizations and administrative practice. Such work will not appeal to all executives and leaders. One can understand and sympathize with a normal human reluctance to come to grips with such questions as the following (extracted from the curriculum of an elite Japanese school of administration): What is the nature of man? What is involved in an organizational system based on the true nature of man? What is the true vision of leaders? How should we view the social responsibility of enterprises? How to get the 'right man in the right place'? (Matsushita, 1980:18-19). Nor may all executives subscribe with facility to the American thesis that '... the philosophical task must precede action. And if philosophers will not become managers, it is certain that managers must become philosophers' (Scott and Hart, 1979:225; Monsen, 1971). But where intellectual diffidence and pragmatic reluctance can be overcome, and for those who seek the power of comprehension, this book would provide aid and conceptual assistance. It does this primarily through a technique of value analysis which can be applied to the resolution of value problems but which can also serve the individual synthesis of working philosophies of administration. The next chapter describes the primary domain of interest, the executive territory, and surveys the characteristics of the executive role as well as introducing the reader to the value-analytic tool. This will be followed by chapters applying value analysis first to the organizational setting and then to the varieties of administrative orientation. This leads finally to a concluding philosophy of leadership which is non-dogmatic but logically consistent with the previously developed discussion and argument.

Administration is at once the oldest, the noblest and the basest of callings. Part art, part science, but always at the centre of the humanities, its potential for good and evil is so striking, so impressive, that it is a cause for no slight wonder why philosophy has been so silent and administrative voices so still. There is work to be done and *Labor omnia vincit.*

2

Administration and Values

Pythagoras was once asked why he considered himself a philosopher. He replied with the illustration of the great fair at Olympia to which all the world came in all its polyglot and motley; some to enjoy, some to work, some to scheme and plot; athletes and entertainers, politicians, artists and artisans; and amongst all the milling horde some few who stood aside, detached observers, spectators who tried to make sense of the whole. These were the philosophers; seeking to interpret what was going on.

The modern parallel is easy to make. We are even more acquainted with hyperactivity than the Greeks. Modern life, in and out of organizations, has a peculiar quality of absorption or attachment whereby the individual consciousness is continually swamped by its content. The dentist concentrates on the point of his drill; the passive viewer is lost in a mindless-communion with his television screen; and the administrator 'loses himself in his work'. The task of the philosopher then becomes that of the rescuing of consciousness; consciousness-manipulation by deliberate withdrawal, detachment and scrutiny of the flux of activity in which it is so easy to become totally submerged. This type of observation goes beyond that of the scientist who is constrained by objectivity and the objective canons of the scientific paradigm. It ultimately invokes subjectivity as well as objectivity. The latter must, however, precede the former. The attempt at some sort of objectivity comes first. First the world must be mapped.

All this implies detachment or non-attachment; a withdrawal to sufficient distance from the absorbing and consciousness-consuming detail of practice to be able to perceive patterns and regularities in the ongoing flux of administrative process. In this chapter we shall first review some of the past attempts at such mapping of administrative process and then develop another projection. This will be necessary in order to readmit and include the subjective or value element which is conventionally slurred or elided in administrative theory. This in turn will necessitate our opening up and examining the value problem, some intensive discussion of value theory, and the development of a value model which can both serve the purposes of subjective philosophizing and reach beyond this into the field of practice. In sum, what will now be undertaken is a detached description of the field of executive action, a superimposition of a logic of process on that field, and the establishment of conceptual grounds for objective-subjective description, and ultimately prescription, in subsequent chapters. In one sense the task of philosophy can be understood as the business of moving, with increasing caution, from ever more verifiable and accurate description to ever more justifiable and defensible prescription.

ADMINISTRATIVE PROCESS

To set up a taxonomy of administrative process has always been a first endeavour of administrative theorists and of administrative practitioners who have succumbed to the temptations of self-reflection. Classically, Fayol, Gulick, and Urwick have bequeathed us POSDCORB (Gulick, 1937). And, by and large, POSDCORB or some emendation of it had stood up. There must be some truth to what has so well withstood the test of time and, of course, the mnemonic does have a persuasive common sense. Planning, organizing, staffing, directing, co-ordinating, reporting and budgeting are the things that administrators do do, though nothing is said of why they are done, nor of the time frame within

which they rest, nor of the contingent connections within
and between the component items.

A more modern version of the theme is that of Litchfield
(1956) who gives us the sequence: decision making, programming, communicating, controlling, reappraising. This is
another superimposition of order which Litchfield extends
to the whole of administrative practice whatever the adjec-
tival subset: public, military, commercial or educational.
Again Thomas (1978) makes the case for a British variant
in the form of SLOCUS (staff and line, organization, communication, span of control). Such schemas are essentially
simplistic taxonomies which are linear and two-dimensional
in scope. But more exotic variants are possible. There is, for
example, Mackenzie's elaboration in the *Harvard Business
Review* (1969) which purports to be three-dimensional and
which ramifies POSDCORB outward from the domains of
the elements (ideas, things and people) through tasks —
continuous functions and sequential functions — to *activities*
each of which can be specified and defined. Thus we have
'praise, renumerate and discipline' for the definition of the
reward activity and 'familiarize new people with the situation' for the definition of the *orient* activity, rewarding and
orienting being but two of the many activities into which
administrative work can be divided. This is a significant
refinement, though what is gained in comprehensiveness may
be lost in complexity. Indeed, on one count or another, be
it brevity, complexity or other defect, the reach for order
seems to exceed the grasp, and so this branch of esoteric
administrative folk wisdom may fail to satisfy. Taxonomy
is a prototypical stage in the development of theory nevertheless. It is an attempt, in the sense described above, to
stand off from and abstract the essential pattern, the essential features and regularities of the map. What is it that
executives do? Those things just indicated; the consistent
and distinctive element of which would seem to be decision
making. Indeed decision is the characteristic act of administration, the heart of its process, and as Barnard has so well
shown this act need not be positive at all. Instead the 'fine
art of executive decision consists in not deciding questions

that are not now pertinent, in not deciding prematurely, in not making decisions that cannot be made effective, and in not making decisions that others should make'. (1972: 194)

But there are other ways of looking at the field of executive action.

NOMOTHETIC AND IDIOGRAPHIC

The scheme portrayed in figure 1 is of some standing in administrative theory (Getzels and Guba, 1957). It depicts, succinctly, from the sociological standpoint, how any organization or social system can be analysed along a formal (nomothetic) dimension and an informal (psychological, individual) dimension. The critical dimension for the administrator is the nomothetic which seeks to link his organization with its goals by way of formal structuring into roles and role-expectations or jobs and job descriptions. By contrast the non-administrative organization member is principally concerned with the idiographic dimension; the nomothetic for him being essentially a matter of constraint which limits his satisfactions while at the same time providing the rational-legal foundation for his contract with the organization. The organization as depicted, of course, does not exist in a vacuum but within an encompassing environment which is also characterized by historical and geographical features and their resultant ethos, mores and values. (Getzels and Thelen, 1960:ch.4)

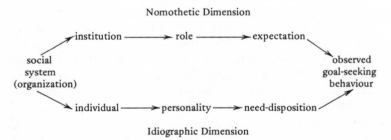

FIGURE 1   *Two dimensions of organizational life*

The task of the executive is thus revealed as one of reconciliation: reconciliation of organization to society and organization members towards organizational goals, reconciliation of individual and increasingly larger collective interests, reconciliations which can, of course, be static or dynamic, creative or uninspired, divisive or harmonious, synergetic or degenerative. The ostensible means for doing all this can be traced to the organizational purposes or goals or complex of goals which serve to focus the interests of all contending individuals and groups. Of course, neither in theory nor practice, is it usual for the goal mechanism to be easily comprehended or understood (Georgiu, 1973:291) and the eternal presence of a cultural dimension merely compounds the complexity. Under this view, then, the administrative process is the complex art of achieving organizational maintenance and growth in a field of conflicting and changing forces.

This may also be shown in figure 2. Once again the prime dimension of executive concern is that which links the organization and its purposes. However the dramaturgical element is now stressed (Thompson, 1961:138) and although the administrative function may be construed correctly as rational-legal or technical-professional, as is done in the classic Weberian bureaucratic model, still the administrator must be aware that he is continually acting a part. This part is conventionally understood as that of the *leader* and the role performance is continuously monitored by a variety of audiences, even when the script must be improvised and the scenarios are totally obscure.

The individual organization member meets with the nomothetic dimension not directly but through his workday encounters with groups, formal and informal, which intervene between him and the executive suite and which modulate his consciousness and experience of the formal administrative dimension. His organizational perspective, in other words, is not that of the administrator. And with respect to organizational purpose he operates at one or several removes. V_3 can be taken to represent the formal value orientation of the *organization.*

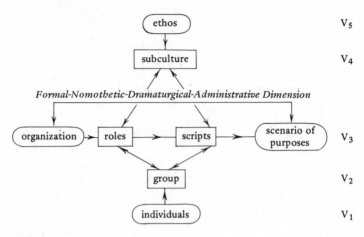

V_5

V_4

V_3

V_2

V_1

FIGURE 2   The total field of action

In a similar way the prevailing ethos (V_5) does not impinge directly upon the organization but is modulated through an intervening subculture. A firm, or a subsidiary of a firm, would differ in significant ways as between, say, California, New York and Frankfurt. Each subculture (V_4) imposes its own local mores and norms, whatever the historical *Zeitgeist* might be. Geography and history thus combine as the spatio-temporal determinants of consciousness in the workplace. Thus, in the permissive, anti-authoritarian climate of the counter-culture of the late sixties, geographic and socio-cultural location still made important differences to school administrators in the way that they were able to run their organizations. And bureaucracy in Turkey can be noticeably different from bureaucracy in Greece, even when both administrations subscribe to the ideal typical organization of Max Weber. Any synthetic view of administrative reality must therefore take into account the modulating or filtering effects of subculture and group (V_4, V_2) upon the major influences of culture and individual psychology (V_5, V_1).

One should perhaps stress that the ethos or culture, the large-scale contemporary pattern of value orientation, abstract indeed though it may be, is a matter for continuous executive monitoring and concern. Thus the counter-culture of the sixties introduced permissive and anti-authoritarian notions into the workplace as well as into the political and domestic arenas. Ecological and ethnic factors which the contemporary administrator must now take into consideration make another illustration.

The rhetoric of organizational purpose reflects V_5 changes. Few large commercial organizations now boldly declare, as they once did, that they exist for the purpose of making money. Rather, they claim to render some kind of public service — the enhancement of life-style through motor vehicle transportation, or improvement in the quality of life through the provision of life insurance protection, or aesthetic advance through cosmetic fantasy — in all of which, of course, the accumulation of profits is a necessary but far from sufficient condition. And although these remarks refer mainly to organizational *rhetoric* it by no means precludes their affecting organizational *logic* and the reality of organizational goals.

The field of executive action is thus totally comprised of five levels of value-orientation and value-functioning: cultural, subcultural, nomothetic, group and individual. These levels overlap, intertwine and interact in dynamic and contingent relationships. It is a matter of some philosophical interest and contention as to whether the scheme of figure 2 exhausts the value possibilities or whether there is, as it were, a sixth level of value (V_6) which is extra-systematic or transcendent. We shall consider this question at a later stage. For the moment it could be noted that history or evolution can serve in this way for the secular Marxist or scientific positivist, while God or Fate might serve for others as explanatory constructs at this level of abstraction. The questions generated by this line of inquiry are of course metaphysical and need not detain us at this point (which is not to say that the executive man of action can wash his hands of metaphysics but that the question at hand is the conceptualizing of empirical administrative process and for this purpose we now construct a third figure).

DYNAMIC PROCESS (P3M3)

Previous taxonomies of administrative process, though they cannot be faulted on the grounds of truth, are open to critical complaint on the grounds of deficiency. (An example would be the failure to allow for fixation or regression in the taxonomic stages.) The model proposed below does not seek to remedy all such deficiencies so much as to draw attention to three neglected aspects: (1) the failure to distinguish between the logically different categories of administration and management; (2) the failure to acknowledge the intrinsically philosophical nature of administration; and (3) the failure to draw some general implications about differential expertise within administrative process.

Let us begin with our axiomatic proposition: administration is philosophy-in-action. Philosophy, whether it be in the mode of articulated policy utterances or of inchoate and unuttered values is daily translated into action through the device of the organization. How? In a sequential twofold way. By means of administrative processes which are abstract, philosophical, qualitative, strategic and humanistic in essence, and by means of managerial processes which are concrete, practical, pragmatic, quantitative, technical and technological in nature. This logic is depicted in figure 3.

Within this scheme the ideal typical sequence is as follows. Organizational values are articulated by top level administration through philosophical processes (argument, dialectic, logic, rhetoric and value clarification). This is the level of *idea*. The idea emergent from this first phase must be translated into some sort of plan and reduced to a written, persisting and communicable form. This form must then be entered into a political process of persuasion. This is the domain of power, resource control and politics, and we have moved from the level of ideas to the level of *people*. Coalitions must be formed, levers pulled, persons persuaded as power and support are marshalled around the project or plan. Each of these three process phases of administration can be subsumed under the rubric of policy-making.

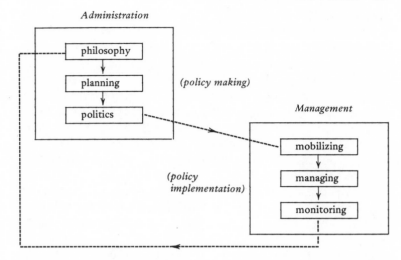

FIGURE 3　The basic taxonomy

When power is aligned and resources are committed, the next stage (still a *people* stage) requires the mobilization and organizing of what economists call the factors of production — land, labour and capital — around the organizational purposes. This phase is critical and involves, metaphorically speaking, a shift of gears from the administrative into the managerial phase. This phase is an intermediate one of art between the philosophy of policy making on the one hand and the science of management on the other; it is here where, if at all, the pieces are put together and philosophy is moved from the realm of ideas through the political behaviour of people into the realm of facts, action and *things*. Implicit in the aspect of mobilization is the motivation of the human resources to the organizational purpose. It is above all on the successful negotiation of this phase that realization or actualization or any organizational goal depends.

Given this transition then the committed and mobilized resources still need day to day, short-term and long-term *managing*. It is here where routinization, programming and the possibilities for factual management science exist. And, finally, there is the managerial phase of monitoring which would include such activities as formal supervision, auditing, accounting and evaluation in the sense expounded by Stufflebeam *et al.* (1971:40), i.e. as the provision of information for administrative decision making, that which appears as philosophy in the model. A feedback loop is shown to relate this final, but still managerial, phase to the administrative circuit. Operations research and systems analysis activate this loop, as indeed does any true evaluation in the philosophical sense when the match or fit between the reality of *things* and the original and continuing project of *ideas* is compared and tested.

It will be seen that these last three stages of process can be classified as managerial and subsumed under the rubric of policy implementation. They are closer to the earth; and to science.

The entire taxonomy is postulated as constituting the necessary and sufficient logic of an administrative theory. It is a superimposition of order in an ideal-type format. It occurs, or seeks to occur, in continuous and overlapping cycles throughout organizational life. This is not to say that stages may not be elided, cast out of sequence, fixated or overemphasized. One can (and often does) plan without philosophizing; one can (and often does) avoid or evade or subvert the monitoring phase; one can even administer (for a while) without managing and manage (for a while) without administering...but the logic persists and, ultimately, *Ordnung regiert die Welt.*

This conception of the field of executive action makes a sharp and robust distinction between administration and management, the former being the more philosophical, the latter the less so but both being inextricably intertwined and interdependent in the overall executive function. And neither category, nor any subcategory of either, can be considered as value-free. It can also be noted that the categories and subcategories of the taxonomy are logically distinct from each other and the most practical implication of this is that expertise and aptitude may be expected to differ throughout the executive cycle. A good administrator need not necessarily be a good manager, and a politically-skilled administrator may be out of his depth in the planning or monitoring functions of his role. Finally, the much abused term leadership, that chief stock-in-trade of administrative rhetoric, may find its operant focus in the mid-phase of the cycle (the *people* phase) as much as or more than at the onset of the process (the *idea* phase).

VALUE PERVASION

Two things now show clearly from the foregoing analysis. First, the central place of decision making in administrative processes, and second, the general pervasion of the administrative enterprise with values: notions of good and bad, right and wrong, benefit and cost, efficiency and effectiveness and so on. These two features are, of course, related in logic since it can be shown that it is impossible to free decision processes of the value component (Hodgkinson, 1978:48-66). The three irreducible elements of decision are facts, probabilities and values. Nor is it at all surprising that the value element should be so salient in an activity which is philosophy-in-action, continuously engaged in the interrelation of ideas, people and things. Administration is distinctive, however, in that, like politics itself, it is an enterprise based on power, in which decisions are made for and about others and in which a primary concern is with the establishment, maintenance and enhancement of power and authority; functions which can never be allowed to rest as given but which must continuously be legitimated through the concepts of organizational purpose and commitment. If morality is interpreted as a concern for *others* then it follows that administration is a peculiarly moral activity.

Again, unlike established professions with their codes of ethics and ostensibly clear modes of value conflict resolution, the practice of administration is more complex and turbulent. It is, as it were, at the cutting edge of action where new possibilities of ethics are raised and old possibilities exhausted. One is reminded, too, of Aristotle's view of praxis as ethical conduct in a political context. Although the issue of professional commitment must be discussed in a later chapter it can for now be conceded that administration is not strictly speaking a profession at all (Waldo, 1980:61-2; Self, 1972—289-99). But it can be taken as an occupation in which some professionally committed people are engaged. It is also an occupation under its own sort of cloud. Traditionally it has appealed to the amoral, the immoral and even the antimoral as is attested by a value-literature peculiar to administration; typical examples of which are to be found in the works of Machiavelli, Nietzsche and the Sanskrit *arthasastra* (Gowen, 1931:171-88; Nietzsche, 1956; Burnham, 1943).

It is perhaps this very feature of administration, the tacit recognition of its significance within the domain of human values, that has led to numerous attempts at eliding or bypassing the problem. One could trace a line from the emergence of modern bureaucratic theory in the work of Max Weber to the systems approach of modern management with its rational planning models and techniques such as PPBS, MBO, MIS and PERT. All such emergent quasi-philosophies of administration are imbued with the spirit of rationalistic positivism (Simon, 1965:45-77) and tend to avoid those value issues which are integral to the executive function. This movement has of course been intimately associated with the growth and development of science, applied science and technology. Its *reductio ad absurdum* would be the administrator as pure technologist, his values and ethics provided by some *deus ex machina* such as the 'will of the people' or the 'will of the owners as expressed through their board of directors'. And if this be not sufficient to achieve an ideal executive value-antisepsis then the empirical findings of motivational psychology can be drawn upon and deployed so as to contain and explain away any aberrations in the desired logical scheme. Thus both ethos and individual can be obviated and the administrator is freed to become a factotum. But, just as war is too important to be left to the generals, so the value problem is too intrinsic a part of the executive function to be left to philosophers. Or even to the mystical 'people' who, in the myth, own our organizations and direct their instrumentality.

THE LOGIC OF VALUE

THE SUBJECTIVE NATURE OF VALUE

The essential point to grasp in thinking about value is that values do not exist *in the world*. They are utterly phenomenological, subjective, facts of the inner and personal experience, ultimately only susceptible of location within an individual cranium, and even at that within the further and deeper mystery of consciousness and mind-brain interaction. We are always inclined to forget that any object in the world such as a gold coin or the Mona Lisa is in truth valueless and worthless save as we go through the phenomenological exercise of imputing value to it. The one is merely a metal of such and such physico-chemical properties, the latter an assemblage of pigment on canvas. In the same way a human being is a bag of skin, and actions within human organizations, such as promotion and dismissal, are movements of bodies, wind playing across vocal chords, redispositions of organic and inorganic matter within the space-time flux. The values which are immediately inputed to such objects, facts and events are *in principle* at the *will* of the possessors, actors, beholders, participants. The world of fact is given, the world of value made (Hodgkinson, 1978:220, Proposition 7). In the same way it can be argued that all moments, and hence all events, are analytically equivalent. Each is valueless and so, worthless or, paradoxically but literally, priceless. Life is a series of moment-fact-events to which subjectivities impute value. And in principle we can do this *freely*.

In fact as opposed to principle we know of course that most value imputations are spontaneous, conditioned and involuntary although capable of explanation through various and elaborate schemes of cultural discourse such as ethics, aesthetics, economics, politics, psycho-analysis and even organization theory (Greenfield, 1973, 1978). Still, the world of fact is given and the world of value made. And administrative artistry, the mystery of leadership, may well involve the overcoming of the former (i.e. reality constraints) by the latter (i.e. value creativity) to the end of new dimensions of co-operative accomplishment, new frontiers, new worlds of possibility. This first and overwhelming characteristic of value thinking is then not without tremendous significance for administrative process. Amazing paradox! That values which are existent, but nonentities, give the world its colour and its entirety of meaning.

TYPING ERRORS

Precisely because of the foregoing subtlety and the protean nature of value we have a difficult and elusive problem. This is the seductive tendency to fall victim to a number of errors in thinking about values. Typical are logical category mistakes or mistakes of classification, what might be called logical typing errors. The failure to get the correct logical *type*. This problem greatly exercised Bertrand Russell, and the principle extends beyond logic and value to the world of common experience. A statement which is true for one level of logical typing may not hold good for another at a higher or lower level. Thus, a statistic of life expectancy might be very precise for an aggregate, but non-applicable to an individual composing that aggregate. And pollsters can predict which party will win an election but cannot predict how any individual will vote. In these cases the two logical types are not normally confused but in value thinking the tendency to conflate categories is always imminent.

   The basic logical types of most interest to the administrator are member or individual (e.g. organizational member, employee); group or class (e.g. informal organization, committee, executives, workers, administrative assistants); and the class of classes (e.g. formal organization or institution). In the matter of logical typing it should be noted that the *class* is of a different order than that of its members. It should also be noted, by way of elementary semantics and common-sense precaution that the *name* is not the thing named but a different logical type, *higher* than that of the thing named (Korzybski, 1933).

The biologist-philosopher Gregory Bateson, in discussing the sorts of confusion arising from typing errors, makes the following acute observation:

> It is interesting to consider the nature of such a concept as a 'crime'. We act as if crime could be extinguished by punishing parts of what we regard as criminal actions, as if 'crime' were the name of a sort of action or of part of a sort of action. More correctly 'crime', like 'exploration', is the name of a way of organizing actions. It is therefore unlikely that punishing the act will extinguish the crime. In several thousand years, the so-called science of criminology has not escaped from a simple blunder in logical typing. (Bateson, 1979:138)

What Bateson has to say may apply with equal force to concepts such as play and work and commitment, all of which have a direct organizational and administrative bearing. And certainly such blunders continually beset the discourse about value or at the very least the risk of committing such a blunder is ever present. For this reason, even before proceeding to a formal definition of the term, it may be advisable to consider a few of the more common fallacies which tend to plague value thinking and value logic, especially in so far as they affect administrative action.

FALLACIES

The temptations to fallacious thinking in administration are legion. This is no doubt attributable to the infinity of dynamic variables which the organization theorist must somehow attempt to comprehend, but the ground becomes more slippery still when one enters what might be called the domain of value logic. Before presenting a formal paradigm of value I would therefore draw the reader's attention to four of the most conspicuous traps to be avoided in seeking one's way through this difficult intellectual territory. The labels given to the four major fallacies are suggestive rather than precise and are intended mainly to sensitize attention rather than sanitize understanding. In the search for logical clarity and precision effort must be relentless and the reasonable must satisfice for the ideal.

1 *The naturalistic fallacy.* The Cambridge philosopher G. E. Moore, author of the Edwardian classic *Principia Ethica*, is credited with showing that notions of the good are irreducible and *sui generis*. In the end the good can only be defined in its own terms. Therefore, values are of a different ontological category than facts. No fact, nor indeed any amount of facts or factual information, can *prove* a value. Or, as the famous phrase has it, you can't get an *ought* from an *is* (Popper, 1948:154).

Now administrators, like lawyers, are particularly prone to consulting the 'facts' of the case. But the world of fact cannot of itself yield any value — a thing is but a thing, an event but an event. Yet since values, as we shall see, constitute a sort of psychological or sociological set of facts within the world the problem is subtle and complicated. And the temptation is ever present to deduce the values from the facts and so commit the naturalistic fallacy.

Nor is Wittgenstein's solution available to the administrator. In his *Tractatus Logico-Philosophicus* he discriminated sharply between the world of value and the world of fact concluding in the end that the former was mystical and that 'Whereof one cannot speak, thereof one must be silent' (1922:Propositions 6.522, 7). Administrators, being men of affairs, cannot be so immaculate; they are forced to speak from time to time and to utter value judgements in action if not in speech — but they must beware the temptations of deriving their 'oughts' from some 'is'. Values are certainly inextricably intertwined with facts but this does not mean that there is any intrinsic or causal relation between the two categories.

2 *The homogenetic fallacy.* Even if values are carefully discriminated from facts there still remains the error of treating them as if they were all on an equal footing with each other, all of a kind, that is, within the same ontological category.

As the paradigm in the next section will show, values themselves are amenable to hierarchic analysis. They are heterogeneous with respect to rank. When this hierarchical distinction within the value concept itself is confused or forgotten the homogenetic fallacy occurs. Values are not all of a kind. This point will be elaborated below, but the essential fallacy here is a typing error of the kind referred to above (see p. 32). Two men may both subscribe to the value of honesty, say, but the subscription (and hence the value) need not be either of the same degree or the same kind. One man's candour can be another man's lies.

3 *The excisionistic fallacy.* This, which is as much favoured by positivists as by administrators, is the error of appearing to solve or resolve value problems by excising the source of the problem and removing the apparent need for its consideration. Thus, if a source of value conflict appears to be located in a particular organization member, that member can be transferred, removed, or even expelled from the organization ranks altogether. The appearance of having solved or resolved a value problem is thus created. But this is delusory. Nothing is said to the *truth* of the rights or wrongs of a case by the mere taking of action or the exercise of power. The dismissed offender may have been right, he may have been wrong. His dismissal says nothing to either possibility. It simply exhibits the distribution of power amongst the actors. The root value question is not addressed, it is avoided.

4 *The militaristic fallacy.* This fallacy, which is itself a version of excisionistic thinking, is named after its most obvious devotees and occurs when ends or terminal values are radically differentiated from means or instrumental values, often to the point where the former are lost sight of through preoccupation with the latter. The fault could, however, as easily be ascribed to technological, bureaucratic, scientific and systems thinking generally, in that all these orientations share a propensity to factor, fractionate and atomize problems to the end that effort can be effectively

and efficiently directed towards behavioural and positivistic objectives. Within administrative literature the position is exemplified by Simon and the logical positivists in general (March and Simon, 1958:130, 169) where value questions are presumed not to exist for the administrator since all critical values are determined extraneous to the executive level of organization by putative policy makers who are non-managerial and non-executive in status. The truth is that value problems pervade organizations throughout all levels of the authority hierarchy and excessive rationality becomes a pathology, a sort of fascism of the intellect where value sensibilities are attenuated or eliminated by an inappropriate military dressage.

These four fallacies have been selected from a potential universe of errors in value logic because of their peculiar salience in administration and their especial applicability to organizational life. It would not be unfair to assert that each is committed with greater and lesser degrees of severity many times each day in the average executive's life. Most often, if not invariably, the error is unconscious and so to maintain a constant level of awareness of these temptations would represent a considerable advance in sophistication, but not an impossible one; and understanding is a first step.

THE VALUE PARADIGM

We may now define our central term, value. This can be done simply. Value is *a concept of the desirable* (Parsons, 1951: 162). Somewhat more exactly, values are concepts of the desirable with motivating force or, concepts of the desirable which tend to act as motivating determinants of behaviour. But now it is becoming more vague and punctured with loopholes such as 'tend to' and with obscurities such as 'motivating'. The point is, of course, that we can have values without their being 'operant'. We can continue to eat gluttonously while subscribing to the desirability of slenderness. In fact it may seem at times as if a central function of value is to interfere with our straightforward enjoyment of the senses. Let us return to this later. For now let us contemplate the simple definition.

Values are subjective because they are concepts. And they have to do with the phenomenology of desire. Neither of *these* things is simple. Though desire has been much studied, introvertedly by philosophers and artists and extrovertedly by psychologists and social scientists, usually under the head of motivation, we are far from clarity and understanding about it. Theories ramify and contest with each other. Errors of logical typing are endemic. Desire manifests itself at different ontological levels and exhibits different relationships to consciousness. It can range from totally unconscious deep psychic drives and complexes to superlatively conscious and highly sublimated intentions of the will. Furthermore, the nature of mental constructs such as concepts is again not fully understood. With phenomenology itself they take us to the frontiers of ignorance and thorough scrutiny would bring the searcher rapidly to intractable problems such as the nature of intuition and creativity, the mind-brain problem, the existence or otherwise of the 'self', and the nature of consciousness. Again one is tempted by Wittgenstein's aphorism, 'Whereof one cannot speak, thereof one must be silent.' But no such resort to silence, however wise, can advance our discourse and discourse is necessary in the field of action. And since Aristotle we have had the notion of *praxis* or practical philosophy whereby men, precisely through their actions, seek to lead or find the good life. The wonder is that with all the infinite ramifications of complexity and mystery hidden just below the opaque surface of language we can still understand and comprehend with practical simplicity and utility the far from simple notion that 'Values are concepts of the desirable.'

With this in mind we now proceed to the paradigm outlined in figure 4. This paradigmatic typology of value emerges because, so far as I have been able to determine, four and only four kinds of answer can be given to the question, why is an object or action or event deemed to be *good* or *right*? The four grounds or justifications for valuing are principles

(Type I), consequences (Type IIA), consensus (Type IIB), and preference (Type III). Let us consider these in the reverse or ascending order.

Value Type	Grounds of Value	Psychological Faculty	Philosophical Orientations	Value Level	
I	PRINCIPLES	conation willing	religion existentialism intuition	I	RIGHT ↑
IIA	CONSEQUENCE (A)	cognition reason thinking	utilitarianism pragmatism humanism democratic liberalism	II	
IIB	CONSENSUS (B)				
III	PREFERENCE	affect emotion feeling	behaviourism positivism hedonism	III	↓ GOOD

FIGURE 4   The value paradigm

Type III preference justifies a value on the grounds, pure and simple, that the object or action is *liked* or preferred by the subject. In this sense all animals possess values and all their values are self-justifying. Human animals likewise have their Type III values and the imponderability of such preferences is recorded in every language: *de gustibus non est disputandum, chacun à son goût, bei mir ist es so Sitte.* I prefer tea to coffee and Turner to Picasso and red to blue and this employee over that one and that's the way it is. Such preferences may be innate. They may also in the human condition be learned. Hence great efforts are expended by commercial and political persuaders everywhere to effect changes in the schemes of Type III preference of their audiences.

Type II values, whether subset A or subset B, are justified upon the general ground of rationality. This can appear first as consensus (IIB), as, say, when one discovers abortion to be wrong (not good) because there is an expressed social consensus manifesting in the form of a given statute or law which so declares (all of this being achieved, presumably, by some sort of rational process such as the assessment of public opinion and its translation through parliamentary and legal channels). Individual preference is here aggregated, averaged or summed. Next, at a higher level of rational process, a claim is laid to establish the value upon an analysis of the consequences of holding it. Murder is wrong (and non-murder right) because the consequences of undeterred murderous indulgence would be unpleasant. An ethic of non-killing is cost-beneficial in other words. Less need for police, prisons, taxes and so on. Honesty is right because it makes for a better, more efficient and effective organization or social context. The test of a value judgement or act is its consequences and much ethical and moral disquisition is devoted to analytical reasoning of this kind.

Type I values are transrational; they go beyond reason. They imply an act of faith or intent or will as it is manifested in the acceptance of a *principle*. Though such principles may often be defended by rational discourse they are essentially metaphysical in origin or location. Often they derive, or it is claimed that they derive, from such rationally intractable phenomenological entities as conscience and intuition. Adultery is wrong at this level because it was so chiselled into the tablets of stone brought down from Mount Sinai. Death on the battlefield for the honour of his regiment and in front of his men is right and good because the ethic of *dulce et decorum est pro patria mori* has been subscribed to by that particular soldier. Poverty, chastity and obedience are good according to the moral insights of some saint or seer and I make them mine by monastic vow. Notice that one may or may not have Type I values, but the resort to a claim of principle is usually reserved for the highest and final court appeal in the attempt to justify or ground a value. Thus we may have organizational loyalty because of affective attachment (III), because of group suasion (IIB), or because of net benefits such as economic return (IIA), but all these pale before the patriotic commitment to membership in a nation-state organization which may make ultimate claims on its membership of the *dulce et decorum* variety but which can only ground such claims in the last analysis on metaphysical or transrational foundations. 'My country right or wrong' is a Type I organizational allegiance.

For each of the value types and levels shown in the paradigm there are corresponding psychological and philosophical correspondences. Type III values are emotive, affective in source, Type II employ the cognitive-rational faculties, and Type I invoke the aspect of the will. A degree of freedom of the will is necessary, one can say absolutely necessary, to make the act of commitment which in turn is necessary to embrace and maintain a principle. On the other hand reason or predisposition suffice for the lower levels of value.

Philosophically the categories shown in figure 4 are roughly indicative of the broad streams of orientation appropriate to each value class. Thus, as will be further discussed below, the logical positivists are inclined to reduce all values to the emotive level of explanation (Level III) and behaviourists generally incline to the side of determinism in their view of the world (Skinner, 1971). At the other extreme (Level I) the existentialists and their philosophically allied cohorts make great play about freedom of will, responsibility to choose or commit or engage oneself, and the attendant agonies of choice. This orientation is shared by those who hold to a religious world-view. The modal level for administration generally is Level II where the philosophical tendencies in so far as they can be labelled at all are inclined towards the pragmatic and the utilitarian. It is understandable, after all, that most executives would have an automatic nomothetic bias by virtue of their role and hence a *prima-facie* concern with the greatest good for the greatest number within the field of their authority and power, and with the pragmatic, getting things done, the art of the possible.

These are the essential elements of the paradigm. Other aspects can and will be added later and other parallels can of course be drawn. The levels correspond, for example, with the Aristotelian good (III), better (II) and self-conscious and free (I). The paradigm will be expanded on throughout the rest of the text and it provides us with our basic logic and our principal tool of analysis. It should be noted that *any* value can be manifested or held at *any* level. Thus Type I honesty would be grounded on principle, Type II honesty would be valued because it has reasoned about or because it is the norm of the group, and Type III honesty would be considered desirable simply because it is preferred to dishonesty (less trouble than having to lie or because that is how one feels at the time the question arises). A preference for tea over coffee may be merely that (Type III tea valuation), or a consequence of living in English society (programmed or socially conditioned Type IIB tea valuation), or because research has shown its caffeine content to be less noxious than that of coffee (Type IIA reasoned tea valuation). And *in extremis* the whole act of drinking tea can be raised to a mystical quasi-religious level as in the Zen tea ceremony (principled Type I tea valuation). Such illustrations could be produced endlessly since all aspects of human action are susceptible of such analysis. Indeed, the crucial thing about any value is its level or type. To fail to discriminate type is to commit the homogenetic fallacy and to clear the path for confusion, argument and the breakdown of communication and understanding.

POSITIVISM

The logical positivists provide us with the classical instance of the homogenetic fallacy, one which the reader must consider with care in view of the influence of this school of philosophy upon administrative thought and management science (Simon, 1965:45; Habermas, 1971; Barker, 1969). In its radical form their argument is that all values are reducible, in the last analysis, to affectivity or emotion. That is, in our terms, there are only Type III values and the other postulated levels are artifacts of fallacious thinking or else some sort of philosophical failure of nerve. Thus, to take the classic case, the value of life or the prohibition of killing is, upon tough-minded ultimate analysis, a matter of personal preference and emotive structure. '*I* do not like killing' or 'Killing, ugh!' (Ayer, 1948:102-20). Legal injunctions against killing and definitions of the crime of murder then become expressions of affect at a higher level (IIB) but still expressions of collective feeling, distaste or non-preference for killing as expressed by way of the statutory judicial machinery of the State. Let's take it further. If the value is to be justified or based on consequential (IIA) grounds, e.g. that the consequences of killing would lead to a state of affairs where life would be mean, nasty, brutish and short, then this would be merely an expression of affect at one remove. A future state is projected and then judged (evaluated) according to singular or collective affect. I (we) don't *like* what the outcome would be. What seems at first sight sweetly reasonable is merely emotion once removed. Finally we would come to the last bastion of the non-positivist, the resort to faith or belief in a principle (Level I). Murder is wrong because it was declared so on Mount Sinai, or because 'conscience' tells us so, or because I choose it to be so and commit myself to that act of choice. But, says the positivist, these are metaphysical grounds and are unverifiable. There is no logic of belief and in the domain of belief one is free to believe *anything*, that there are fairies at the bottom of our garden, that the Prophet Jones has the right to command us to drink cyanide, that one has free will, anything, and therefore one value is *as good as any other.* Moreover, one's beliefs are doubtless simply reflections of one's affective structure and emotive disposition. And once again one is back at Level III. In short, so-called Type I values are Type III affect at a transrational and logically unverifiable remove while Type II values are Type III affect which has been rationalized. Man is not different in kind from other animals since these also clearly have Type III values but he is peculiar in his delusion about ethics — that there is some sort of ethical principle in the universe, a category of 'ought' which somehow imposes obligations on the human animal in a way not shared by his fellow creatures.

Such is the case of logical positivism and it is formidable. In fact, within the boundaries of argument established by the positivists it would seem to me to be irrefutable. One can only rebut it by referring to one's own phenomenological and, therefore, admittedly unverifiable experience of the tension between the postulated levels of value and by taking a position outside the limits of positivist discourse, that is, in the region of Wittgenstein's 'silence'. To do so is to affirm that man is different from other animals in *kind*, not simply in degree, a proposition which does not sit well with those of positivistic tendencies. It must be left for each reader to arrive at his own conclusion about this fundamental philosophical cleavage. This book is, however, non-positivistic and seeks to both transcend and subsume the positivist position within an encompassing value paradigm.

METAVALUES

In addition to the concept of value as discussed above it may be useful to introduce the notion of metavalue (Hodgkinson, 1978:180). A metavalue is a concept of the desirable so vested and entrenched that it seems to be beyond dispute or contention — one that usually enters the ordinary value calculus of individual and collective life in the form of an unexpressed or unexamined assumption. In administration and organizational life the dominant metavalues are efficiency and effectiveness. No one is ever likely to suggest that an organization should be run less efficiently or less effectively. Examples of personal metavalues would be survival and fulfilment. An example of an academic (and bureaucratic) metavalue would be rationality. Metavalues are special values which are not only deepseated and usually unexamined but are also powerful unconscious structuring influences on individual and collective value hierarchies. If human beings were perfectly rational and their metavalues were known it would be possible to infer a deductive logic of behaviour which would be scientific and highly predictive. The logic of the value paradigm would argue, however, for a complex mixture of potentialities, the components being subrational, rational, and transrational. The paradigm has concealed or implicit within it a second-order valuation, itself a metavaluational structure, which establishes a rank of *quality* from I down to III, hence the deliberate numbering. Type I values are tacitly and implicitly presumed to be in some way 'better' or 'higher' than Type II and these in turn than Type III. This is upon the logic that reasoning is in some way superior to feeling, Aristotle's rational animal discrimination, and that the autonomous action of a free will with its power of commitment is in turn superior to ratiocination and calculation. 'They say that the power of the senses is great. But greater than the senses is the mind. Greater than the mind is Buddhi, reason; and greater than reason is He — the Spirit in man and in all.' (*Bhagavad Gita*, see Mascaró 1962, 3:43). Or as another translation of the Sanskrit would put it (Prabhavananda and Isherwood, 1949:72) 'The senses are said to be higher than the sense objects. The mind is higher than the senses. The individual will is higher than the mind. What is higher than the individual will? The Atman itself.'

It should be clear, none the less, that such second-order valuation is not only idiosyncratic to and metavaluational with the author, but it cannot, in accordance with Gödel's principle (1931:173-98) find its justification within its own system. It is axiomatic and extrasystematic but also fundamental to the value logic expounded in this book. Other formulations would be possible in the same way that there can be non-Aristotelian logics and non-Euclidean geometries. The paradigmatic pattern is commended none the less on the belief that it has most to offer by way of explanatory power and is most coincident with ordinary human affairs and praxis, especially as these unfold in organizational activity.

CREDO: *I believe in the potentiality of individual free will, in partial determinism and degrees of freedom, and in the possibility of enhancing human autonomy, for ourselves and for others.*

It is this which distinguishes man from animal, in kind as

well as in degree. It is this which can make administration the greatest human art.

ILLUSTRATIONS

It is important to grasp that the value paradigm can be applied to any action or event. And to understand that any value can appear at any of the paradigm levels. Take, for example, an ethical value such as honesty. If, say, in the process of evolution an especially gifted individual — saint, prophet or seer — should gain the moral insight that there is an intrinsic and integral moral order in the universe in the scheme of which honesty is a crucial and fundamental part, then he will certainly underwrite this value at a Type I level within his own form of life[1] and he may very well feel called upon to propound it to others as an ethical imperative. Thou shalt not lie! Conceivably with the passage of time, such a commitment might lose its moral force for *others* but still people might adhere to the value of honesty on the calculated grounds that a society in which people were habitually dishonest would be inconvenient, unpleasant and cost-ineffective. Such would be a rational IIA commitment. And if, to descend further, the value of honesty is held merely because that is the norm of expectancy in the group or groups circumscribing the actor's form of life then it is consensual (IIB) and largely a matter of social programming, the whys and wherefores of the value having been but lightly considered, if at all, at the rational level. Finally, one may be honest or choose to be honest simply because that is one's preference of the moment. This is Type III and the commitment here is at its least stable and its associated form of life least affected.

One can note at this point that the behavioural indices of value structure can be very misleading. Type III expressions

---

[1] The expression 'form of life' here and elsewhere is to be understood in Wittengenstein's sense (Pitkin, 1972:132-9), that is, as patterns of human existence extending beyond the individual into networks of linguistic and social relations in the one direction and into ontological origins in the other.

can be more vociferous than Type I, and so, for instance, it would be critical for an administrator, such as a school superintendent dealing with a parent protest, to know the correct value *type* of the protest. Irate parents may merely be letting off Type III steam but if their concern affects their depth value structure (Type I religious commitment against sex education, say) then the impending trouble may be severe and the administrator's head may be at stake even though the behavioural sound and fury may be less than in a Type III furore. The quality of a value as it manifests itself within a form of life will vary with its typological level and in the discrimination between levels rests the fine art of administrative value analysis.

The typology applies to all valuation and value action. Instances have already been given from the realm of domestic life (see p. 41 above) and these could be extended to include any aspect of human affairs. Thus, in the sexual conduct of life, homosexuality may be merely a matter of affective preference (Type III); or it may be the norm of one's group to be homosexual or heterosexual (Type IIB) and hence right or wrong as the case may be; or homosexuality may be held to be wrong because the social consequences are seen to be deleterious or right because they are advantageous (IIA). Arguments may always be proferred both ways, e.g. homosexuals do not reproduce themselves and this can be interpreted as a threat to the family institution or an advantage in conditions of overpopulation. Finally, homosexuality can be argued for and against at the Type I level as when human rights activists take one side and religious fundamentalists take the other. Let us revert, however, to administrative illustrations and consider the archetypal administrative decisions of hiring and firing.

Where an organization member is hired on the essential basis of affective preference, because he seems to be a nice fellow, or because she will improve the office ambience, then it is Type III. Such patrimonial and arbitrary decisions would be rare in any complex or bureaucratic organization and instead there would be an attempt to achieve some degree of overt rationality. At the very least there would probably be a search for consensus on the candidate (through the cross-verification of preferences in a search committee, or by more informal 'soundings') and the decision would thus be raised to the level of IIB. More likely still the process would be embellished by deliberate scrutiny of credentials and some sort of cost-benefit analysis of fitting potential candidates to the role. When this is done a degree of rationality may be achieved sufficient to label the decision as IIA and, indeed, one could make the case that this is perhaps the modal level within modern organizations. Which is not to say that many ostensible IIA hirings are not in fact expressions of IIB and even III emotive preference. When, in addition to the foregoing, and subsuming these levels of valuation, elements of principle are introduced such as, say, a man's ideological status in the Soviet context, or scholastic standing and excellence in an academic context, and these matters of principle become overriding in the value calculus, then the appointment decision is Type I.

Consider in this regard the appointment (or promotion) of a Pope. The College of Cardinals is totally engaged as a search committee. Elements of Type III preference are subsumed in the search for Type IIB consensus and this in turn is subsumed into the Type IIA deliberations about the prospective impact of a candidate on the total organization. Finally, the cardinals invoke faith and conceptualize the final phase of the value logic as the Holy Spirit operating through the political process and the individual searchings of conscience. An extreme but instructive illustration of a Type I administrative decision.

The logic applies similarly to the firing or dismissal process. A Minister of the Crown is removed from office (actual case) because he has been travelling by air economy class and pocketing the difference between this and the first class fare to which his rank entitled him. Surely a venial and trivial offence. But the principle of Caesar's wife is used as the ostensible ground for his public (Type I) dismissal by his cabinet and political colleagues. Ministers should be seen to be without stain or blemish! Of course, to shift from actual to hypothetical, it may have been the case that the *real* reason for firing was concern for the party's prospects in the next election (Type IIA) or simply group displeasure, enmity and negative affect (Type IIB). Again it could be argued that the modal level in modern organizations is IIA and this could be reinforced by the omnipresence of grievance procedures and job security provisions which demand defensible *reasons* whenever dismissal or letting go occurs. Unions, guilds and professional associations will not normally countenance incompatibility (IIB or III) as a ground for firing and so the pro forma practice of window-dressing administrative decisions of this type is now well entrenched. An effort is invariably made to come up with 'reasons' which at least give a surface appearance of IIA justification; and, again, none of which is to say that the sophisticated executive will not be able to discern the IIB and III valuations which are subsumed (or which may be the 'real reasons') in the overtly IIA or I firing deposition.

It is also interesting and suggestive to consider colloquial rationales from the standpoint of value analysis: 'He's abrasive and arrogant but he's what our organization really needs' versus 'He's a really nice guy but we had to let him go'. The executive dismissal of General MacArthur by President Truman would appear to span all four levels of the paradigm from the Type I principle of the integrity of the constitutional office of President of the United States ('The buck stops here') through Type II political-rational considerations (MacArthur was a potential candidate himself) to Type III affect ('I told the son of a bitch he was fired').

Throughout these illustrations it should be noted that it is the dominant characteristic of the decision, the salient valuational stress or emphasis, which determines the level of assignment in the value typology. Once again the possibilities for typing errors are rampant but clarity of analysis demands that the true level of value be discovered for each of the critical values entering into a decision calculus.

MOTIVATION

If there is one concept which can compete with value in

generating intellectual distress and philosophical confusion it is probably that of motivation.[2] In the organizational literature much theorizing and endless empiricizing has been devoted to this topic (Steers and Porter, 1975). It constitutes the theme and focus of much of the journal literature and dwarfs by comparison the study of values. Indeed it overshadows to the point of invisibility the topic of ethics and morals when this is even considered worthy of study at all by administrative aspirants, theorists and practitioners. Why this anomaly?

Probably because empirical behavioural science is more at ease with a concept like motivation which has at least a connotation of driving or being driven (and hence a suggestion of determinism) than with a concept like value which, sooner or later, implies a freedom of actors to choose, and hence introduces a factor of uncertainty and indeterminism which is antagonistic to the project of predictive science. Motivation has deterministic overtones and augurs more positively for the possibility of control in human affairs. But we must beware of the lust for simplification, the tendencies to reduction and the homogenetic fallacy. Human nature is clearly mixed. It is obviously susceptible to much motivational determinism; it can often be overdetermined; but still it retains the possibility of being free.

The value paradigm subsumes and transcends motivational analysis. It permits us to dispense with the motivation terminology. This is so because motivation can be treated as a *source* of values. A fund from which concepts of the desirable can be drawn, or a spring from which they can be thought to well up. Thus Type III values may derive from the unconscious dynamics of depth psychology. Or from simple hedonics — the innate tendency to seek pleasure and avoid pain. Type II values can flow from the 'motivation' to rational analysis or collective judgement, much of which if not all may indeed be social conditioning. And Type I values can be said to emerge from a uniquely human motivation towards transrational commitment. (It is at this point that

---

[2] See R. S. Peters (1960) for a definitive philosophical analysis.

the hard-line behaviourist would become distinctly uncomfortable.) Again, to take the Freudian obsession, there is no question about the omnipresence of the primal urge but this motivational drive can translate out at all levels of the desire paradigm. As hedonic gratification behaviour (Level III), as all manner of stylized mating rituals from sock hops to coming out parties (Level IIB), as legalized prostitution (Level IIA), and as the practice of clerical celibacy (Level I). It should be clear from this illustration alone that the concept of motivational impulse *per se* is not refined enough for value analysis and at the most general level this critique can be launched against all the grand reductionists and motivational theorists. Marx and Freud committed the homogenetic fallacy. In the last analysis all is neither sex nor power nor property, though the associated psychological drives unquestionably provide us with primary and major sources of our complex value orientations and patterns of the desirable. In our discourse motives can be treated as subsumed, explicitly or implicitly, within the concept of values.

A further complexity is added, however, by the status of motivation (rather than values) in the administrative and organizational literature. This probably derives from the identification of the executive role with leadership, and all the confusions this concept in turn is heir to. Conventionally, this leads to an emphasis on the administrator's responsibility to 'motivate' his subordinates. His essential task is often seen as that of maintaining a kind of hedonic balance of trade within his organization or, as Barnard would put it, maintaining an economy of incentives such that organization members would choose to remain in rather than leave the co-operative system (Georgiu, 1973:300, Barnard, 1972:93).

There is truth to this picture of organizational life as there is truth to the principles of economic science but the realities tend to frustrate simplistic explanation. Given a real freedom to move between and within organizational envelopes — a possibility immediately contradicted in a condition of neo-feudalism — then there would certainly be an inter- and intraorganizational market of motivational forces tending always towards some hypothetical state of equilibrium at which the motivational price tag for any given class of organizational member, including administrators, could be determined. But such theorizing is not helpful even if the perils of reductionism and the homogenetic fallacy are avoided. The push-pull of affective striving in the organizational market-place is a partial truth. The philosopher Barrett has recently argued that 'the sense of meaning is the primary fact in motivation' (1979:293) and the motivational literature itself acknowledges the operative presence of so-called higher motivations. For administrators this is exemplified in the work of Herzberg (1959, 1966) and Maslow (1954, 1968).

Maslow's famous needs theory postulates an hierarchically ordered set of human motivational needs ranging from the lowest level of physiological and security needs through higher level needs for social acceptance and status to a highest level need for self-actualization; a quasi-mystical state of affairs in which 'peak experiences' occur and all the potentialities of the individual are maximized.[3] Similarly, though without Maslow's apex of self-actualization, Herzberg distinguishes between lower level and higher level needs. The former he calls hygiene needs, embracing such organizational aspects as supervision, pay and working conditions, while the latter he terms motivating needs: promotion, achievement, responsibility, challenge and the like. The parallel between such motivational schemas and the value paradigm is indicated in figure 5. In general the argument of motivational theorists tends to rest upon the hierarchical assumption that lower level needs must be satisfied before higher level needs can emerge. One cannot be a philosopher while one has toothache. Needs must when the devil drives, and so on. In terms of the value paradigm, however, the interpretation is more subtle and difficult. The assumption here is rather of dialectical tension, continuously between the socially generated Type II values and the individually seated self-indulgent Type III values; occasionally between Type I and lower levels.

---

[3] See Low (1976) for a further sophistication of this hierarchy to which he brings insights from both Zen philosophy and management practice.

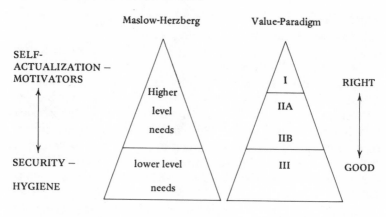

FIGURE 5   Motivation and values

All men who are neither saints nor psychopaths nor super-men experience this first type of phenomenological tension between what is moral or right or socially approved and what it is that they would rather do. Moreover, man is a rational as well as a social animal and the same dialectical tension constantly reveals itself in the internal interplay between the affective and cognitive sides of our nature. Type I values are more difficult. Their character is trans-rational. In theory they need not occur within an individual's value system but when and if they do they inform that system with a power of override. That is, they have a dominant character of hegemony by which they tend to subordinate, realign and synthesize lower-type values and their contending motivations within the individual form of life. Saul on the road to Damascus acquired a Type I value commitment and experienced the phenomenon of religious conversion. (All authentic religious or secular 'conversions' imply an infusion of Type I values.) Type I values entail deep-seated commitment and powerfully determined motivation. When they are present in a field of action the value calculus is radicalized. Motivation, as it were, becomes supercharged and reason may become subservient to intuition.

From what has been said it follows that the terminologies of motivation and value are to some extent interchangeable and reinforcing. To avoid confusion, however, the discourse of this text will for the most part be confined to the language of value rather than that of motivation, it being understood that motives are sources or originating factors in our value systems. They can be taken as elements which are subsumed within the general language game of values.

PRAXIS

What was always implicit should now be explicitly clear. The field of executive action and the administrative endeavour which embraces it make philosophical demands. It is the highest function of the executive to develop a deep understanding of himself and his fellows, a knowledge of human nature which includes motivation but reaches beyond it into the domain of value possibilities. After all, the very stuff of the administrative fabric, the warp and woof of organizational life, is protoplasmic — human nature in all its rich diversity, complexity and frequent simplicity. Administrators are voyeurs extraordinary.

Of course, different kinds of men will come to the role of administrator, men with different characters and characteristics; men, that is to say, with different patterns of values. And their roles will be embedded in different types of organizational context, again with different patterns of values. But whatever the variations of context and role, the philosophical theme will persist and certain philosophical skills will be desirable and appropriate even for rudimentary survival. At its lowest level, organizational life is a sort of daily combat. Even here, however, the deadliest weapons in the administrative armoury are philosophical: the skills of logical and critical analysis, conceptual synthesis, value analysis and commitment, the powers of expression in language and communication, rhetoric and, most fundamentally, the depth understanding of human nature. So in the end philosophy becomes intrinsically practical. The cartography it provides becomes the administrator's most vital navigational aid. But skill in the use of this armamentarium does not come automatically. It is far more likely (with one proviso) to be acquired through experience and the natural acquisition of seniority. For this reason there may well be wisdom, and a sort of natural justice in the practice — once universal but now most obvious in Japan — of promotion on the sole basis of seniority. The proviso, of course, is that experience be consciously reflective and not the mere passage of time.

It is here that Aristotle has taught us a valuable lesson, a lesson which, strangely, seems to have been forgotten in the West but one which urgently needs to be relearned. It is that man has three distinctive ways of knowing; three approaches to the world, three modes of action. They are *theoria, techné*, and *praxis. Theoria* or theory represents our knowing function in its purest form as it seeks to abstract, generalize, induce and deduce from a world of sense data which is given and which needs to be explained. It is this state of mind which has dominated in the search for first principles. In its higher reaches it offers the prospect of *sophia*, that transcendent wisdom of which *philo*sophy is supposed to be the lover. Nevertheless, this crowning glory which has done so much, which has given us science and explored the limits of cosmic and microcosmic space, which has unravelled so much of our chemical nature, has yet failed to provide us with the theory of action or the theories of organization and administration.

What theory has endowed us with most lavishly is *techné*, the mode of knowing which yields productive arrangements of matter and material, indeed, all the arts, crafts and products of man. From this root stems technics, technique, technology, applied science, applied theory. From this cognitive mode comes so much of the structure and quality of modern life; from moonshots to multimedia, from periodontics to pantyhose. Technology liberates as it constrains, imprisons as it frees, seems to possess the peculiar capability of delimiting our horizons at the same time as it expands them, promises the stars then locks us in our bureaucratic cells. In Aristotle's thought *techné* gave rise to *poiesis* which was a way of treating the reality of the sense world so that artifacts, objects and constructs were produced. Its exponent was *homo faber*, the productive or creative man: man as artist and artisan and, nowadays, man as applied scientist, technologist, manager, auditor, accountant and clerk.

These distinctions are commonplace and well understood. In fact they have become oversubscribed with the dichotomy between theory and practice so well entrenched in modern society that it has led to some dangerous divisions in professional life between theorist and practitioner, researcher and developer, academic cloister and field experience, planner and public and, of course, in our terms between administrator and manager. Such divisions can lead to worse than mere failure of communication but they stem from a failure of conception. What is missing here is Aristotle's third term, *praxis*.

No direct equivalent exists in the English language for this term but it deserves a better fate than to have been appropriated solely by the Marxists where it is understood as action with reflection (that is, with the right ideological consciousness). Aristotle intended the term to mean ethical action in a political context or, simply, purposeful human conduct which would be an amalgam of theory (rationality, science) and values (morals, emotions, ethics). *Praxis* was thus a complex and subtle but none the less essential concept. It suggests a duality in action, two 'moments' of consciousness or reflection on the one hand and behaviour and commitment on the other. The contemporary contrast between behaviour and action comes close to this distinction but is cruder and more dualistic. Behaviour is discernible movement while action is movement with identified intent. Strict behaviourists might see no need for any present or potential voluntarism in this distinction but the concept of praxis would insist upon some freedom of choice at the phenomenological level. Praxis would then imply the conscious reflective intentional action of man. Applied to administration it would mean the combination of management science with ethics and value theory. In the model of figure 3 above it would refer with especial force to the bridging sector of administrative process, that which linked administration to management in the general sense and politics to mobilizing in the particular sense. Praxis is thus a concept uniquely applicable to administration: it could be regarded as the quintessence of administration. But it is a concept which would make intellectual and spiritual demands and perhaps this is why it has become lost to usage. Its principal demands would be within the domains of consciousness and values and about these topics much more has yet to be said. In the end, however, praxis is what must be explicated because it is the true link between theory and practice, *theoria* and *techné*. It is, as is administration, philosophy-in-action.

Considerable attention has been given in this chapter to the problem of value. This accords with the Aristotelian notion of praxis. Praxis can be conceived as part of a *theory of practice* (Culbertson *et al.*, 1981) which would have two divisions, the first a retrospective and inductive treatment of the realities of administrative cases, which would be called analysis, and the second a prospective and deductive treatment of the realities of administrative futures, which would be called praxis. The value paradigm presented in this chapter is intended as a conceptual tool both for analysis and for praxis. The need for such a valuational approach to administration is intensified in an era of pluralism and value confusion which is at the same time an era of intensifying organizational feudalism. Increasingly the quality of individual life is organizationally determined and this renders philosophy of administration all the more imperative. In the next three chapters, we shall make use of the paradigm as an analytical principle for the study of organizational contexts and thereafter for the study of administrative forms of life. Taken together these sets of stages and actors comprise the total range of praxis possibilities and prepare the foundation upon which a philosophical theory of commitment can be constructed.

3
Realities

THE REALITY PRINCIPLE

Life is, in fact, a battle...Evil is insolent and strong; beauty
enchanting but rare; goodness very apt to be weak; folly very
apt to be defiant; wickedness to carry the day; imbeciles to be
in great places, people of sense in small, and mankind generally,
unhappy. But the world as it stands is no illusion, no phantasm,
no evil dream of a night; we wake up to it again for ever and
ever; we can neither forget it nor deny it nor dispense with it.
(Henry James)

The James quote is neither hyperbole nor morbidity. It is
literature and truth. Not the whole truth of course but an
important part of it and perhaps the most fundamental part.
Also a part which we would rather ignore, elide or forget. A
stranger on the planet would have difficulty in finding evidence of this side of organizational life if he were to confine
himself to the orthodox literature where, for the most part,
it passes without mention. As if it were enough to have
daily to experience ennui, frustration, anger, defeat and
occasionally pure evil and malevolence without having also
to write about them and incorporate them in the technical
or scientific literature. Because of this we should begin our
philosophical journey at the point of lowest ebb. If philosophy means the examined life then we should examine all
that goes to form that life. Especially should we hone our
remembrance of the harsher realities. Philosophy begins in
the dirt.

None of this commits us to a naively negative position on human nature; nor to pessimism about organization and administration. It simply serves as a logical and righteous point of departure. If we can get beyond it, fine. If not, *tant pis*. At all events we shall have done our philosophical duty.

To begin with, the affective experience of life in organizations is also in accord with the value paradigm. At its lowest level this is hedonic, men seek to gain pleasure and avoid pain. Or, to put it otherwise, they seek to maximize their own welfare within a set of game rules or constraints such as the one provided by the organization to which they owe their allegiance and within which they play out their games. If one accepts this assumption — that they are in it for what they can get out of it — then the utility function this implies can be looked at in various ways. Sardonically, it can lead to an ethics of the trough. Life, played out through the forms of organizational careers, is a struggle, by hand and mind, of each against all for a better place at the trough, a better share of the rewards-system pie, a ruthless but covert pursuit of self-interest within the organization game, a steady and relentless effort to maximize perquisites, power and status, which ends only with ultimate expulsion from the organization by dismissal or retirement (or else by transfer, voluntary or forced, to another organizational context where James's battle continues). When Clausewitz stated that war is a continuation of policy by other means he implied that the condition of institutional peace was warfare on a normal scale.

Before writing off these views as overdrawn, or accusing James of middle-aged anhedonia, or pleading guilty to the charge of overweening cynicism, it might be as well to consider the formidable strength of the arguments from the negative. These, after all, have been encapsulated and enshrined in the Buddha's First Noble Truth: life is suffering. And to the naive counter that life also contains pleasures and delights, the Buddhist responds that all pleasures are themselves tainted sources of suffering for they are transient, fleeting, consummated only in the knowledge that they are passing, leaving behind as traces only the seeds of craving for painful repetition. It is of some passing interest, too, that the Lord Buddha commenced his career as an administrative cadet but refused steadfastly to found an organization or to make any organizational commitment at the end of his great philosophical experiment. His followers, of course, being lesser men, proceeded forthwith, as did those of Jesus Christ, to establish notably successful forms of organization. But this is not yet the place for us to consider the implications of Buddhist logic for organizations, though it may be appropriate for us to recognize the profundity of the First Noble Truth. At the least, there is a reasonable likelihood that it does bear organizational and administrative implications. If unhappiness is the normal condition of man then this norm surely deserves administrative recognition. A recognition not to my knowledge conceded by any of the contemporary authorities in the field with the possible exception of Argyris who at times appears to argue convincingly that human personalities and human organizations are fundamentally incompatible (1957, 1964, 1973:141).

Most authorities, however, appear to assume an essential benevolence about organizational life and at least a presumption that costs to the ego are outweighed by benefits to the collectivity through goal accomplishment and capital growth (Handy, 1976; Katz and Kahn, 1978; Likert, 1967; McGregor, 1967). Administrators likewise tend to be portrayed in the orthodox literature in unrealistic terms. The classical school tends to have them either as moral neuters (Simon, 1965; Weber, 1947, 1956) or as moral paragons (Barnard, 1966; Drucker, 1967; Vickers, 1965). The modern school, with its emphasis on human relations or 'resources' tends to portray them as a sort of moral chameleon. Democratic leaders brimming with energy and creative problem-solving skills (Miles, 1975). All of these stereotypes carry truth but none can be fairly considered in isolation from organizational context and it is to the realities of this that we must now turn. What is there in the infinite variety of organizational life which can be distilled into general statements that can serve as ground for philosophy? Let us begin with the negative, the affective, and some of the Type III aspects of organizational reality.

ORGANIZATIONAL EVIL

That organizations can be construed as moral primitives has been explained at length elsewhere (Hodgkinson, 1978: 171ff). The crux of the argument is that only an individual can possess consciousness and will. Only an individual can experience value. What passes then as group decisions and collective judgements and actions are at best pseudo-conscious, quasi-willful and typologically distinct with respect to value (see chapter 2). It follows that organizations *qua* organizations cannot be morally responsible. Nevertheless organizations are collectively more powerful than individuals and they do act in the world. Though such action be directed to ostensibly benevolent ends its potential for corruption cannot be ignored. Perhaps the most vehement case has been made by Simone Weil. She takes as her starting point the fact that man in a state of nature would be at his least free, because in primitive conditions he would be driven to satisfy his elemental needs at the mercy of natural forces. He would be in slavery to an environment beyond his control or power to command. He would be determined rather than determining.[1] But evolution and the course of history tend to ensure that man will enlarge his degrees of freedom, in the sense of control over his natural environment, by means of co-operative enterprise and ever more complex forms of collective effort and organization, culminating in the inventions of the nation state and modern bureaucracies in the public, private and international sectors. Nature is at last vanquished or, at least, multiple levels of organization and culture are interposed between ordinary man and the brute realities of nature. Yet paradoxically, Weil would argue, one form of oppression has been merely exchanged for another, where man the administrator, the ruler, the executive has become the new oppressor:

[1]　See Sahlins, 1972, for the contrary anthropological position.

In short, wherever, in the struggle against men or against nature,
efforts need to be multiplied and co-ordinated to be effective,
co-ordination becomes the monopoly of a few leaders as soon
as it reaches a certain degree of complexity, and execution's
primary law is then obedience; this is true both for the management of public affairs and for that of private undertakings. There
may be other sources of privilege, but these are the chief ones;
furthermore, except in the case of money, which appears at a
given moment of history, all these factors enter into play under
all systems of oppression; what changes is the way in which they
are distributed and combined, the degree of concentration of
power, and also the more or less closed and consequently more
or less mysterious character of each monopoly. Nevertheless,
privileges, of themselves, are not sufficient to cause oppression.
Inequality could be easily mitigated by the resistance of the
weak and the feeling for justice of the strong; it would not lead
to a still harsher form of necessity than that of natural needs
themselves, were it nor for the intervention of a further factor,
namely, the struggle for power. (Weil, 1965:504)

That is, man first overcomes nature by organization. But
organizations are hierarchical power structures. And power
is corrupting. So:

Power, by definition, is only a means; or to put it better, to
possess a power is simply to possess means of action which
exceed the very limited force that a single individual has at his
disposal. But power-seeking, owing to its essential incapacity
to seize hold of its object, rules out all consideration of an end,
and finally comes, through an inevitable reversal, to take the
place of all ends. It is this reversal of the relationship between
means and end, it is this fundamental folly that accounts for all
that is senseless and bloody right through history. Human history
is simply the history of the servitude which makes men — oppres-
sors and oppressed alike — the plaything of the instruments of
domination they themselves have manufactured, and thus reduces
living humanity to being the chattel of inanimate chattels. (Weil,
1965:508)

Which is, of course, to put it rather strongly, probably too
strongly. Men are not intrinsically or innately evil as a species,
but as a species they are perhaps subject to a sort of second

law of moral thermodynamics which tends to become especially visible in certain organizational forms of life. Experience of this reality can be registered from a number of standpoints.

Firstly the individual experience of organization membership means, even in the very best of worlds, a loss of autonomy. The voluntary joining of any organization entails a psychological contract. In exchange for a presumptive net benefit the joiner agrees to forgo certain privileges such as complete control over his own time and what is otherwise an independence of authority. The notion is summed up in Barnard's concept of a zone of indifference and Simon's equivalent zone of acceptance. Within these zones the organization member obeys without question, and ceases, strictly speaking, to be an effectively free moral agent. (He might of course restore his moral autonomy by constantly subjecting his zone to critical reflection and review but this would be to subvert the whole point of organizational hegemony which is simply to remove the very need for any such inefficient, ineffective and authority-threatening review in the first place.)

In the mythical market-place of economic theory there would be a freedom to trade in psychological contracts and to establish equity and equilibrium through an interplay of organization-member supply and demand. But this is the stuff of theory not reality. In reality the facts are that, however and by whatever means the individual came to the organization, once he is in he is subject to a sudden inelasticity of commitment. One is reminded of the romantic recruiting pitch for the French Foreign Legion which went, Join the Foreign Legion and Forget! To seek release after entry upon the grounds that one had forgotten was unlikely to result in a termination of contract. Similarly the romantic rebel who joins a terrorist organization such as the IRA is likely to find that his zone of acceptance has been arbitrarily expanded to the point of near-complete loss of autonomy with or without his consent.

Even in the most innocuous of organizations circumstances rapidly combine to overdetermine the new recruit's zone of acceptance. Constraints multiply. Autonomy dwindles. If he is lucky he will be left to dwell at or near the centre of his zone of indifference. But it will be the rare case, and the rarer with ascent of the hierarchy, that the individual is not pushed to or across the boundaries of his zone in some sort of moral compromise or adjustment of Type I or II values. When that occurs it follows that one of the easier modes of psychological adjustment is to reduce or eliminate any value dissonance by conscious or unconscious extension of the area of one's zone of indifference or acceptance. And so the organizational impress can grow until, in the extreme case, it is not mine to question why. My organization, like my country, right or wrong! The study of numerous case histories in public administration and elsewhere support the general notion of organizational impress as a potent and submoral force. The metavalues discussed in the previous chapter provide a theoretical basis to substantiate such ideas.

Secondly, it is not only the individual member of an organization who is subjected to the collective or bureaucratic impress. Organizational clients also experience from time to time a frustration of their egos and an overriding of their personally perceived claims to special service, concessions or attentions. Hence the common-language, pejorative sense of 'bureaucracy' and such epithets as 'red tape' Such experiences are too familiar a part of modern life to require elaboration. Certainly in and of itself this general frustration of the ego is not evil — particularly when from a third observer's standpoint the collective is right and the individual is less right — but it can give rise to a sort of evil through a void of sympathy or compassion at the organizational level. Organizations are not conscious. They cannot feel. Though potent they are faceless. And this, in turn, gives rise to a reactive version of neurosis at the individual level which Thompson labels *bureausis* (1961:170ff). This latter kind of personal response to organizational reality can lead to violence and antisocial aggression along with other varieties of human malfunctioning. Once again, with or without justification, the organization is experienced as *oppressive*.

Thirdly, the experience of evil can become a stark reality

within the executive suite on those occasions, should they arise, when an administrator's Type I values are threatened or contravened. The conflict thus engendered can be severe enough to force the administrator's resignation or else initiate a power struggle of proportions massive enough to change the face and character of the organization. Martin Luther's break with his organizational hierarchy is a classical instance of this, but common experience informs us that organizations can be felt as morally primitive and oppressive at less than the Type I level. Typical are the day to day pressures of group decision making, collegial arm-twisting and political expediency which would surely contribute to a sense of moral queasiness were that not so easily and at once suppressed by the bromides of the pragmatic pharmocopoeia always ready to hand. Politics is the art of the possible. Live and let live. If you can't beat 'em, join 'em. *Chacun à son goût.* Business is business. Get through the day.

Lastly, the general experience of organization dysfunctions is well attested and documented under the general heading of bureaupathology (Thompson, 1961:152; 1976:90, 92; Crozier, 1964; Blau and Scott, 1962; Etzioni, 1964 *inter alia*). This subject need not be enlarged upon here. It may suffice to note that the accomplishment of organizational goals is inevitably accompanied by (a) side effects of process which are foreseen and unforeseen and which may be benevolent or maleficent and (b) side effects of product or result which are subject to the same strictures. Purposive actions are like drugs; there are always side effects, and these are compounded as the complexity of the field of action is enhanced. Yet collectives legitimately subsume individual interests under a general goal paradigm (Georgiu, 1973). The trade-off for a general efficacy in goal accomplishment inevitably entails some loss of human quality in the workplace. At its worst this loss can be psychologically destructive but more probably it is psychologically abrasive. The abrasion is intensified the more organizations approach the extreme of morally primitive, goal-seeking golems (Ladd, 1970).

THE ORGANIZATIONAL IMPERATIVE

Given the above discussion it might seem that wisdom would at least lead to caution and sensitivity in our organizational arrangements; yet there is stronger evidence of the contrary. Scott and Hart (1979:43-6), who have shown how organizations are increasingly dominant in our lives, have analyzed the concept of the organizational imperative. This is specified as being made up of two propositions and three ethical values. The two propositions are: 'Whatever is good for the individual can only come from the modern organization,' and therefore, 'All behaviour must enhance the health of such organizations.' The three ethical rules are: the rule of rationality (the task of administration is to maximize efficiency defined as the ratio of output to input); the rule of stewardship (administrators owe primary loyalty to the organizational imperative, that is, their first obligation is feudal fealty); and the rule of pragmatism (administrators must be expedient and must focus on short-term reality to the exclusion of long-term idealism).

The result of subscription to this philosophical aggregate is deep-seated commitment to rationality, managerial efficiency, organizational culture and values, in-group membership and pragmatic factoring of problems down to the 'engineering' or technical level. In our terms, that is, a general withdrawal from the administrative towards the managerial end of the spectrum. This tendency, Scott and Hart would argue, is now endemic in American culture. It has led to a wholesale shift from individualistic values (belief in an innate and fixed human nature, individuality, individual indispensability, community, spontaneity and voluntarism) to the values of the organizational imperative and Organizational America (belief in infinite human malleability, obedience, individual dispensability, specialization, planning and paternalism). In other words the culture of the new feudalism is materialistic, positivistic, conformist and scientific (or in a single word, bureaucratic).

More support for the general thesis of organizational

imperative is to be found in the brilliant series of experiments conceived and conducted by Stanley Milgram (1963; 1965; 1974). In passing, it can be noted that these experiments are non-repeatable, having been conducted in the period just before the professional ethics of social psychology changed so as to prohibit such deception of human subjects. In brief, what happened was that naive subjects were required to administer supposed electric shocks to a supposed victim upon command of various authorities. The victim was a confederate of the experimenters. The research appeared to show conclusively that a willingness to obey figures of authority in an organizational hierarchy was much greater than had been supposed. In other words the zones of indifference and acceptance were substantially large, administrators had a most significant power base, and the overriding of ordinary moral scruples could easily be accomplished in an organizational context. Approximately two-thirds of all subjects (conflating differences across experiments) committed normally intolerable acts of violence upon their fellows. Such a finding can be read two ways. The pessimists about human nature will deplore the implication that two-thirds did not appear to have a conscience while the optimists will applaud the result as proof that conscience exists since a third of the subjects successfully resisted the experimental persuasion. (The true interpretation is probably less black or white than either of these alternatives since even among those subjects who went 'all the way', shocking the victim beyond the point of danger to life, there were considerable affective misgivings and after-the-fact evidence of some sort of struggle with conscience or scruple.)

Whatever the interpretation which is placed upon the Milgram studies by philosophers it is important to consider the conclusion of the researcher himself. Professor Milgram was led in the end to postulate what he calls an *agentic state.* This is a psychological set or condition into which a subordinate rapidly falls when placed in a context of formal organization. It is a condition of ready obedience and willingness to be commanded. All that seems to be required is that the trappings and attitudes of authority and office are appropriately presented. These trappings include all the outward and visible signs of formal organization, symbols and badges of rank, a hierarchy of command, power and authority...even the mere capacity to assume an authoritative posture and speak with an authoritative voice. Man falls easily into the agentic state because, it can be supposed, the history of the species has time and again reinforced the greater survival capacity of the collective over that of the individual. Man, unlike cat, is a social animal. From hominid to *Homo sapiens* he has survived through cultural means. There is, therefore, a strong suggestion of bio-ethical merit in submissiveness to authority. Indeed, our entire culture and civilization rests upon a presumption of legitimacy in our institutions. Formal organizations from superstates to kibbutzim are the constituents of our reality, and therefore all formally identified functionaries from meter maids to kings induce a spontaneous reflex of subservience. This is a fact of great significance for those who are concerned with the actual design of power-authority systems, that is, administrators. The experimental evidence of agentic state is clearly an important factor in such design. In the event of emergency such as war or crisis this factor can be overwhelming and in the conditions of neo-feudalism or Organizational America it can be overdetermining. What then is its moral significance?

To put it simply, it is easy to accept authority, easy to design the façade of authority, easier to obey than disobey, easy to seduce commitment, easier to slip by stages from passive condonation to taking the line of least resistance, to the compromise of reason and principle (see discussion in chapter 7 on the degeneracy of value) to, in the end, active participation in organizational wrongdoing, malevolence and evil. And easiest of all is to overlook the existence of this slippery slope, for not to see it is a standard ego defence mechanism. All the more then that administrators ought not to ignore it. It is but one of many organizational pathologies to which they should become sensitive. These pathologies are legion. They stem from human nature itself. That nature is not fully or properly understood but it can be conceded, at the Type III level at least, that the historical record alone gives conclusive evidence of aggressiveness, malice and vice (together with more positive qualities, of course, but they are not our concern here). These negative attributes are compounded and magnified in the organizational setting for the simple reason that organizations are foci of power and repositories of power, property and status. Set against organization, the individual dwindles to minute proportions, to inconsequence, invisibility and impotence.

At the macro- or organizational level the useful term 'bureaupathology' has been coined to refer to those things which can go wrong when ostensibly benevolent and rational complex organizations set out to function and accomplish their purposes in the real world (Thompson, 1961:152). Technically, the term seeks to identify and describe those dysfunctions which are commonly associated in the public mind with the pejorative sense of bureaucracy: bigness leading to inertial inflexibility, obsolescence, impersonality, intraorganizational and interorganizational imperialism, and so *ad nauseam*. Dickens expressed his perception of the problem in Victorian times through his entertaining description of the Office of Circumlocution. Kafka took a much more sinister view and in general the expression of antagonistic sentiment about complex organizations has continued unabated as the Orwellian deadline of 1984 approaches. Indeed the consensus of the arts about the organizational imperative is striking both in its consistency and its negativity. Clearly there is some reality there which tends to threaten and offend artistic sensibilities. That this reality might be grounded in Type III affectivity does not, of course, suggest any conclusiveness of argument. The Type II arguments for the efficiency and effectiveness of classical Weberian bureaucracy are, on the contrary, overpoweringly persuasive, but in the value conflict between Type II rationality and Type III affect it is clear where the lines are drawn between spokesmen of the humanities and the proponents of political practice.

We need not here examine the plethora of bureaupathologies.

It is enough to acknowledge their existence and ubiquity. But one of them can perhaps be singled out because of its central importance to administrative philosophy. It has to do with the problem of generalism — and administrators, let us remember, can be said to have made a specialty of generalism. Organizations are hierarchical power structures. The conception of power and authority is conventionally pyramidal and is loosely expressed in the theoretical notion of line and staff. The classical power hierarchy is the administrative *line* of command which runs from apex to base of the organization, carrying veto power with it all the way. In Scott and Hart's terms it runs from the significant people of the executive suite via the professional ranks of staff expertise through to the insignificant people of the lower organizational echelons (1979:95ff). Now, traditionally the lowest ranks were made up of workers with general or undifferentiated skills but in a technological society, where even private soldiers tend to be specialized, this classical pattern no longer holds true. The quality and quantity of specialization increases with ascent of the hierarchy, particularly at the staff or professional levels. These strata tend to be occupied by organization members with a special kind of power, the power of expertise which is sanctioned by some sort of professional cachet. In other words this power is kept exclusive by means of professional or guild credentials. Such power holders can often be 'cosmopolitans' (Gouldner, 1957:281) whose feudal allegiance to the organization may be suspect when contrasted with the local affiliation to the organization of both the significant and insignificant people. This gives rise to a very general source of conflict where the expertise required to perform the organizational tasks rests with the *staff* while the power of command and veto rests with the *line*. Executive authority is thus dependent on the acquiesence of lower levels of hierarchy and this creates the potential for a variety of pathologies not the least of which is dramaturgy or role-playing (Thompson, 1961: 58ff, 138). Such a divergence — inevitable under modern technology — between the myths and the realities of power and authority is perhaps the most significant and ominous of the defects concealed under the organizational imperative.

NEGATIVITIES

In addition to the bureaupathologies which are manifest at the macro-level there are, of course, the infinity of psycho-pathologies which inhere in the individual as an attribute of human nature and which manifest themselves at the micro-level. Even to enumerate the latter would be a vexing task but it were best to leave such work to specialists such as clinical philosophers of administration and those social and political scientists who have a bent for such sordid exploration. It is certainly not work for the tender-minded nor for the squeamish and perhaps that is why in modern times it has not been systematically and comprehensively undertaken. Our task here, however, is not to present the full compendium of administrative malfunctions attributable to defects of character. That kind of encyclopedia would range from the managerial lapse (a snow plough is ordered to clear the runway; the sense meant is *get off* the runway; the operator interprets it as get the *snow* off the runway; a plane crash results; lives are lost; true case) to pure forms of administrative malevolence (the final solution of the Jewish question; true case). One can simply acknowledge the realities of administrative evil which are, after all, common enough to be almost taken for granted in the workaday world.

By way of general illustration let us focus on two ubiquitous examples. These stem from the administrative realities of confidentiality and time constraint. It is widely accepted that both managers and administrators are busy men with heavy workloads, and full, often overfull, schedules and calendars (Mintzberg, 1973:28-38). Whether or not such a pace and rhythm really and truly ought to be need not be questioned now. What matters is that the effective result of this common reality conduces to superficiality and its corollary, secrecy. Proper and adequate time and energy are not devoted to problems, proposals, projects and personnel. Instead there is the illusion of concern. Bad policies, plans, decisions and actions frequently result, bad not merely in the organizational sense of inefficient and ineffective but bad also in the moral sense. This is an administrative parallel to Sartre's bad faith and inauthenticity. It is also a sort of Marxian false consciousness wherein the pressed executive deludes himself into thinking that he has an adequate grasp of the subtleties and complexities of the problem situation.[2] Since superficiality cannot be openly acknowledged, elaborate organizational devices are created to disguise it. Behind screens of secretarial and support staff, behind praetorian guards of lieutenants and assistants, behind façades of pomp and circumstance, proper channels and due process, the administrator can project the image of gravity necessary to assure the naive enquirer that all is known that is to be known and all is being done that has to be done. He is, after all, the *leader*, the wise one. But to maintain this façade it is necessary to have a system of organizational confidentiality and administrative secrecy. Administration has its inevitable freemasonry, of course. Communications have to be passed in the faith that discretion will be exercised. Sometimes this is done overtly, 'Eyes only', 'Strictly between you and me'; but often it occurs casually, spontaneously and tacitly, in the corridor, in telephone talk, in a moment snatched at the beginning or end of a meeting, in informal contacts at a conference or convention. Thus old boy networks operate and thus the goodwill and trust requisite to any organizational functioning is built. The danger in all this is that the communication which passes tends to be superficial because of constraints of time and the pressing nature of administrative activity. And the danger in *this* is that such information can and does enter into decision making as a crucial or determining value factor. In this way careers can be determined and fates decided in a furtive or casual or mindless manner. Hannah Arendt has written about the banality of evil and the phrase applies with force to many of the

---

[2] A brilliant and sustained illustration of this pathology is given in Solzhenitsyn's *August 1914* where a staff officer reveals the unwitting inadequacies of his superiors and of the entire administration.

informal exchanges, especially about personalities, which are so common and so functional a part of organizational life that they are simply taken for granted. Often, too, there is a sort of robust *macho* quality to these exchanges which cements the understanding that they occur between hard-nosed movers and shapers of the world, a tough-minded elite without pretensions to intellectualism or culture, these being effete mysteries which would entail administrative impotence and futility. Those who can, do, those who can't, think.

It also commonly goes without saying that executives are ambitious about their own careers. This is not only con-doned, it is admired, even deemed necessary although it is generally expected that this personal characteristic should be palatably disguised. Naked hunger for power and advance-ment should be suitably clothed in socially approved rhetoric. Clever ambition requires social skills and the ability to read or sense values from V_1 to V_6 and Type I to Type III. It also requires more than a modicum of aggression. That modern organizational norms require the concealment of this Type III drive, at least in formal discourse, and since those norms also encourage the display, dramaturgical or otherwise, of calm and cool it is not difficult to trace the psychological syndrome which results in the executive ulcer. More philoso-phically, it is important not to underestimate the possibilities which may combine to induce the discharge of aggressive energies directly against opponents in the settling of scores. The luxury of indulging personal animosities is a lively con-comitant of power. And the exercise of aggression can take many forms — from golf to the guillotine. As Herman Melville remarked, 'Who has but once dined his friends, has tasted whatever it is to be Caesar.' The administrative reality com-mits its actors to much dining, and much besides food to digest.

It is of course facile to sketch by innuendo a portrait of the administrative form of life in which human nature is habitually and pre-eminently corrupt. Machiavelli has done it for all time and in later pages we shall pay homage to him. But the very ease with which this can be done, and the easy acceptance it always seems to command, speaks volumes, to the philosopher at least, about the negativities of the administrative role. Yet, by and large, the orthodox literature on organizations and the administrative profession does not reflect this sense. Self, for example, in a classic contemporary work on public administration acknowledges careerism but concludes in the positive (1972:234-5). Therefore let us merely acknowledge the potential for organizational evil at the micro-level of administrative character and return to the more general macroproblem of organizational oppression.

If organizations are oppressive, or even if they are only perceived to be so, then this negativity can probably be traced to the twin roots of power and instrumentality. The first of these, power, is essential to any form whatsoever of collective organization and Milgram only confirms in the laboratory what philosophers from Plato and Machiavelli to Marx and Lord Acton have long contended, that power can corrupt and oppress. To quote Weil again:

> ...the powerful obtain through persuasion what they are totally unable to obtain by force, either by placing the oppressed in a situation such that they have or think they have an immediate interest in doing what is asked of them, or by inspiring them with a fanaticism calculated to make them accept any and every sacrifice...
>
> The powerful, be they priests, military leaders, kings or capitalists, always believe that they command by divine right; and those who are under them feel themselves crushed by a power which seems to them either divine or diabolical, but in any case supernatural. Every oppressive society is cemented by this religion of power, which falsifies all social relations by enabling the powerful to command over and above what they are able to impose...(Weil, 1965:508)

We need not arrive at Weil's polemical conclusion that 'It would seem that man is born a slave, and that servitude is his natural condition' (510) to acknowledge the negativity she is describing. Within the wisdom of the humanities, if not the social sciences, it has long been recognized that enslaving extends to the powerful as well as the powerless. One can become addicted to the wielding of power and obsessed with its maintenance and acquisition. The *ab*use of power is at once oppressive but so too can be its mere use; yet power is basic to — it is the lifeblood of — administration: therefore the façades of authority, legitimacy, persuasion, influence and credibility which must be carefully erected about it. The justification of these is a central task of administrative philosophy. We must at least know, even if we do not show, why the negative is made to appear positive.

The second root cause of organizational oppressiveness lies in the nomothetic dimension and the V_3 value domain (figure 2 above). The organization is an instrumentality for seeking collective goals. It follows in logic (but at a different level of logical type!) that all organization members, including administrators, are instrumental to the organization. When human beings are treated, and they must be so treated under classical bureaucratic and organization theory, as instruments, objects or things, then more than logical confusion can arise. There can be psychological distress. Psychological reactions might include (1) alienation (see below), (2) dependence (see Argyris, 1973), (3) identification (as, for example, with the stormtrooper at the Nazi mass rally or, more hypothetically, how a Japanese assembly-line worker might feel at the morning singing of his company song — this could also be called the 'hive effect'), (4) impassivity (that is, no reaction at all). All of these reactions can be interpreted as negativities. There is a fifth possibility, *Stoicism*, a cultivated acceptance of our reduced logical status in the scheme and process of things, but this is more philosophically than psychologically grounded and in any event would take cognizance of the negativities just described.

The catalogue of evil given thus far is illustrative and suggestive rather than exhaustive or definitive. It is intended to remind us of realities which must be comprehended within administrative philosophy. Such comprehension would be prerequisite to any sophisticated theory of commitment. One must also acknowledge that for the most part organizations function more than they malfunction and that any social cost-benefit analysis would find a net balance in their favour taken overall. One has to assert with rather less confidence

that administrators are, in the aggregate, more whole than
unholy — the world would be worse than it is were this
not so — but this does not give us *carte blanche* — as it
might seem from the orthodox literature — to withold
scrutiny of ethical and value questions, to be valuationally
neutral and philosophically void.

ORGANIZATIONAL REALITY

Let us continue with our exploration of the negativities.
They form a part, not the whole of reality, but a part which
it is our philosophical duty to observe lest we be charged
with tendermindedness, non-comprehensiveness or a failure
of skeptical nerve. What is meant by *reality*? What is meant
by *organizational* reality?

To ask about the nature of reality is of course to plunge
into the philosophical deeps. Its equivalent is the Roman
administrator Pilate asking, What is truth? Strangely enough,
such metaphysical and arcane questions are very much alive
in what is usually considered to be that most eminently
practical of fields — administration. There is, for example,
in contemporary organization theory a heated and pro-
tracted debate about the ontological foundations of the
discipline. Dichotomous schools have emerged: the orthodox claiming the authority of empirical science and the
heterodox marching under the banner of phenomenology.
The former is perhaps best represented by the prestigious
journal *Administrative Science Quarterly*. A perusal of its
contents over the last quarter of a century would reveal at
once the emphasis on quantitative methodology, empirical
research and statistical analysis, all subsumed within a general
tradition reflecting Frederick W. Taylor's belief in the possibility of scientific management (1915, 1964; Litchfield,
1956). The heterodox position is best represented in
the work of T. Greenfield (1973, 1978a, 1978b, 1980;
Feyerabend, 1975) the flavour of which is caught in such
titles as 'Organizations as Social Inventions', 'Organization
Theory as Ideology', 'Reflections on Organization Theory

and the Truths of Irreconcilable Realities', 'Organizations as Talk, Chance, Action, and Experience'....It is a position which insists on *experience* as the essence of reality while the opposing position subordinates experience to *behaviour*. One position can be characterized as objectivist, the other as subjectivist. The former appeals to the scientific proclivity and asserts that reality exhibits qualities of order, structure, determinism, consistency and predictability within which laws can be discovered and the control of men by man achieved. The latter appeals to the aesthetic proclivity and asserts that the aforementioned qualities are a façade, an appearance, behind which there is a truth which is imponderable in essence, an existential reality which is unique to each individual, which is phenomenological and noumenal, which has as its most distinctive component the possibility of free will. Once free will is admitted to the scheme of things to however slight a degree the camel's head is within the tent. At best one can then seek in human affairs only a moral as opposed to a scientific order. Hence, the control of men by man is never fully achieved and the ultimate goal may become instead the control of man by himself, that is, self-control. Wisdom rather than knowledge, philosophy rather than science, is perceived as the aim of administration. The former school of thought leads to general systems theory and managerialism while the latter does not know where it is heading; the one can dispense with and dispose of the value problem in administration as Simon, Katz and Kahn, and the logical positivists generally, have done, the other is profoundly bothered by problems of will, choice and morality. And, of course, both have profound implications for praxis.

The simplest truth about reality is that it is complex. Both schools would agree on this. Because it is complex, the possibility exists for category mistakes and the confusion of logical types. Much of the conflict between the contending schools of thought on organizational reality would seem to be traceable to logical typing errors. To avoid such errors I would again suggest a triplex analysis. Reality is a triple conflation of three logically distinct categories. We may assign numbers to these categories so as to correlate them with the value types. In this scheme reality III would be the empirical domain of science, the deterministic world of cause and effect, the world of hard edges, tangibilities and the stuff and furniture of experience. Here propositions can be predictive and verifiable, taking the form of 'laws' perhaps, such as $I = E/R$, or $e = mc^2$. It is a reality we all have to live in, and, generally, the more science can tell us about it the better.

The second reality, reality II, would be the appropriate province of social science. Here propositions are less rigorously shaped, more probabilistic, cast in such forms as 'Organizations which have a high degree of goal specificity will have a greater degree of effectiveness than organizations which have a low degree of goal specificity.' Or '$B = f(P,E)$': 'Behaviour is a function of personality and environment,' or, 'If I fail to pay my workers they will cease to contribute to the goals of my enterprise.' In this reality there are degrees of freedom; its realm is only partly determined. It is in part imponderable and the propositions of its 'language' may be called hypothetical. Again, and in general, the more propositions, verified or unfalsified, that social science can deliver about this reality the better.

Finally we must acknowledge and construe reality I, the phenomenological realm of individual experience which, at least in potential, is voluntaristic or free. Its commergence with the shared realities of II and III will produce quite different *mises-en-scène* for the psychotic or for the normal adult, for a child, indeed for any two persons. Propositions touching upon this realm, therefore, while constrained by the 'lower' or 'harder' realities and falsifiable by them, are more evocative or philosophical: they function only through the eye of the beholder and the mind of the reader and are dependent for their ultimate worth and validity upon the value orientation, life experience and phenomenological status of the recipient. They are, as it were, raw material for philosophy, and their function is as much affective as cognitive. We need more propositions and more ordering of propositions at this level. There is at present no philosophy of administration, at best only crude philosophies of success and power; what humanism there is is both inchoate and impotent. And we need to get clear about the language games of the three realities, so that, as Wittgenstein would say, our intelligence is not bewitched by language.

The way in which this logical ordering accords with the general taxonomy of process can be seen in figure 6.

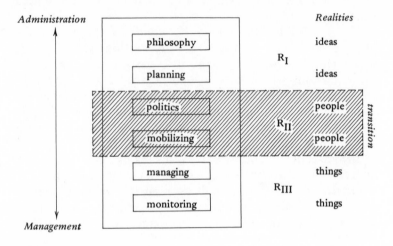

FIGURE 6   *Reality correlates*

Reality, like value, is triplex: (1) *internal*-mental; (2) *internal/external*-social; (3) *external*-material. All of these emerge from a ground of consciousness, variable with the individual, and all, like the Trinity itself, coexistent and, in the last analysis, ineffable. But administrative practice and organizational life cannot deal with the last analysis. In the long run, as Lord Keynes used to say, we are all dead. It's the short run that counts. And a chief characteristic of short-term reality is Type III affect.

ALIENATION AND ANOMIE

The sociologists Cohen and Taylor have thrown an interesting light upon organizational reality in a remarkable study subtitled *The Theory and Practice of Resistance to Everyday Life* (1978). They had set out initially to discover how convicts serving life sentences and long-term prisoners without hope of parole managed to cope with the realities of their enforced institutional life. How did they get through the day? The answer is provocative. In their research they found that people within institutional walls coped in much the same way as people outside those walls. Psychologically speaking, the escape attempts within paralleled the escape attempts without. Or to put it another way, we are all serving a life sentence. The major difference between walled and unwalled servitude is that the paradigm of resistance and escape is more amenable to direct observation in the former, more concentrated situation. We are all confined and oppressed in some way by organizational and institutional life. From the standpoint of the affective ego, life-experience itself can be a frustrating confinement with but limited modes and means of escape. For example: the 'high's' of alcohol, drugs, sex; the anodynes of television, media, conversation and gossip; the 'enclaves' provided by hobbies and holidays, the attitudinal postures of irony and cynicism, perhaps even philosophy and religion. But however and whenever we 'escape' or 'resist' we must always return to the phenomenological reality of the walls of our respective cells. Life is an open prison.

The degree of openness seems to vary as between free and work time, for the latter is an obligation imposed by our organizational authority and our particular feudal realities. A dominant characteristic of this organizational time is routine. Routine is the hallmark of 'paramount reality' as Cohen and Taylor describe it (p. 19; also Berger and Luckmann, 1972:35) and we are constantly confronted in the 'inner theatre of the mind' (69) with the 'nightmare of repetition' (46) and the never-ending problem of the 'mental management of routine' (25). 'Paramount reality is a world of timetables, routines, duties, responsibilities, fixed times, fixed places. We have to learn that our temporarily extended free areas are only "binges", "arousal jags", "crazy interludes", "mad flings", "escapes". They are not stageposts on the way to some alternative reality. However consoling they may be, they still remain compartmentalized features of everyday life.' (p. 140.) This passage brings home to us once again, this time from the perspective of sociological research, the oppressive quality of the organizational form of life. We think the organization serves us but the paramount reality is that we serve it. We think we design our own life plans and command our fates but we must set these aside under the paramount constraints of attending meetings, punching clocks, writing letters, catching planes and being on parade whenever the paramount reality of the organization requires it. This reality too is triplex: a composite of R_{I-III} in which ideas, people and things combine to yield an affective colouring or aesthetic ambience and a Type III value orientation which, upon reaching a critical threshold, demands action in the form of resistance or escape attempts. Discontent is a normal condition of man. The escape from the organizational prison, *if it is felt as a prison*, is usually into a free area, escape route, or identity site outside the ambit of organizational life:

> Some very odd and apparently completely dissimilar areas of life come under our heading of free areas: from collecting bus tickets to undergoing psychoanalysis, from taking a package holiday to going on an acid trip, from playing roulette to joining a commune. They all share a similar escape meaning: they are routes out. They also share a particular tension between the known and the unknown, the safe and the dangerous, the innovatory and the conventional. When we opt for any of these activities we might be buying some quite standard elements of everyday life. The time and money we invest in a hobby might only buy what looks to others like another job. (Cohen and Taylor, 96)

But what about inside the organization, on the job? Is it possible that work itself can be an escape attempt and the organization an identity site? Surely. And can the ego rejoice in its subjection to paramount reality? Yes. This holds good not merely for the immature personality type that Argyris describes as infantile (1973:142); we shall attempt to show later that it would also apply to definitely 'adult' personalities who are capable of sophisticated forms of commitment. The individual may escape *into* the organization and the organization can be a haven, a place of warm security and predictability; its impersonality, order and routine a source of psychological consolation and philosophical meaning.

From what is escape being sought? From the full range of human unhappiness: tedium, ennui, frustration, unwanted responsibilities, guilt, despair, anxiety, insecurity, inadequacy, impotence, grief, meaninglessness, a vexing wife, a tormenting mistress, millstone parents, disappointing children, failure, loss of youth, disease, suffering, aging and death; the Buddha's First Noble Truth. So man in his discontent seeks anodynes and finds them within and without the organization life. Always these anodynes are limited and always they have side-effects. It is the ones *within* the organization that are of most interest to us: religious commitment to work, devotion to duty, mindless absorption in task, sabotage of the system and of individuals within it, politics, intrigue, slander and, occasionally, the escape into administration. Those who can, do; those who can't, or won't, administer, for administration can be perceived as an escape from alienation. Its career path (if not blocked or frustrated) leads to presumed hierarchical summits of power, status and liberty of action: a way out!

Much of the classical discourse about resistance to everyday life has been conducted about the terms 'alienation' and 'anomie'. The concepts originate with Marx and Durkheim respectively (Laslett and Runciman, 1967:134-56). Alienation at first referred to the loss of relation between a worker and the product of his labour under systems of capitalist organization. By extension it has come to refer to loss of relationship generally between man and other men. Our society is often perceived as alienating; bureaucracy, technocracy and the new feudalism provide an excess of formal over informal organization, of *Gesellschaft* over *Gemeinschaft*. Those who react against this perception would seek to restore the values of community to the workplace, to reinvest the organization with human meaning.

Anomie has undergone a more radical extension of meaning. At first it referred to *loss* of regulation (Durkheim, 1957:12) leading to 'weariness', 'disillusionment', 'disturbance, agitation and discontent', 'anger', and 'irritated disgust with life' (Beehler and Drengson, 1978:404), even in the end to suicide. It now refers also to a condition arising from an *excess* of regulation, such as might be imposed by a complex bureaucracy, but the induced Type III feelings would be the same. Anomie and alienation, these are names for pathologies of organizational role and organizational life, for a modern sickness of the soul which can infect even the administrative ranks. Yet it must be remembered that it is within the very logic and character of organizations to have this potentiality, to so structure socio-psychological reality that men are alienated and deprived of their intrinsic worth and meaning. Acknowledgement of this potential is essential to administrative philosophy.

The administrator may have to act within an organizational imperative but this is not to say that he cannot have a private agenda. No organization is that alienating. If he wishes, he can subscribe also to an administrative imperative which would impose upon him a duty to reduce alienation and oppression, to mitigate and alleviate organizational oppression. Such a commitment would be optional, and it would be meliorative rather than curative; a matter of morality and ethics rather than management theory. It would impose a more complicated praxis and demand a heightened awareness and deeper sensitivity to the psychological substrata of the administrative field.

Such praxis in turn would have to rest on a philosophy of man, some set of beliefs or presumptions about human nature. For example, it could be maintained that man is by nature sexual, violent and greedy. Social evolution attempts to civilize this primitive nature through the respective institutions of marriage, warfare and commerce. Administrators are by role and function supporters of the social order because of their automatic organizational and nomothetic commitments. It would follow in this illustration that they would have a disciplinary and tutelary obligation. And from such premisses and tacit logic there would emerge an administrative or leadership style which would affect the levels of anomie and alienation and the entire psychological climate of the organization. Different initial premisses would lead to different organizational forms of life. The basic premisses are limited. Despite thousands of years of philosophy and thousands upon thousands of words, the alternative positions do not exceed three, ensconced in the contemporary literature of administration as Theories X, Y and Z (McGregor, 1960:33-57, Ouchi, 1978, 1980).

Theory X accentuates the negative: It takes as its basic premiss about human nature that man as worker (man as organization member) has an inherent disinclination to work. He will avoid work if he can and, therefore, needs to be coerced in some way into doing it. And, of course, he will need supervising. Moreover, man the worker, the organization member, prefers direction and the security of authority to responsibility and the insecurity of risk taking and decision making: the X-man is dependent or infantile in Argyris's sense. To maximize the productivity of X-men one judiciously applies the techniques of scientific management, time and motion study, cost accounting and the latest findings of social psychology and motivation theory. There should be one best way of doing any definable work, and systems analysis and operations research should enable management to discover that way. If the work can then be machined, programmed, or robotized so much the better; if not, then the human element must be employed and controlled. What is curious about Theory X is that it invariably tends to be applied to lower echelons and workers rather than higher echelons and management-administration, but perhaps this is natural in view of its emphasis upon themes of coercion, resistance, power, supervision and control. But it should not be overlooked that if Theory-X presumptions about human nature are good, then in strict logic we should also expect to find instances of the X-administrator and the X-manager. We know from practice and experience that such people exist, but it is a peculiarity of the orthodox literature that it is blind in this respect. As for scientific management, that its assumptions flourish can be seen from ample evidence in the real world, the McDonald hamburger operation being an obvious instance. The assembly line principle, however modified and overlaid with veneers of human relations and job satisfaction theory, would appear to be of universal application and efficacy. It is also fair to say that the tenor of Theory X is in resonance with the themes of the present chapter.

The presumptions of Theory Y are diametrically opposite. Work, if satisfying, can be play; man will exercise self-direction and assume responsibility, if he is committed; he can find opportunity for fulfilment in organizational life and can be left to work without supervision. Such optimistic presumptions are more in accord with the tenor of the following chapter and will be dealt with there.

Lastly, there is the unspecified and somewhat promissory Theory Z which would seek to reconcile or combine Theories X and Y. This with the necessary changes having been made can be taken to provide the set of operating premisses about human nature appropriate to chapter 5.

Philosophically speaking, the utility of such stereotypes as X, Y and Z lies in the simplification of analysis. Each represents only a part of that complex whole which is the truth, but each, however partial, is itself *true*. It is true that some men and some administrators lead lives of quiet desperation and it is true that some men and some administrators abhor their work, to the point that their shrunken horizon of fulfilment consists merely in getting through the day. It is furthermore true that the context of organizational life can often be characterized by routine, a routine leading some to infantile dependence and others to dullness, boredom, ennui and even a sense of mental and spiritual suffocation or exhaustion. These negative realities are to be found not merely on the assembly line or the desk arcade or the factory floor. The highest ranks of organizational hierarchy are not immune. Executives too may feel the gray lassitude of ennui. When major challenges have been met, problems resolved, structure established, decisions routinized, power grown secure, they, like Alexander, may suffer from a deficit of

worlds to conquer. In time novelty wears off, things run
down, men get older on the job and even the salt of achievement can lose its savour. X-analysis compartmentalizes the
negative. And underlying Theory X, a partial truth, is the
more general truth about human beings that their nature
seeks a dynamic balance between stimulation and quietude;
between stress and the absence of stress; between work and
play.

The quality and weight of experienced reality is a function
of consciousness. It differs for each individual. What is X for
one is Y for another and Z for a third. The same R_{II} reality
which is a source of ennui for one is threat for another and
security for a third. For some, routine is security; repetition
and sameness are the source of psychological comfort; the
organization is home. In a pluralistic society where values are
in conflict and cultural transmission mechanisms are breaking
down, the patterned order of the neo-feudal organization
may well be an enclave of psychological stability. For here, as
in the microcosm of a ship, each man knows his role, has his
place, is guaranteed economic sustenance and social identity
in return for his fealty. Even in the old mediaeval feudalism
this was so. Not all serfs felt downtrodden and many was the
burgher who relished his small privileges, styles and titles.
So it is that some administrators exhibit what could be
called a managerial bent, and practise the retreat into managerialism. There is security in moving material from the
in-basket to the out-basket, in observing established procedures, attending regularly scheduled meetings, making the
same motions, mouthing the customary clichés. One knows
where one stands and one avoids thinking about what one
is worth. Sufficient is it that in one place at least there is
order. *Ordnung regiert die Welt.*

Alienation, anomie, security — all this is a matter of affect,
of Type III value orientation. Our felt world is a function of
our Type III values. Organizational reality is a complex social
construct depending on individual phenomenologies (V_1). It
is the peculiar and especial task of the administrator to
observe, discover, sense, intuit, assess and seek to understand
this value fabric. To do this is an art. It cannot be empiricized

although attempts to do so have been bravely made under such rubrics as the study of organizational climate (Halpin, 1967). And just as there is climate so there is organizational weather; this too is a qualitative reality and a knowledge of these things is as essential to administration as their corresponding R_{III} phenomena are to the aviator and the navigator.

FÜRSTENSPIEGEL

The foregoing discussion has been cast, as it were, in the passive voice. We have been speaking about the things that organizations do to us. But there are action and interaction as well as reaction: people do things to organizations and to each other. Human nature is aggressive. It has its active voice. Men may often be the tools of organizations but the converse is also true. Organizations are the tools of men. States are the tools of princes. The ways in which administrators act and react in the organizational setting again depend upon questions of character or human nature. The anthropologist Kluckhohn (1961) has shown that across times and cultures human nature has been conceived within three distinct value orientations as: fundamentally bad, fundamentally good, fundamentally mixed. The last is perhaps the view most amenable to *our* time and place and it is the position subscribed to in this book. Nevertheless it should be noted that the other two positions, though extreme, are tenable and they each have been persuasively defended by authorities of repute. That man is fundamentally bad or evil is in accord with Theory X and has the support of the historical record from Babylon to Hiroshima, from Dachau to My Lai. If I am not mistaken it is the essential view of Christianity, once the veneers of modernism and liberalism are stripped away. Man is born in sin — original sin in the myth of the Garden — and cannot achieve salvation or redemption without Divine Intervention and grace. It has atheistic support also. Sigmund Freud has postulated an unconscious dominated by the id and has referred to civilization as a repression of natural humanity; civilization is a neurosis. Anthropologists and philosophers such as Lorenz and Schopenhauer would concur. Spare the rod and spoil the child. Theory X is well grounded.

The polar opposite of this, that man is fundamentally good, accords with Theory Y. It too has its supporters among liberal philosophers everywhere and most notably among modern psychologists from James to Maslow. William James in discussing human impulse said that every desire had a right to be gratified and if not, why not? (1970:195). Rousseau said that man was born free but was everywhere in chains — espousing the doctrine of the noble savage and the corruptiveness of society. The refrain would be echoed in the writings of Carl Roger and Erich Fromm. In the literature of administration its exponents would include Herzberg, Maslow and McGregor. Theory Y also appears to be well grounded.

Simple introspection should be sufficient for most readers to acknowledge elements of both X and Y within their own natures so one might ask where does this lead us? The answer is that it can lead into some very dark corners and if one were to pursue the thematic of X it would lead, from the administrative standpoint, towards the doctrine of the *arthasastra* and the literature of *Fürstenspiegel*. The latter is a German word which translates literally as 'a mirror for princes' while the former is a Sanskrit term for the writings and doctrine of 'success'. Together they can be taken as a science or proto-science by means of which the adept can gain, consolidate and maximize power. In other words, a manual of leadership. The tradition is very ancient, lost in the mists of time, and it is not very public. For good reason! It would not do if this knowledge were common knowledge. The ignorant must be allowed to keep their illusions. Indeed, sustaining those illusions is a prime responsibility of every prince and administrator.

At the heart of *arthasastra* and *Fürstenspiegel* lies the positive notion that moralities are relative and manipulable. There is no absolute morality and certainly no Kantian imperative. They do not commit the homogenetic fallacy and they recognize that the whole is greater than the sum of its parts. In this sense they are logically sound although ethically contestable. The *arthasastra* in particular (Zimmer, 1956:35-8) is the most sinister. To function best this 'technology of success' requires strict codes or morality for *others*. The proponent himself is amoral or antimoral. His end is his own political success and every means: deceit, treachery, lies, violence, crime, infinite duplicity are justified simply on the positivist criteria of efficiency and effectiveness. His façade, of course, will reveal none of this. Outwardly he will cultivate the smiling or self-effacing image of the trusted leader — father of his people — a pillar of moral integrity and credible righteousness. The adepts of this wisdom will also tend to support public and organizational morality in a real sense because it facilitates their own anti-moral praxis. In the extreme, and for him ideal, case, the seeker of success would be the *sole* immoralist — a one-eyed man in a kingdom of the blind. That the victim have a healthy body is best for predator and parasite alike so the social conditioning and programming provided by public morality and organizational norms is desirable in that it renders men predictable and manipulable. The ruthless administrator will therefore enforce the Type II codes and even enunciate and espouse the highest Type I sentiments. Moral image and moral credibility are always a matter of prime concern to administrators, for the assignment and deployment of power is dependent on trust.

Nicolo Machiavelli is the great Western authority in this field, and the classic exponent of its arts. His thought remains a living force in administrative praxis. His great text *The Prince* is still fully applicable to the realities of organizational and political life and it has always been a source of some wonder to me, as a teacher of administration, that experienced practitioner-students often come visibly alive and receptive when introduced to *Fürstenspiegel* and Machiavelli, as if, like Molière's character, they are astonished to discover that all along they have been speaking prose. Or as if they have at last come upon an oasis of meaning amid the aridities of management science. The ancient maxims of power are very much alive. They resonate with modern audiences in a way which contrasts with the reception of conventional, value-neutered organization theory.

The principles of success as discerned in the mirror for princes are universal as well as ancient. In French there is the expression '*droit de gérance*'. The administrator in the last analysis must always have the power to enforce his will. The modern major-general, well schooled in all the social-science findings, may elicit and solicit input from all parties and ranks to a dispute or decision, but at the end of the day will act, in accordance with his own will and motivational complex.

In German there is the term *Realpolitik*, the politics of what really happens. Bombing Hanoi on Christmas Day by virtue of one's clear-eyed comprehension of the logic of power, eliminating one's opponent by betrayal, bribery or deceit, obtaining funds or promotion or perquisites by flattery, obsequiousness, manipulation; these things occur. To be ignorant about them is to be unsophisticated, politically virginal, administratively inept.

REALGRUND, REALETHIK

One's attitude to power is critical. It is a nice test of honesty towards self to ask of one's own valuation of power at which level of the value paradigm it rests. Is one, for example, rationally committed or *more than* rationally committed to the acquisition of power, authority and influence? Power is important because in an administrative career the stakes (and risks) can be high and the tenure insecure. The realities of power in a given setting affect the value complex from I through III for each individual actor. Any specific organizational context represents a *Realgrund*, a backdrop of organizational reality for a given actor at a given time. While always in flux *Realgrund* is a phenomenological constant for any particular administrative act. It represents the ambience or ethos and the value dimensions V_5 through V_3 in figure 3 above. Similarly, the $P_3 M_3$ process cycles constantly within and against this *Realgrund*.

Although *Realgrund* exists tacitly, for the most part unanalysed, often subliminal, it nevertheless implies value conditioning and value imperatives which constitute *Realethik*: the ethics of what one does and ought to do given the realities (not the ethics of the textbooks nor even the ethics of one's own value matrix — instead an ethics known and understood tacitly). The *Realgrund* of Victorian Imperial India yields the *Realethik* of the 'Honour of the Regiment'. The *Realgrund* of 1944 yields the *Realethik* which sanctions simultaneously Auschwitz, Dresden and the Manhattan Project. It is not commonly exposed to rational scrutiny until after the fact. Moreover, it invariably contains a contra-ethical element in that every administrator born or yet to be born owes at least a silent tribute to Machiavelli. *Fürstenspiegel* seeks to bring *Realethik* into the light. To do so is, however, difficult and even dangerous. A secret revealed is a secret destroyed, and organizations, like their component parts, have to maintain appearances, images and façades. So masks cannot always be stripped. And it may be debilitating to look in the mirror. A totalitarian regime, for example, which purports to represent the most just Republic, could not allow such exposure. It would constitute an intellectual threat to the very bases of the State. Still, the *Realgrund* is always there and a *Realethik* runs with it.

As with the systems of reality discussed earlier so there coexist in conflation several systems of ethics: cultural, sub-cultural, organizational and individual. All together play out, act, react and interact. Among them, unstated and often not capable of being stated, is the *Realethik*, the ethic of the agentic state.

In this chapter we have sought to pursue the theme of motivation into the working field of executive action: the organizational environment. This field is complex enough in the realm of fact; it is infinitely more complex in the realm of value. We have considered some of this complexity from the standpoint of Type III values, for Type III values, affective values, are the ordinary component of psychological experience and the major characteristic of qualitative reality. They are the least common denominator in the logic of value. Every value implies an equal and opposite disvalue. I have chosen to dwell largely upon the negative rather than the positive, because positive affect, having to do with what is good, can in a sense be left to take care of itself. I have also been selective about negative affect — nothing has been said, for example, about the problem of envy which to my knowledge has not been properly studied in organizational contexts and which must rank on a par with problems of ennui and spiritual fatigue — nor about insecurity of rank and tenure and the associated galaxy of dysfunctional negativities. The complex of Type III values which characterize the realities of organizational life is indeed too profuse to be adequately dealt with in this space and within the limitations set by a general philosophical exploration and statement. But the values are there and they are real. Each organization, each informal organization, and each suborganization establishes its own Type III ambience. The burden of this chapter does not deny that, for many, this ambience will be net positive. Those who administer and those who are the subjects of administration may both find affective gratification in their organizational life. It can be emotionally satisfying. *Tant mieux*. It is good that some feel this way for organizational society and organizational feudalism increasingly determine our forms of life.

But the very prevalence and salience of organization create an obligation of watchfulness and suggest a duty of care to be aware of the pathologies, negativities and realities indicated in this chapter. The list, micro- and macro-, is far from exhaustive; it is merely indicative. The organizational imperative would seem to be strengthening and this may be inevitable given our present world culture. So the onus is intensified for those who would defend the idiographic, the individual, the unique and the free. Some of these defenders must be themselves administrators else the defence will fail. Our organizations beset us and threaten us. They abrade the ego. And yet:

CREDO: *The frustration of the ego, and its discipline under a collective and hierarchical regimen, is an essential part of organizational life. It can refine the ego; it can be a means of spiritual growth.*

4

Ideologies

THE TRANSMUTATION OF VALUE

Most of man's inhumanity to man has been caused, is being caused and will be caused by Type I values. One can say that Type I values are the fundament of all ideologies, sacred and secular. They are the values men are willing to die and kill for: affect transmuted by will and transcending reason — affect invested with a quality of *belief*. How do these special constellations of the desirable and the undesirable come about to lodge in men's hearts and take over their spirits? It is beyond my capacity to answer or explain, it is such a great mystery in its inner workings, yet there seems to be a discernible pattern at the surface level of observation and one can dare to hypothesize about the dynamics.

All sentient and motile creatures exhibit and presumably experience Type III affect. This quality of affect permeates organizational life as was shown in the previous chapter. It is part of animal as well as human nature and the reader will recall the logical positivist argument from chapter 2 which would effectively equate man with the rest of the animal kingdom. To understand value then would be to understand emotion, affect. Something which science can quite readily concede it does not yet approximate. But with man there would appear to be something peculiar which distinguishes him from other animals, and this distinctiveness is not merely a matter of his cognitive capacity, ability to reason and use language, but something having to do with his capacity for free will, choice and commitment. This enables him on occasion to accomplish a sort of transvaluation of value or transmutation of value. Upon this rare occurrence specific values and their attendant value clusters may become activated as central value features of the ego structure, integral to the personality of the value-actor. In philosophical terms his central life-meaning, his *Weltanschauung* becomes bound up with some set of Type I values.

To illustrate: most men have some natural affect towards their country of origin, birthplace and *patria*. Normal manifestation of these Type III or IIb values are to be found in displays of nationalistic, ethnic or patriotic pride the world over. Occasionally, however, by way of history or socio-cultural programming perhaps, this Type III affect reaches for some a point of intensity such that the psyche is galvanized, polarized, structurally reordered about these values and we observe the patriot, the fanatic who is prepared to lay down his life for Fatherland, or 'Ireland', or Tenno Banzai, or whatever the trigger stimulus might be. (Note that, semantically, the terms 'patriot' and 'fanatic' are euphemestic and pejorative variants of a single phenomenon: Type I commitment.)

Likewise martyrs and saints are created in the name of religion. And likewise some men expend their lives on the battlefields of art, science, letters. What is being considered here is not ordinary dedication or commitment...that too can lead to great things...but the supernormal or transcendent. It is as if by psycho-mechanisms yet unknown a Type I value is engaged at once, or else, by some process of intensification of affect, a critical mass is attained and there is a psychological locking-in or irreversibility which entrenches the value which then becomes a powerful determinant of the form of life. This is not to say that Type I commitments cannot degenerate or disappear but that they are highly resistant to any such conversion. Thus Type I values are emotive but they engage the will and hence become transmuted or transvalued. Furthermore, they do not necessarily engage the rational faculty because they are *trans*-rational. Figure 7 lists some of the factors and characteristics which discriminate between Type III and Type I values. It is an important administrative skill to be able to make this discrimination, because any value can appear at either level.

Type III Factor	Corresponding Type I Quality
subrationality (infrarationality)	transrationality (suprarationality)
preference	intuition
impulse	choice
transience	permanence
intermittence naturalistic compulsion (habit)	persistence transcendental freedom
abandon	commitment
affective programming (heteronomy)	conscience (autonomy)
instinct	belief/faith
weak or normal motivation	super- or hypermotivation

FIGURE 7   Factors discriminating between affective and conative value

It would be possible in principle, in theory, for a human being to live his life without having Type I values. If the logical positivists are correct, this is, in fact, the case. On the other hand, if we are prepared to suspend belief in strict positivism (itself an ideology) and entertain the logical and ontological distinction of type just made, then we will have a means for explaining many sorts of behaviour not other-wise explicable and we shall also have a conceptual tool for the analysis of ideology.

Ideologies are quasi-philosophical systems of thought and belief which structure meaning for man in the world. Their genesis and etiology lie in Type I values but once extant ideologies do not necessarily elicit Type I adherence from all of their adherents and without such commitment somewhere an ideology withers and disappears. The term 'ideology' includes all religious and political philosophies which go to compose any given culture. Thus, anti-Semitism was an ideological component of the Third Reich and romanticism was a Napoleonic (as well as Nazi) ideology. And, too, rationalism is an integral feature of the ideology of modern organizations. We cannot and need not examine the whole of the rich ideological spectrum but can instead concentrate upon those ideological features which seem especially pertinent to the administrative form of life.

RATIONALISM

Science is the religious orthodoxy of our age. Our culture — the culture of developed nations and economies in the late twentieth century — has been profoundly affected by the values of reason. That is desirable which is logical, empirical, mathematical, technical, explicable in terms of cause and effect, in a word, scientific. A corollary, of course, is a bias toward the material, since science treats of the sensible world[1] and when this bias becomes raised to ideological proportions it acquires an -ism suffix and becomes materialism (as in dialectical materialism, for example, which purports to be a scientific treatment of history). The parent and presiding value in all this is rationality which appears in its most impressive form in the institutions of science and technology. The term 'rationality', with its connotation of logical cognitive processes — ratiocination — is to be distinguished from 'reasonableness' on the one hand and 'rational*ism*' on the other. The former implies a satisficing, a pragmatic making-do in a real world where the ideals of logic inevitably fall short, while the latter implies an overemphasis in the value domain upon reason, an excess, as it were, of rational rectitude. The antecedents of rationalism are especially European and can be traced from classical antiquity through

---

[1] One acknowledges of course that science nowadays treads very subtly in the realm of matter but however attenuated the frontiers of physics become some substratum of ultimate 'hardware' is usually presumed. At least, the more mystical interpretations of physical reality do not yet seem to have funded any corresponding public ideology.

the Renaissance and Enlightenment to the industrial and technological revolutions of the last two hundred years. The root value of rationality is deep seated and connected, doubtless, with an underlying philosophical conception of *truth*. If what is true is assumed to be what is in accord with reason, then the value of rationality is reinforced, driven upwards perhaps to the metavaluational level. And if the implementation of the value in the course of time results in material cultural transformations — as is the case with modern technology, bureaucracy and large-scale complex organizations — then inertial forces are formed within the culture which must tend to further reinforce the value and entrench its accompanying ideology.

RATIONALISM AND ADMINISTRATION

To the extent that ends and means are connected by any kind of causal logic, and because efficiency and effectiveness are always metavalues of goal-seeking organization, it is fair to say that the spirit of rationalism has always invested administration and co-operative endeavour to some large extent. But this relationship has intensified over time. We can fix a date for this intensification with the work of Frederick W. Taylor around the turn of the century. Taylor (1915, 1964) has acquired a conventional status as the 'father of scientific management'. This status is well earned. Indeed, Taylor's essential logic — that there must be one best way of performing work — still goes unrefuted. If a task can be specified; if an end item can be defined; then there *must* be one best way of specifying the causal linkage of means to that end. Therefore, appropriate *rational* investigation by problem factoring, task analysis, operations research, time and motion study and so on must ultimately lead to the solution of any set problem. In short, work and its management can be scientific. Only a philosopher would quibble with this (perhaps becoming fixated and frustrated over the word *best*) but no conceptual perplexity need deter or decelerate the administrator who has unreflectively underwritten the metavalues of efficiency effectiveness and taken his ends as given.

This principle and spirit of rational enquiry was reinforced by technological advances in the early twentieth century and soon approached an intellectual critical mass when combined with theories of bureaucracy as propounded by Fayol and Weber. With the advent of assembly lines, the massive military logistics of World War I, and the rapidly growing public sector services then and thereafter, the Reality III conditions were set for mass acceptance of rationalist ideology, and these in turn were reinforced by the inter-war Reality I movements of behaviourism and logical positivism. Large, complex modern organizations are *a priori* rational. They are also *a fortiori* rational*istic*.

Since no action is without countervailing reaction Taylor's thrust to scientific management generated its own counter-ideology in the form of the human relations (now human *resources*) movement, a movement which drew heavily for its academic sustenance upon the famous series of experiments known as the Hawthorne studies (Roethlisberger and Dickson, 1939; Mayo, 1933, 1947, 1949). This reaction decelerated but never derailed the original ideological thrust, which found new allies in the positivism and behaviourism that came to characterize philosophy and psychology in the middle part of the century. The second World War again posed impressive problems of administration and management and provided impetus for the development in the post-war decades of general systems theory (von Bertalanffy, 1968; Beer, 1959; Buckley, 1968; Laszlo, 1972). The influence of this latter movement has been great enough to justify a rank of ideology in its own right. Offshoots and variants such as Management by Objectives (MBO), Program Evaluation Review Technique (PERT), and Planning, Programming, Budget Systems (PPBS) are now standard features of the curriculum in schools of management and administration. Since all of these deal with the realm of value as well as the realm of fact the naturalistic and militaristic fallacies are committed daily. Computer technology has both facilitated and entrenched such developments. When US Secretary of Defence Robert MacNamara introduced

the techniques and the spirit of this ideology into the conduct of the Viet Nam war he initiated a controversy in the
field of philosophy of administration which is far from
concluded (Gabriel and Savage, 1978). And in educational
administration the term hyperrationalization (Wise, 1977:
43-57) has been coined to describe the dysfunctional quality
and consequences of excessive subscription to this type of
ideological persuasion.

At its core general systems theory is simply the unexcep-
tionable endeavour of seeking to introduce logical rigour
into the understanding and conduct of complex human
affairs. Divinely simple and divinely defensible — God is
not only a mathematician, He is a systems theorist. Even
our $P_3 M_3$ model (see p. 26) is but an attempt to super-
impose rational order upon a multi-levelled systematic
complex. (It does, however, seek to avoid the homogenetic
and militaristic fallacies so frequently overlooked in rationalist administration generally.) Moreover, the influence of
logical positivism upon contemporary administrative thought
is conceded to be powerful and pervasive (Culbertson, 1981:
25-43). Since logical positivism is quintessentially rationalistic,
the inference is not itself unreasonable that modern administration is in the grip of a rational scientific ideology. If this
is not obvious it is because rationality is also a metavalue. It
goes without saying (without conscious reflection or critical
concern) that no administrator is going to contest for long
against a rational argument; and since most of organizational
decision making and policy analysis is conducted within a
language game of rational discourse — usually in the terms
of cost-benefit calculus — then the ideological impress becomes overwhelming. Often it would require a high degree of
philosophical skill to even perceive the problem,[2] much less
expose the weaknesses and fallacies that lie concealed within
the discourse itself. These fallacies (see pp. 33-36) are so

---

[2] '...someone unpractised in philosophy passes by all the spots where difficulties
are hidden in the grass, whereas someone who has had practice will pause and
sense that there is a difficulty close by even though he cannot see it yet.....How
hard I find it to see what is *right in front of my eyes!*' (Wie schwer fällt mir zu
sehen, was *vor meinen Augen liegt!*) (Wittgenstein 1980:29, 39).

embedded in rational, quasi-rational and pseudo-rational administrative praxis that they pass unnoticed into the flow of events.

BUREAUCRACY

Bureaucracy is a complex but common term which has a range of meaning from the pejorative connotations of Type III affect in the public mind to the ideological connotations of Type I principle embodied in the sophisticated work of Max Weber. In general it implies the application of rationality to administrative affairs. As Frederick Taylor was to the factory floor so Max Weber became to the office complex. Weber's scholarship was monumental, his influence profound. Perhaps he should be included amongst those four horsemen of the modern apocalypse, German-speakers all, who stand at the threshold of modern times: Einstein in physics, Freud in psychology, Marx in politics, and Weber in administration. His ideal-type theory of bureaucracy foreshadowed the growth of the Organizational State. Administrators everywhere in public or private sectors of the economy, in developed or underdeveloped nations, espouse the concepts that Weber formulated; and a whole genre of social science literature is given over to the attempt to reconcile the purity of Weberian theory with the imperfections of reality and praxis (Merton, 1952; Blau, 1955; Crozier, 1964; Downs, 1967; Thompson, J. D., 1967; Thompson, Victor A, 1961).

Though there be discrepancies between theory, practice and praxis there are plain facts before our faces. Bureaucracy works. It satisfies the pragmatic criterion despite the rhetoric of individualists, reactionaries and entrepreneurs. Everywhere around us are large functioning bureaucracies: ministries, hospitals, school systems, police forces, armies, research institutes, post offices and publishers; even farms and shopping centres; NASA, KGB, UNO, IWA, BBC...all exhibit common bureaucratic properties. Were our sense of wonder not anaesthetized by familiarity we should be full of awe at these marvels of co-operative endeavour which all miraculously *work*. Planes fly, trains run, meals are served, bells ring and schoolchildren learn to read and write, presses roll and felons are convicted, heart surgery is carried out, dancers dance and far planets are photographed, the dead are buried and new protoplasm flows into the system. How wonderful! How *negentropic*!

Perhaps it were good for us, sophisticated administrators though we be, to pause just once and marvel at how well it all does work...in spite of us...or even that it works at all! That there is order!

It seemed to many, certainly it seemed to Weber, that the principle underlying all this negentropy, this informed complexity, was one of rationality. *Zweckrationalität* and *Wertrationalität* in Weber's terms: the logic of purpose and value. Certainly rational bureaucracy and its shadow side of irrational bureaupathology is the mark of our ethos, our *Zeitgeist*, the spirit of our times. And it has ideological resonances which are revealed in the following words of Marx:

> The bureaucratic spirit is an out and out jesuitical, theological spirit. The bureaucrats are the state Jesuits and state theologians. Bureaucracy is *la république prêtre*. (1927:456)

Weber contrasts bureaucracy with the lesser evolved forms of patrimonial, traditional and charismatic organization. What seems most easily and most generally to distinguish bureaucratic from non-bureaucratic forms of life is a quality of *community* present in the latter but missing in the former. Classical feudalism is credited with this quality. It is well-known to those who have experienced the microcosmic feudalism of shipboard life. In the military it is a vaunted characteristic of the regimental system as opposed to more rationalistic alternatives. Where community exists some sort of binding affective ties extend across the network of hierarchical relationships in such a way as to give rise to a sense of belonging, ego-endorsement, ego-commitment. Sociology has taken such subtleties seriously and established the well-known distinction between *Gesellschaft* and *Gemein-schaft* (Tönnies, 1955). In this the former term refers to mere formal association and incorporation while the latter extends beyond nomothetic bloodlessness into the reaches of community, human warmth, social binding and what the Germans call *Gemütlichkeit*.

The philosopher-administrator must seek, as part of his continual coping with a value flux, to reconcile in his praxis the *Gemeinschaft-Gesellschaft* dichotomy. This means that he himself must have a standpoint. For these extremes imply divergent ethics and different Type I values, different ideologies in effect. *Gesellschaft* is square in the line of rationalism, bureaucracy, technology, systems theory, Theory X and the subordination of man to work, organization and State while *Gemeinschaft* signals the converse. The one is for the great vision of planning, the other for incrementalism and muddling through. The one appeals to the amateur in each of us, the other to the professional.

PROFESSIONALISM

So advanced is the new feudalism and the Organizational State that it would be possible to treat professional*ism* as an ideology in its own right. However, it is so closely allied to and springs so full blown from the parental matrix of rationalism that it can be treated under that general head. Certainly its influence is sufficiently universal that it might almost pass unobserved as a characteristic feature of modern organizational contexts. Professionalism is the manifestation of rationalism applied to patterns of work.

The topic is of such significance that we shall have to return to it later. It, too, has engendered a literature of its own and scholars dispute about the meaning of the term. For our purposes the criteria of a profession as opposed to any other rubric of work would include at least the following:

1 An esoteric body of knowledge. An expertise not immediately or readily available to anyone.

2 Guild command of entry to and egress from the ranks of the profession. The right to include and exclude.
3 Pretensions to an ethical commitment. A putative ethical concern.
4 A significant degree of institutional and intraorganizational autonomy. Often sanctioned by the metaorganization of the State or, at least, by an organization independent of the organization or setting within which the profession is to be practised.
5 Some dignity of style and title implying a certain status within the social structure of deference patterns.

The professional status of administration need not delay us. Clearly it is not a profession on these criteria but these criteria refer to a Weberian ideal type. Given that ideal type, it is possible to discern a general tendency of aspiration towards professional status within the multiple forms of work life. The question can then be asked, how is professionalism implemented? And invariably the answer is, by *credentialling*. The mark of professionalism is the establishment of a credential, or better, a chain of credentials which entitle the holder to the professional rights and privileges. This is a characteristic of neo-feudalism, analogous to the system of charters, grants and titles of the Middle Ages. Credentials are formal documents (degrees, licences, diplomas, certificates) issued by State-empowered authorities to establish the status of an aspirant or license a practitioner in some technology or art. From the driving licence and the school leaving certificate to the post-doctoral diploma they are characteristic of bureaucratic rationalism. They tell us whom to trust to do what. To be without credentials in a bureau-feudal environment is to risk being outcast, endangered and unemployable.

It is also a mark of our times that along with currencies devalued through inflation we can find a parallel inflation and devaluation of credentials. A BA degree may have little market value as a terminal credential though, paradoxically, its value can be increased if it is regarded as an instrumental credential or prerequisite part of a credential chain. More and more areas of work formerly open to all (child care, insurance, real estate sales) aspire to professional status. Paper barricades must be scaled to gain the perquisites within. In Shaw's opinion, all professions are conspiracies against the laity.

In all of this, administration remains anomalous and distinctive. It is still one of the few fields of endeavour in which the ambitious can make a career without regimentation by diploma. Yet this assertion itself is no longer as true as it once was and inevitably in all the subcategories of administrative enterprise the influence of credentialling grows, so that the MBA and MPA degrees, the law school or business training, the background in economics, become increasingly established as part of a system of proto-professional controls. Only at the political level is it still widely possible for the pure amateur to gain access to organizational power, but at this level (the school or hospital board, the Minister of the Crown) he is likely to find himself well buffered from the organization he ostensibly controls by echelons of credentialled personnel who consider themselves to be professionals.

STATISM

The logical sequence is straightforward. Scientific and technological expansion imply specialization. Increased command over nature admits of larger projects in time and space. Growing populations conduce to complexity of organization and articulation. Bureaucracy and professionalism, nomothetic rationalism and general systems theory, *Gesellschaft* and the organizational society emerge. This historical logic also entails a central feature, the evolution of the nation state. Although overlaid by the tides of political imperialism and their transmutations in the form of ideological and economic imperialism the nation state remains the central fact for contemporary forms of life, in that it defines each human being in terms of rigorous *nationality*. Despite an evolution and accretion of supranational organizations and linkages — UN, EEC, NATO, OECD, OPEC, international conglomerates and cartels — the State remains the dominant power in the lives of individuals and groups. It provides the elemental credentialling. For most, that initial determination of identity will last all of their lives; for a minority, emigration or political upheaval may allow a change of label; but for all there is some sort of value initiation, a definite cultural programming, into a relationship with a metaorganizational State. That State is sovereign within its territory and is the ultimate source of power, authority, property and laws. Its sovereignty is such as to place it beyond good and evil, the pursuit of its self-interest being fettered only by the weakest of moral constraints such as those embodied in international law. Within its own domain it legitimizes and delegitimizes all institutions and, hence, all organizations. Through its fiscal, welfare and public administration systems it pervades all social life and intrudes directly into private lives. The power is absolute. The military, for example, are endowed with the right to expend citizens' lives. Neither is life itself in the last analysis private, for here too, as with property, the State has its rights of eminent domain. From cradle to grave the modern State is so much with us that, paradoxically, we are apt to be unaware of or insensitive to its intimate relationship with our very selves. Even our minds, which we take to be our most intimate attributes, are products, upon analysis, of formation by the State. Lifelong monitoring and documentation are norms of the overlooked and invisible ideology of statism.

All of this entails, the rhetoric of anti-bureaucratic politicians notwithstanding, a growth in public administration and State bureaucracy. The empirical evidence for this is incontestable. Whether the State itself be communist, socialist, fascist or capitalist, the intrinsic logic of administration remains the same and leads to the unexamined ideological framework which we here call statist.

It is possible to perceive, for example, simply at the economic level of analysis, a dimension of unity in the world order. One finds in effect only variations in the degree of regulation of capitalism. The factors of production are everywhere the same and include, in addition to the classic ones (land, labour and capital) the resource known synonymously as entrepreneurship or *administration*. States are metaorganizations run by administrators. The State itself being an unconscious abstraction, it is not possible for it to have either values or ideology. The latter repose in the persons of administrators and to the extent that these are commonly informed by a vested interest in the metavalues of the State there comes about an undeclared statist ideology.

Again, at the organizational level of analysis there is the discernible unity exhibited across bureaucratic systems. A world order based upon economic interdependence and bureaucratic administration is far from inconceivable. It may even be emergent. But its antecedent phase seems rather to be a neo-feudalism structured upon States and groupings of States. If a new order, a world bureaucracy, were to evolve, it would fit nicely with the Weberian prognosis and would be well rooted in rational ideology. Intellectual origins and foundations could be found in the work of Marx, Lenin and Taylor. But behind any analysis of bureaucratic rationalism — the study of structure and function in State administration — lie disturbing and perennial questions of political philosophy, and, therefore, of administrative philosophy.

Is man, *collectively* the creator of the State, also subordinate to the State, in some sense *for* the State, the whole being greater than the sum of the parts? Or conversely is man, even though almost totally dependent upon the State, for *himself*; the State for *man*, the individual being somehow more than the whole of which he is a component part? In administrative terms, do organizations subserve their members, or conversely? If organizations subserve goals, what are the *goals* of the State?

The answers to these questions are ideological. Statism, the unwritten ideology of our times, might seem to speak for the hegemony of organizations. Yet this is oversimple and probably fallacious. The problem of the relationships between metaorganization, organization and individual is perennial and universal. Yet, though ancient, it is embedded in logical confusion. Its very statement broaches the homo-genetic fallacy. Each part of the problem represents a different level of truth. How are we to reconcile the shifts of level which occur as debate about respective rights and obligations becomes heated? We shall return to this question later. The point to be noted at present is the historical growth of an incipient ideology of statism wherein adminis-tration could be invested with commitment in the service of ever-larger and more complex collectivities. Welfare economics gives a clear illustration of this ideological develop-ment. It would be difficult nowadays to find an administrator who did not tacitly *believe* that all children had a *right* to State education, all sick a *right* to some measure of State medicine, all destitute or deprived a *right* to some measure of State support. *Beliefs* and *rights* are the stuff of *ideology.*

Statism is important for administrative philosophy not only because it can fund an ideological commitment but also because it affects forms of life generally. It stresses, as the example shows, that we are owed certain rights by the State: health care, education, defence, justice. In return we owe certain duties to the State: service, law observance, allegiance, wealth. This equation of rights and duties is rarely in equilibrium; it tilts to one emphasis or the other in accord with V_5 ethos. But in certain ways, subtle and obvious, the relationship tends to militate against the indi-vidual, to render him more malleable and more amenable to more government. Thus one can come to prophesy more neo-feudal dependency and perhaps even the advent of the Organizational World State where power would be diffused not merely amongst the component nation states, but also among the bureaux of supranational and international organizations. In the shape of this world to come Marx would have to yield to Weber as the more prophetic thinker. There has been no withering away of the State. On the contrary, that chief instrumentality of statism, bureaucracy, has become more efficient, more effective and more universal. A quasi-profession of public service is everywhere an estab-lished vested interest and the elementary political arithmetic and geometry of this administrative system ensures the propagation of a subtle ideology of statism. This ideology is subtended from and subsumed by the parent ideology of rationalism. It is in accord with a scientific-technological era. It determines the ethos under which men act. It structures organizations and helps to determine the quality of work life. For some it will create a value context leading to Type III reactions of alienation and anomie while for others it will accord with commitments, occasionally even at the Type I level, to the value of rationality. Whatever the individual response, the cultural envelope of the nation state cannot be ignored as an important factor of organizational context, the moreso because it can so easily be overlooked.

HUMANISM

A grand dialectic pervades the ideological aspect of organizational context. On the one hand there is the historical progression from scientific management through to bureaucracy and systems theory. On the other hand there is the stream of thought embodied in the work of psychologists such as Maslow, McGregor, Herzberg and Argyris. Both of these streams, the one essentially rational, the other essentially emotive, endorse philosophical models of man which are antithetical to each other. And both represent incontestable truths about the human condition. One implies a work ethic and possible ethic of duty and self-abnegation while the other implies a hedonistic or gratification ethic and a possible ethic of self-fulfilment or self-transcendence. And both streams of the dialectic must be re-evaluated in the light of the post-Christian ideologies of our times. Such ideologies as are expressed, for example, in Lasch's *Culture of Narcissism* and the Scott-Hart study of *Organizational America.*

The basic pattern of the dialectic is, however, the contest between rationalism and humanism. Traditional humanism is characterized by an overt faith in the beneficent nature of man. Maslow is the most transparent exponent of this ideology. In his administrative text *Eupsychian Management* he goes so far as to propound the notion that the fundamental *raison d'être* of organizations is to provide opportunities for their members to self-actualize, that is, to maximize their individual inner potentials. That such psychological potentialities might be for evil as well as for good is either ignored in the Maslowian polemic or else discounted on the grounds that any bad manifestations of human behaviour are explicable as 'needs deficiencies'. Hitler would presumably have actualized otherwise than he did if he had been nurtured differently and had not suffered certain critical deprivations. This is of a piece with the contemporary ideology which stresses the power of social conditioning and the arguments for diminished moral responsibility in criminal law. Terrorists are to be excused, or at least explained, by reference to their socio-political environment and history. Change but this and all will be well again. A paradoxical ambivalence towards free will is as typical of this ideology as is its devotion to the homogenetic fallacy and is illustrated by the belief that if the members of a society (organization) are not morally responsible, its architects (rulers, administrators, leaders) somehow *are*.

Nevertheless humanism forms a powerful countervailing force in opposition to the cynics, the hard-headed realists, and the tough-minded devotees of Theory X. Ideologies are greater than sentiment and they change the world. The humanistic ideology has led to the growth of academic subdisciplines in the field of administrative studies such as organizational development (OD), personnel management and industrial psychology. Moreover, from the time of the Hawthorne studies on there has been extensive research in the social sciences directed to problems of human motivation and work performance. The human relations movement generally has profoundly affected what Herzberg and others call QWL (the quality of work life). Indeed the mere existence of such an acronym in the language of organization theory makes its own point. Human relations theory is now sometimes referred to as human resources theory (Miles, 1975:41) in a semantic effort to escape unfavourable connotations associated with certain excesses with which the earlier movement had been charged. These referred to possible manipulation of individuals by the techniques of group dynamics, group assaults on individual integrity through encounter techniques, T-grouping and the like. There was a phase in the counter-cultural period, in America at least, when a powerful vogue existed in administrative circles which often obliged executives to undertake some form of 'sensitivity training'. That vogue has passed and possibly a reaction has set in, but many cadres remain who have been exposed to fairly radical dimensions of humanistic psychology. And the entrepreneurial side of the human relations movement remains well established, most executives having invitations to seminars, workshops and conferences crossing their desks with notable frequency.

The philosophical roots of humanism go back to antiquity. In modern times Rousseau, Marx and Mill are representative of the political wing while in administration there are the idealistic thrusts of Mary Parker Follet, Likert and McGregor. Theory Y is entrenched as an administrative ideology. It countervails against the intrinsic pessimism of the equally entrenched Theory X. Nevertheless, this dialectic between X and Y can itself be subsumed under the overarching ideology of rationalism, because organizational humanism does not purport to be irrational or anti-rational. On the contrary, it seeks to establish its own claims to rationality through motivation theory and empirical research. But the two lines of rationality and logic arrive at different termini. Carried to its extreme the Taylorian view of man leads remorsely to a work ethic with a Kantian stress upon duty, submission of the part to the greater interests of the whole, and ultimate acknowledgement of the primacy of history, State, organization and work over the hedonic gratifications of the individual. Carried to the other extreme, the Maslowian view of man leads inexorably to an actualization or fulfil-ment ethic with the Kantian stress now upon individual integrity, assertion of the primacy of part over whole and the individual with respect to the State — a celebration of the ego and the hedonic.

Expressed in terms of political psychology, the dialectic

appears as the continuous oppositional interplay between conservative/radical and liberal/centrist, between liberal indulgence and reactionary discipline, between tough- and tender-mindedness (Eysenck, 1958), and between compromise and principle. Historically and culturally one can observe the movements of this repetitive ideological ballet. The V_5 ethos (see p. 24) of any period tends always in one direction or the other. In the sixties there were widespread convulsions of anti-authoritarianism and sporadic violence against established institutions and patterns of authority. In time these yielded to various forms of conservative reaction. Of course, history does not simply repeat itself; it moves dialectically through phases of thesis, antithesis and synthesis. It would be the interesting task of the historian of ideas to trace, for example, the influence of positivistic philosophy and behaviourist psychology upon the evolution of 'playboy' philosophy and modern hedonism. Such a study would not be able to neglect the work of industrial psychology and administrative thought. Lasch (1979) and other social commentators (Wolfe, 1980; Naipaul, 1981) have suggested the emergence of a 'culture of narcissism' which characterizes our times and which implies a deep-seated but tacit ideology of self-indulgence, self-interest and self-gratification. But lines blur. The units of this kind of social analysis are large or vague; the implications for administrative praxis real, but confused and unclear. Workaholism, for example, an overcommitment to work behaviour can as well find its ideological support in narcissistic humanism as in a fulfilment ethic or the simple pragmatics of success. Nevertheless, the administrative philosopher has a duty of perspicacity. An awareness of the ideological substrata of the *Realgrund* of his own organizational reality is desirable. The central values of the currently obtaining humanism (there will always be *a* humanism) effectively determine that reality.

When rationalism preponderates over humanism, or conversely, there will be a reaction. The more severe the preponderance, the more excessive the reaction. Thus the aberrations of narcissism, hedonism and what has been

called the playboy philosophy are quasi-ideological phenomena which could be analysed as reactions against the
regimentation of a rationalistic culture. They are defective
from the humanistic standpoint in that they effectively
fail to replace *Gesellschaft* by *Gemeinschaft*. Instead their
long-term effect would seem to be a worsening of the states
of alienation and anomie. Nevertheless, they march under
the broad banner of humanism and contribute in their way
towards the dialectical equilibrium. Converse restorative
movements would occur as mass sensibility reacted to excessive emphasis in the humanistic direction.

It is worth noting, however, that human fulfilment is in
principle attainable within either of the great contending
ideological streams. Neither side can establish a monopoly
of human values. Nomothetic organization can provide its
members with satisfactions and life-meaning, its administrators with personal fulfilment and sense of purpose, as well
as can the cozy warmth of communal enterprise. Except to
their adherents, ideologies are neither true nor right in any
objective or absolute sense. They just are, they exist as facts
within the domain of values (value-facts), and they affect
organizational life. In the dialectic between humanism and
rationalism, between expression and discipline, one can
see reflected the tension between the idiographic and the
nomothetic: the individual and the collectivity. How is this
everlasting dialectical tension to be resolved? How is it to be
coped with in praxis?

CREDO: (Proposition N = 1) *No   one   is   indispensable.
Everyone is irreplaceable.*

These two truths expose the paradox of organized life.
Each has a different logical status and the confusion of these
levels engenders the homogenetic fallacy. At one level it is
true that for societies and organizations to survive they must
have replaceable parts. At another, and higher, level it is also
true that the price of this survival capacity is a continuous
flux in *quality* since no individual can be removed from an
existing order without some change in the human chemistry

of the aggregate. The antithesis to this proposition (N = ∞) would be that everyone is indispensable and no one is irreplaceable. It conjures up the nightmare vision of an insect world, a hive mentality, a philosophy of administration neither rational nor human, a Satanic positivism.

Neither of the great ideologies need be inconsistent with Proposition N = 1. It accords with both the phenomenological and the objectivist views of organization theory. But it creates its own sort of professional onus. The administrator who would claim to be a humanist and who is not a mere dilettante would be required to make some serious study of that sprawling body of knowledge which deals with human nature. He should be acquainted and knowledgeable (which probably also means schooled) in the administrative ramifications of personality theory, group psychology and motivation — as well as the more antiseptic pursuits of quantitative analysis and systems theory. As a reasonable man and a political man he would seek to attain as much of the legitimizing cachet that a rational ideology could provide. And as a man of wisdom he would intuit when to rest upon one level of the proposition or the other.

TRANSCENDENTALISM

> You see, gentlemen, reason is an excellent thing, there is no disputing that. But reason is nothing but reason and satisfies only the rational side of man's nature while *will* is a manifestation of the whole life, that is, of the whole human life, including reason and all the impulses. (Fyodor Dostoevsky)

Man cannot live by the bread of rationality alone. Nor is it enough for him to wallow in emotive gratification. There is a *tertium quid*. This makes demands which upon occasion can be so prepotent and insistent that they override all else. I refer to the mystery of the will and its entailments: faith, belief, conviction and commitment. That is to say, to the transcendental, the higher irrational, the *transrational*. Religions have the power of evoking Type I commitment.

The truly religious have no difficulty in contravening the Type II values of organization or their own Type III values. On the battleground of struggle between soul and world they follow the colours of a Type I ideology. When called upon, they will fall and die around those colours. It is as if the zealot asks for more than the world has to offer.

Religions, of course, can be of God or Mammon — sacred or secular. Men worship power and fame and their own career success, glory, honour, sexual gratification and wealth, the Nobel Prize and the Knight's Cross with Oak Leaves — many things. Where Type I values exist — and they can only exist within an individual consciousness — they will tend to colour the organizational context in which that consciousness interacts with other selves so as to give it a charismatic quality. The transcendental or religious values need not be shared by members of the organization for the effect to be present, but when shared fully there can be a galvanizing and synergetic effect upon organizational performance, an *esprit de corps* which multiplies the power of the administrator. Even when they are not shared at all I would argue that the mere presence of a single actor with Type I commitments is enough to radically affect the organizational character, such is the potency of Type I value and the mystery of social chemistry. It is not understood how the phenomenon of transcendentalism affects the quality of organizational life, but affect it it does.

In the Christian phase of Western civilization the Church was a general source of ideology which helped to determine organizational contexts in a variety of ways. No doubt it served in some ways to ameliorate work conditions and one would like to think that it contributed to an infusion of hierarchical *noblesse oblige*. However, the historical aspect which is perhaps of most interest to administrative theorists is that occasioned by the Reformation. The accompanying Protestant work ethic is well documented in Max Weber's *The Protestant Ethic and the Spirit of Capitalism*. Certain sects — Calvinists, Quakers, Mennonites, Mormons — then as now, became noted for the display of such qualities as frugality, diligence, honesty, trustworthiness, devotion to duty and work responsibilities. These values have a direct bearing upon organizational life and administration. I strongly suspect, although I cannot refer to the evidence, that even today in a putative post-Christian era, the fundamentalist sects are disproportionately represented within the ranks of successful executives. Of course, this might simply be a reflection of the fact that one set of characterological qualities conducive to administrative success closely correspond to those endorsed by some species of Christian ideology. But the *arthasastra* also leads to success (perhaps more directly) and all ideologies are influential in some way. The Christian influence upon collective enterprise can be damned (Nietzsche) or praised (Rowntree). The judgements are beside the point; the point is that any discernible religious ideological effect, Christian or non-Christian, upon the organizational context would be essentially dependent upon Type I commitment. This commitment can reach the organization in three ways: most forcibly through the person of the administrator, forcibly through the persons of other organizational members and, weakly, as a diluted permeation from the general socio-cultural environment (V_5, V_4). Religions, sacred or secular, can constrain administrative options. They can infuse direction and inform conduct. They clearly must be considered within any administrative philosophy. They may even, in determinate cases, form the essential structure and function of such philosophy.

This ideological terrain has not been properly charted. Christianity represents but one mode of transcendentalism. Others are too numerous to survey here though I shall comment briefly on some sundry -isms which do seem to have a peculiar affinity for administration.

MILITARISM

Certain constellations of values when subscribed to at the Type I level can result in the ideological world-view we can call militarism. These values would include, indicatively: order, honour, discipline, hierarchy, duty, power, loyalty, symbols. The linkage to statism is easily achieved and self-reinforcing through Type I, II and III associations with nationalism or patriotism. Nowadays, the ideology is sometimes disparaged as fascist, but in truth its values transcend any particular theory of the State. Indeed, the belief that human institutions rest ultimately upon the use of force or violence is itself without colour, race or creed. Moreover, militaristic ideology needs neither nation state nor armed force for its functioning. The Society of Jesus gives a clerical illustration of this point and, without question, private sector industry and commerce can be thoroughly expressive of the militaristic spirit.

At the organizational level this ideology resonates strongly with systems theory and such administrative credos as Management by Objectives. As noted above (see p. 35) it generates its own value fallacy in the notion that any specified goal can be obtained by analytic factoring of administrative problems. Militarism needs neither display of uniforms nor parades; its influence is plain enough in organizational behaviour, particularly in large bureaucracies. It can be regarded as a subform of rationalism. Given the contemporary ethos its surface manifestations usually exhibit a heavy overlay of humanistic influence and this would hold even within military organizations *per se.*

STOICISM

It might be more appropriate to refer to this form of value-subscription, with its attendant world-view, as Orientalism, since its most lucid expressions are to be found not in Western but in Eastern philosophy.[3] Doctrines of Zen, of Buddhism proper and of the Hindu doctrine of *karma yoga* as expounded in the *Bhagavad Gita* convey the essential values and principles to which, of course, commitment at the Type I level must occur if administrative ramifications are to be at all significant. The basic ingredients of the ideology are detachment and concentration, two attitudes which, on first

---

[3] The *Meditations* of the Roman emperor Marcus Aurelius constitute a most notable Western exception.

sight, appear to be in contradiction of each other. The first means that egoistic self-interest is submerged in collective responsibilities; the second that egoism is transcended through concentrated absorption of mind in the tasks at hand. That there are paradoxes here, both of philosophy and psychology, is at once conceded but the key elements of work and duty each have profound moral and aesthetic implications. This ideology has intriguing elements which will lead us to consider it again later in the book. It is one which is perhaps more widely prevalent in today's world than might at first be obvious. In the West it may have suffered a decline along with the Victorian *Zeitgeist* but in the East there is the singular and important instance of modern Japan, and in the Communist societies generally there is at least a *Realgrund* amenable to stoicism in our sense of the term.

IDEALISM

Idealism as an ideology must be distinguished from idealism as a philosophical system. The technical details and sense of the latter need not delay us. Ideological idealism is a way of treating values. When concepts of the desirable are regarded less as end states to be consummated and more as ultimates or absolutes which can never be achieved but nevertheless are functional as criteria, as guides or directors of behaviour, then we have the idealistic posture: pie in the sky, and not necessarily by and by. Global values such as Justice, Truth, Beauty may be entertained as criteria for forming lower-order value judgements. The idealistic spirit thrives upon the unattainable but tries to use it as a guide to action. It follows that in the ideological sense idealism is a universalistic posture which can inform any other ideology and reinforce it. Only when allied to an idealistic *philosophy* can it be properly considered as autonomous.

LIBERALISM

The ideological status of liberalism is peculiar. Again one must distinguish between the well-articulated political

theories which are grounded in liberal philosophy and a constellation of what may be called liberal values with their
associated attitudes and beliefs. Given our understanding of
ideology and of the philosophy and values of liberalism, it
is questionable whether the latter can enlist the intensive
Type I commitments necessary to gain thorough ideological
status. As we shall see in the following chapter, some form
of Type II commitment is more likely to be the mode. On
the other hand, it cannot be denied that liberal values have
enjoyed a long period of cultural ascendance in the West
and have come to constitute, with some prevalence, a political orthodoxy since the end of the last world war. Liberalism
has, therefore, clearly affected the *Realgrund* of societies
and their constituent organizations. Nevertheless, the values
endorsed by liberalism (e.g. compromise, egalitarianism,
utilitarianism) are subsumed under the broader ideological
sweeps of rationalism and humanism. Moreover, its general
Type II orientation is itself a deterrent to Type I transcendentalism.

The liberal view accords with Theory Y and affects
administration through that vehicle. As a broad-based cultural orthodoxy it affects the organizational context through
the V_5 ethos. Its transcendental effect can, on the other
hand, be largely discounted — an assertion which would not
hold for its opponents in the political dialectic: conservatism
and radicalism (Eysenck, 1960:265).

THE LURE AND THE PERIL

...It is the *map-maker* who actually creates the world in which
the navigator is going to navigate. This world may or may not
correspond exactly to the real world. (de Bono, 1979:56)

What I have tried to do in this chapter is to sketch the rough
outlines of a map. The broad terrain is discernible: large
continents like rationalism, humanism; the high ground of
transcendentalism; the shifting boundaries of militarism,
idealism — but in this map of human motivation, commitment

and values, much is obscure, uncharted, dangerously unknown. The psyche has its observable surface and its inscrutable depths. The administrator seeks knowledge of both. And this is dangerous, for while knowledge is power, power can corrupt.

Certain values, Type I values, have for certain men the magical property of transmuting their forms of life, investing them with meaning, giving to them an absoluteness which carries them beyond the relativity of individual circumscription. The ordinary ego of workaday selfishness and common sense is somehow transcended. The terms 'charisma' and 'fanaticism' enter into this discourse. When an actor becomes committed in this Type I way, he affects his field of action. When an administrator is engaged at the Type I level, he determines the quality of his organization. Such influence, whether directly or at many removes, can be powerful and overwhelming. Those who surrounded Hitler, Churchill, de Gaulle, Henry Luce, Alfred Sloan, experienced this reality.

There is a lure in all this, and a peril. The lure is in the transcendence of Type I values, their suprarationality, and their ideological capacity to provide authority, meaning and simplistic responses to life's complexity. There is all the appeal and exaltation of saint and superman, martyr and man-on-horseback. For man does not live by bread alone, he craves religion. He is not content to forever question, he craves answers.

The peril lies in the real-world effects of Type I commitment. Values translate into behaviours and behaviours into material consequences in the world of men and things. The historical record is bleak. Wherever Type I values are evidenced, in nationalist fervour, patriotism, religion, there also is evidenced disorder and human suffering, wars, inquisitions, persecutions. Man's inhumanity to his fellows thrives upon ideology. We burn at the stake not out of Type III subrationality or Type II rationality but because of Type I transrationality.

In administration men are led to exceed themselves in the co-operative cause when fired by ideology. And other men are broken on the wheel and crushed beneath the organizational juggernaut. Powerful commitment is double-edged. The sophisticated administrator approaches Type I values with excitement tempered by caution. The practical import of this chapter is this, that ideologies enter into reality through individual actors and organizational psychology. The administrator who is concerned about praxis is aware of this and learns the art of value-observation — inward to the world of the organization and his own person, outward to the world and its subtly changing ethos. He cultivates his sense of historical and personal perspective and he understands that one must not only be aware of, one must also *beware* of Type I values. He knows that ideologies (R_I) have the power to create hells $(R_{II, III})$ where none have previously existed and at the same time to provide men with the courage to bear these hells and even invest them with fulfilment and meaning. He must, therefore, monitor constantly his value environment and be conscious of his own values, his own form of life. His praxis would reflect this belief:

CREDO: *Wisdom is a particular ability to look at the world and to look at one's looking.* (de Bono, 1979:67)

5

Pragmatics

'Do the duty that lies nearest thee,' which thou knowest to be a duty! Thy second duty will already have become clearer. (Sartor Resartus)

'VIA AUREA MEDIOCRITAS'

There is a middle ground between the commitments of ideology and the fluctuating turbulence of affectivity. This is fortunate for human nerve and tissue. Even at best the demands of ideology are rooted in abstraction and men do not live in intellectual abstractions, however much they may subscribe to them or be governed by them. As for affect, men cannot constantly be engaged in the internecine warfare of the ego. Between the Type III realities and the Type I blueprints there lies the vast region of normality — the everyday, workaday world of organizational life. A banal world, perhaps, but one in which man is at relative ease: habituated, conditioned, programmed, modest and content.

We are concerned here with the valuational character or 'colour' of organizational settings. This coloration coexists with any given set of organizational facts. At one extreme it gives us the Realities, at another the Ideologies, and in between the realm of pragmatics and common sense. Type II middle ground is characterized by sense rather than sensibility, by reason, reasonableness and the organizational metavalues. The affective tone may be neutral and void of ideological override, it may even be tedious, banal and enervating, but it is tolerable and comfortable, a context within which the ego can subsist without excessive wear and tear. Instead of the ultimate values of Level I and the proximate values of Level III there are the *ap*proximate values of Level II. These are themselves subject to the criteria of consensus and consequences, criteria which are essentially pragmatic or utilitarian in their philosophical orientation. Level II is the region of the golden mean and within this region organizations approximate their goals, organization members approximate job satisfaction and administrators (some of them) approximate their ideals.

To put it yet another way, between the realms of sense (III) and Being (I) there is the vast region of thought (II). Action is always an amalgam of all three but it is the area of thoughtful process which is being singled out for analysis here. The Type II values associated with this area are themselves characterized by some element, however fallible or however exact, of cognitive calculation. Since rationality is so fundamental a human attribute and since organizations subserve human interests, it follows that this context — the pragmatic organizational setting — is the most ordinary, the most typical, and the to-be-expected pattern of organizational life within which the administrative actor must perform. For that reason alone it is important to the philosophy of administration.

Man is a rational and a social animal. These attributes determine co-operative action since they enable a value consensus to be reached about ends which can then be approximated or attained through a logical sequence of means. The socio-rational instincts result in a world of experience which is not philosophical at first blush but is rather a field of behaviour where, in the short term at least, action is favoured over reflection and doing over being. Problem finding, problem creating and problem solving characterize this activity which is, in a word, the pragmatic. The pragmatic spirit assumes that emotions can be subordinated to rational manipulation and control. It abjures the ideological and treats the intellectual as a suspect domain.

It worships the great god Common Sense and it rejoices with Aristotle in the Golden Mean.

CONSENSUS ORGANIZATION

The basic element in individual experience is affective-sensory. We feel first, think later. Phenomenology is affectively coloured, which is to say that it is characterized by Type III values. The translation of these *individual* qualities into a collective or organizational expression is on the face of it most easily accomplished through *consensus*; that is, the working aggregation or averaging of the component individual values. In principle such a consensus is possible for any group, although it should be noted that averaging in a strictly mathematical sense does not occur. What does occur is that within phenomenological boundaries concessions are made and victories achieved without disturbance to the overall zone of indifference. The consensus is easier where Type III values are the components and most difficult where Type I values are present; indeed, in the latter case, a working consensus may become impossible since conflicting Type I commitments may be irreconcilable. (Compare political contexts where a detente is impossible: Northern Ireland, Israeli-PLO relations.) Because of this the pragmatist seeks to avoid engagement upon matters of principle, he searches instead for the politically possible. Indeed, the political arts of discovering, sensing, interpreting, manipulating and using consensus are at the heart of administrative process. Consensus invokes the processes of compromise, co-operation, trade-off, negotiation, conciliation, dealing and bargaining which occur whenever parties possess differential power and seek divergent ends. So long as these ends can be encompassed within the scenario of purposes or goal matrix of the organization the pragmatic administrator has room for manoeuvre. The resultant values are neither ultimate nor proximate but approximate, and it is for this reason that Type II administration functions best when there is a lack of clarity about goals, a certain semantic obfuscation and an absence of ideological commitment. In the pragmatic organizational context no one is ever entirely satisfied but neither is anyone dissatisfied to the point of sabotage or disruption or separation. It is, therefore, a constant aim of the administrator to maintain and enlarge the zones of acceptance and indifference. Consensus is the lowest common denominator of administrative process. Anything less is mere compulsion. This context (II_B) is the norm and the basis of the ordinary world of administration and management. In contrast with Type I and III contexts it minimizes stress and strain. The soldier marches with his eye on the pack of the man in front of him, the bureaucrat moves paper from in-basket to out-basket, phones ring, secretaries type, machines are assembled, customers are served, all of which is evidence of tacit working agreements about values. Such agreements between role incumbents are not scrutinized or raised to the level of consciousness in the normal working mode. This is not necessary. Things work. They go on. That is enough.

Shifts in consensus occur in the same subliminal way. The equation of human chemistry can alter subtly or radically as individuals move into and out of organizational roles. The skilled administrator monitors these movements and senses when changes in consensus transpire. At the societal or macro-level the skilled politician does likewise and finds the correct language game in which to couch the rhetoric which will manipulate the collective energy. Adolf Hitler, Abraham Lincoln and Winston Churchill excelled at this.

At the largest level it may well be that value polarities oscillate rhythmically and historically between extremes (left and right) but this movement takes place at different levels of consciousness and expression. Thus, at a given time the overt orthodoxy (liberalism, say) is being undermined by a resurgent conservativism, a movement which would enable the politically astute to profit. These macro-level (V_5) changes would impinge upon organizations at the V_3 level and again the administratively astute could find opportunities in the lag and lead of the value polarities (the point being, of course, that there is always more to consensus than meets the eye). To identify the *true* consensus is the mark of administrative genius at best and great pragmatic leadership at least. Nor is this task simple; surface harmony can disguise decay in the polity while volatile group behaviour and rebelliousness can distract observation and distort perception of the underlying unity and moral integrity. Of interest in this regard is Speer's account of the first time he saw Hitler and heard him speak:

> Finally, Hitler no longer seemed to be speaking to convince; rather, he seemed to feel that he was expressing what the audience, by now transformed into a single mass, expected of him. It was as if it were the most natural thing in the world to lead students and faculty of the two greatest academies in Germany submissively by the leash. Yet that evening he was not yet the absolute ruler, immune from all criticism, but was still exposed to attack from all directions. (Speer, 1970:19)

Nevertheless, subtleties of perception to one side, it may be asserted that organizations demand some minimal degree of value consensus in order to be viable; there must be a level II modicum of general agreement about the way things are and the way things work, what the organization exists for and what the roles within it are intended to accomplish, the *status quo* and the *modus operandi*. But in the most common of organizational contexts pragmatism prospers and all is usually well enough.

THE PRAGMATIC CONTEXT

Consciously or unconsciously the pragmatic attitude subordinates or excludes the extremes of Type I and Type III valuation. This attitude, revealed and reflected in the context of the organization, is one which endorses practicality, possibility and workability. The test of truth and value is, will it work? There is an emphasis upon the short run, upon getting through the day, even upon the moment. Problems of value are muted or elided since value direction is always available, either as given in the positivistic sense or through reference to the working consensus. As Scott and Hart put it:

The organizational world of management is one where complex problems of short-term duration must be dealt with expediently in order to advance the a priori propositions (of the organizational imperative). Pragmatism demands that managers direct their energies and talents to finding solutions for practical, existing problems within an immediate time frame. The language, reward systems, and activities of management demonstrate this concern for the present. Its attention to putting out fires, meeting competition, adjusting to inputs from the public, insuring the smooth day-to-day running of departments, and short-range planning horizons indicate its devotion to securing an orderly, purposeful world composed of interesting, narrow puzzles to be solved. This pragmatic puzzle-world encourages managers not to reflect on larger, less immediate issues of long-range effects or needs. (Scott and Hart, 1979:45-6)

This pressure to pragmatism, the pragmatic impress, prevails within most administrative contexts of any degree of complexity. Consider an illustration from educational administration:

...the administrator finds himself at the intersection of conflicting expectations and forces, and that a great deal of his time and effort are required to deal with these conflicts. There are several ways in which to attempt to do so: to mediate; to try for compromise; to ignore and hope it will go away, but thereby risking intensification or extension of the conflict; to resolve by application of power. Whichever method is selected, the controlling ingredient seems to be the political one. It's less a matter of doing what's right, than of doing what's possible, or even what's expedient. The administrator gives up what he might like to do, hoping that the opportunity will come again at a better time.... he concludes that principles and values can only be partially realized, and almost never in the short run, or that it will never be possible to do more than mediate among the demands of others, withdrawing personally from the arena except to act as referee and arbiter to see that the rules are followed. (Enns, 1981:5)

The pattern and the context is familiar. The pressures are relentless. The organization is a forum for contending interests, a market-place of values. Within this context the pragmatic pressure to action deflects any tendency to Type I ideology and overrides the narcissistic hedonic motivations which characterize the Type III context. The pause for reflection is not allowed. Stimulus begets unmediated response. Principles and ideals tend to be treated with grudging respect, if at all. Even within a field where philosophical commitment might be thought to be of the essence the pragmatic impress acts to elevate, in our terms, management over administration.

> An observation made by Marquis and Goldhammer (1961) seems to me to be relevant in this look at ethics in the educational professions. They noted that in North American society action is generally valued over contemplation, doing over being, achievement over reflection. Men and women of action are admired in business, the professions, and even in the arts. In education administrators have been more highly regarded than scholars and philosophers, and even among the latter, systems emphasizing action (e.g., pragmatism and behaviourism) are preferred over others. I suggest that because this is so, educators and policy makers have tended to be more concerned with 'What gets the job done? than with 'What is ethical? (Enns, 1981:5)

Stage and actor, context and experience, are interactive. As goes administrative behaviour so goes the quality of work life. In this most prevalent, typical and common of organizational styles, the chief characteristic is busyness. This has been well documented in a classical contemporary study *The Nature of Managerial Work* (Mintzberg, 1973) and repeated studies have tended to support and strengthen the original thesis. The busy-syndrome includes a preference for oral contact — face to face or by telephone — and a fragmented schedule of interruptions and tasks which are undemanding in terms of critical analysis, concentration or philosophical reflection. The syndrome is self-justifying and guilt-assuaging; the administrator (more accurately, manager) is worthy of his salt because his activity and busyness fulfils the role-expectations which the pragmatic context generates. So the pathology of retreat to managerialism becomes entrenched, and administration as we have defined it withers.

Instead, intellectual or philosophical or humane activities are avoided as stress-producing, and superficiality blossoms. In such a context the maxims and contradictory proverbs which pass for administrative theory and were held in such disdain by Simon (1965:20-44) become the preferred mode of administrative philosophy. Hands-on down-to-earthedness and commonsensicality are the preferred mode of rationality, and, in the realm of policy making, muddling through and disjointed incrementalism (Lindblom, 1959: 155, 1979) triumph over rational comprehensive planning. Such are the natural if not inevitable tendencies of consensus organization.

RESULTS ORGANIZATION

The pragmatic coin has two sides. The one — consensus organization — establishes an ambience of Type IIB values the mark of which is working compromise or *modus vivendi*. The other — results organization — is concerned with Type IIA values and the achievement of the organizational purposes. It sets the *modus operandi* and seeks to justify the maintenance of the organization through accomplishment and growth. The values which build this ambience are characterized by rationality and the analysis of consequences of action. The test, for either side of the coin, is pragmatic. Does it work? Do the subscribed values and value commitments result in organizational maintenance and growth? That is, are the basic metavalues fulfilled? In Barnard's terminology, is there adequate efficiency and effectiveness? Again it can be noted and should be stressed that results organization is the modal, ordinary, common form of organizational life. The simplest distinction between Type I and Type II organizations is that the results sought in the former are distinguished by virtue of Type I commitments to principles or values of ideology and faith. The Type II organization is less religious, perhaps even a-religious, and its *raison d'être* is quite simply the well-being, usually the economic well-being of its component members.

In the pragmatic Type IIA context the basic criterion for action and for the establishment of priorities (policy) is the consequences and results of proposed and present action. Implicit in this analysis is a healthy sense of *cui bono*? Who will get what from whom? And how will the pie be divided? Because of this spirit of libertarian self-seeking, and because pragmatics tend naturally to the material and the objective as opposed to the non-material and the subjective, it follows that the philosophical infrastructure behind the IIA context is typically that of utilitarianism. The greatest good for the greatest number becomes the eminent maxim. Sometimes indeed this becomes metavaluational and the organization comes to be regarded as a self-validating moral agency. What is good for General Motors is thought to be good for the country.

In results organization, the metavalues of maintenance, growth, efficiency and effectiveness become imperative. They also provide a protocol for the resolution of value problems. First, defend one's vested interest in the organization (as defined by the larger organizational envelope or by some subunit within that membrane) against any threat. Second, extend and expand that interest wherever opportunity allows. (This is corollary since growth is itself a form of defence. The more territory one commands the more one can afford to lose.) Third, act so as to minimize costs while maximizing results. (The principle of rational efficiency.)

These canons when consistently applied to value judgements, choice and action go to establish a working context in which men are neither angelic nor demonic. There may be a constant falling short of the metavalues but the practical, stochastic processes of day to day problem solving and muddling through keep organizations intact and produce a complex web of commitment which allows them to survive, to maintain themselves and, where possible, to grow.

Results organization represents a world of work which can be divorced from 'private' life. Interests, that is to say, can be compartmentalized. Some theorists have observed that this can obscure the individual's relation to the final organizational achievement or the larger consequences of organizational action. Using the term 'fragmentation' Silver and Geller (1978:125) say that this permits the individual to function effectively and happily in a limited context, without ever being aware of the larger purposes of the organization, and without having to accept any personal responsibility for the organizational results. This is true, but again distinction must be made between Type I and Type II organizations. The SS operations in World War II and the US Air Force operation in Viet Nam illustrate the distinction. The stratojet bombardier concerned about promotion and pension rights is in a quite different category from the death camp *Sturmbannführer*. Not simply by virtue of differential psychological distancing — air-conditioned antiseptic technological comfort in the first instance and dirty hands-on contact with human misery and suffering in the second — but because the SS provided an ideology, while the USAF is essentially Type II, where a pragmatic, econometric model provides an ambience of liberal uninspired reasonableness.

In the IIA context, language games can assume considerable importance. Should the consequences of organizational action conflict with environmental ethos (V_5) or offend latent public or political sensibilities (as in the Viet Nam example) there will be a resort to some form of Newspeak. 'Body counts', 'terminations', 'special treatments', 'preventive strikes' and other euphemisms are freely coined. But even where there is no threat to any zone of consensus and where the organization's purposes and pursuit of these purposes are impeccable, there is still a tendency to regulate language. Thus there is a general conditioning to accept a need for cost-effective rationality in business organizations, and the business-like model extends across non-profit organizations to assume a universal norm. The jargon of accounting and systems theory ('bottom line', 'up front', 'in place', 'heading up', 'track record') enters into administrative speech patterns and thought processes (Cutt, 1980). So, too, does language reveal the pragmatic spirit: 'play it by ear'; 'go with the flow'; 'take it from where it's at'. The language games change continuously but a familiarity with them helps to establish the players' mutual legitimacy and credibility. They have a shibboleth function and serve notice as it were of a freemasonry of understanding wherein rational and ethical absurdities are tempered by pragmatic commonsense. Sometimes a tacit managerial conspiracy to subvert administration. A modest unspoken agreement to tread the middle path between the extremes of high and low commitment. A sensible subscription to satisficing results. This too is characteristic of the Type II ambience.

CREDO: *Pay-off is the ultimate test of any organization. This is more than a belief, it is a tautology.*

THEORY Z AND THE GOAL PARADIGM

Theories X and Y comprise stereotypes and polarities which suggest that a Theory Z, if there were truly such, would occupy a middle ground, a golden mean as might be expressed by Class II values and their corresponding organizational context. In such a context the consensual (IIB) values would be reconciled and aligned with the consequential (IIA) values and the mechanism for doing this would be the scenario of purposes (see figure 2, p. 24). In other words, the organization's goals or the results which the organization is expected to achieve would elicit the necessary commitment from the members of the consensus, not in any simplistic or quantitative sense — although the quantitative indices of accounting and econometrics cannot be ignored — but in a sophisticated and qualitative sense in which the task of the administration is to achieve the necessary identification between self-interest and organizational interest. The clearest evidence for the existence and empirical success of such a Theory Z comes from contemporary Japan (Ouchi, 1980; Drucker, 1981) where organizational contexts are overtly feudal[1] and

[1] Note that Japanese major corporations ensure life-long employment and career patterns as opposed to the (still) more fluid and mobile West. Also that historical feudalism is a recent feature of Japanese culture.

explicitly paternalistic. Here it would seem that administrative behaviour is characterized by a sort of *noblesse oblige* which requires intensive and extensive communication with all ranks of the organizational membership — from floor-sweeper to president — in order to establish consensus, commitment and co-ordination. A time-consuming endeavour of heroic proportions which would be alien to even the most participatory and democratic of organizations cast in the Western bureaucratic mould. Nevertheless, it would appear to pay high dividends, at least in the V_5 context of Japan. The Western tendency, on the other hand, is to flirt with the militaristic fallacy and to separate more sharply ends (results) from means (consensus). The emphasis is upon IIA consequences and instrumentality, whereas in the Japanese administrative philosophy the organization itself is an end as well as a means. It is so to speak, non-disposable, and the concept of organization extends backwards and forwards across time to include valued cadres of past and future workers.

It is possible then for an organization to have intrinsic as well as extrinsic value. The mechanism for relating these two kinds of value is the scenario of purposes, the goal paradigm. While it is conceded that organizations are goal-seeking entities it is, in fact, very rarely the case that there is simplicity, unity and clarity of goal or function. To say, for example, that a corporation exists to make a profit or an army to keep the peace is deceptive. These aims are but part of a complex goal pattern, necessary but not sufficient to give administrative understanding. Along with them there coexist and interact the private agendas, the individual idiographic values which are traded daily in the organizational market-place. In Barnard's terms, each organization becomes an economy of incentives and disincentives and the goal paradigm (Georgiu, 1973) must be understood at a sophisticated level.

This sophistication is perhaps most practically evident (whether consciously so or not is another question) in the Type II context. Whereas Type III contexts presume a hedonistic self-interest which must be disciplined by the nomothetic-administrative arm, with ensuing alienation, and whereas Type I contexts presume an ideological commitment to organizational purpose with ensuing heroics, the Type II organization strikes an intermediate balance of interactive value trading. It presumes a fundamentally rational self-interest and a fundamental, though only partial commitment to the organization's overt goals. It would seem then that any effective Theory Z would be marked by a salience of Type II values. It would accord with utilitarian and pragmatic principles but be void of ideological fervour. The motivational tone would be warm rather than hot or cold. Results organization would represent its typical form of life and the dominant metavalues would be efficiency, effectiveness, maintenance, growth and rationality. This is indeed the type of organizational context which is most common. By and large it is what we are most used to.

MAPPING

It is now possible to arrange the notions developed thus far in the diagram of figure 8. The taxonomy continues from the point where figure 6 leaves off. The declension from administrative to managerial logic is again apparent and the possibilities of logical confusion through the homogenetic fallacy become evident. Figure 8 also sums up the discussion of chapters 3 through 5. The analysis is based upon the value paradigm. The general applicability of this paradigm is useful in that, once grasped, it can assist the administrator in the value analysis aspect of decision and policy making.

This kind of value logic is of course *analytical* while reality, in contrast, is synthetic. Reality conflates the categories; so real contexts are never pure, and are always mixed. Moreover they are dynamic. Sands shift. Nevertheless a certain stability will tend to persist over the short and mid-term since values themselves are highly resistant to change. The perceptive administrator-philosopher will be able to discern the quality of context within which he is acting. For the non-administrator this quality will be a phenomenological reality, a felt experience perhaps subliminal, perhaps painfully or pleasantly a part of his fabric of awareness. Within and against these contexts administration works itself out.

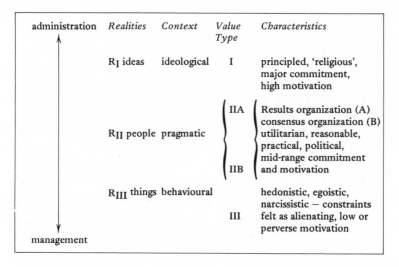

administration	*Realities*	*Context*	*Value Type*	*Characteristics*
	R_I ideas	ideological	I	principled, 'religious', major commitment, high motivation
	R_{II} people	pragmatic	IIA	Results organization (A) consensus organization (B) utilitarian, reasonable, practical, political, mid-range commitment and motivation
			IIB	
	R_{III} things	behavioural		hedonistic, egoistic, narcissistic − constraints
management			III	felt as alienating, low or perverse motivation

FIGURE 8   *Organizational contexts*

THEORY AND PRACTICE

The omnipresence of the Type II context means the hegemony of management over administration. This gives rise to some interesting but vexing questions. Consider, for example, the division, both logical and psychological, between theory and practice. Within the Type II contexts, theory and philosophy are discounted while practical sense and sensibilities − know-how, can-do − are at a premium. This, after all, is the ignoble but ordinary world of sordid managerial detail where the object of each exercise is to make it work, where for manager and managee the problem is often simply one of coping: with quotas, targets, committees, stress, deadlines, bottlenecks and the minutiae of technical details and human interactions. How to get through the day is the question. Reasonableness, compromise and workability are the values.

Philosophically speaking, this context with its resultant managerial postures is vapid, even anti-intellectual. Practical men of affairs who have to meet a payroll and whose continuous obsession is with the steering of their organizational ship through the shifting shoals of internal and external threat may not be well placed for philosophical activity. They are too constrained under the impress of the metavalues. So where and how does philosophy get done? And who does administration as opposed to management? Can *any*body do it (without benefit of preparation or special knowledge)? To this last question the simple empirical answer would seem to be yes, because this is the way the world works and not only can *anybody* do administration, anybody *does* and, often enough, does it very well at that. A more sophisticated answer would invoke the distinction between administration and management, for while anyone may do the former it is not at all clear that anyone has an automatic birthright to the latter. Management implies at least some body of expertise or preparatory knowledge if only the *in situ* knowledge of a particular real organization and its context. And this again strengthens the managerial bias of pragmatism, to the detriment of theory or philosophy. The question which pragmatics studiously avoids is this: is there some way of preparing administrators (not managers) to do administrative (not managerial) work better, more wisely, more *philosophically*? Such a question would be alien to the pragmatic spirit.

A sanguinity about the amateur status of *administration* coupled with evolving claims to the professional status of *management* typifies this context. This is the normal way of things, the common, typical attitude. It might be that this attitude were defensible if it were simply a matter of the division of theory and practice. But it is not. There is a much more subtle, more important, and (as we have argued above) thoroughly overlooked division: the division between practice and praxis. That this distinction is overlooked is apparent when one of the leading administrative theorists effectively ignores it when discussing how administrators could be prepared. He assumes five analytical skills to compose the essence of administrative work. These are '(1) The analysis of *expertise*. The management of knowledge. (2) The analysis of *coalitions*. The management of conflict. (3) The analysis of *ambiguity*. The management of goals. (4) The analysis of *time*. The management of attention. (5) The analysis of *information*. The management of inference.' (March, 1974:28)

All these are surely desirable administrative skills but they neglect entirely the analysis of *value* (The management of *meaning*) with all its ramifications of ethics, morality, purpose, policy and philosophy.

Logical and critical faculties are rightly emphasized but the problem of value and value analysis is slighted. Yet the world of administration is primarily a *value* world, the components of fact and logic are subordinate and secondary. March succumbs to the militaristic fallacy as Simon has done before him. In a rightly ordered world praxis would supervene practice, and theory, to the extent that it existed, would fund both. It is easy, indeed it is the line of least resistance, to avoid praxis at the expense of practice. Pragmatics confirms and assists this trend.

And what of Theories X and Y in the pragmatic context? It could be argued that these polarities are both subsumed and transcended. They disappear or evaporate in practice. Is this median path, then, the practical realization of a Theory Z where stochastic processes assure the ultimate triumph of rationality along with ever-progressive improvement in the quality of work life? Or does it devolve eventually into the merely minimal achievement of metavalues through some spirit of antagonistic co-operation? Good logic and sound sense, a healthy grasp of the realities; all these would be well enough did man but live by bread alone. He does not. His value complexity extends beyond this simplicity. Pragmatics will bring us through the day but it will not take us where we want to go.

CREDO: *Common sense is a necessary but not sufficient condition for right administration, for praxis.*

CRITIQUE

It is well to remember that what has been discussed up to now is contexts-of-action rather than action itself, stages and sets rather than actors and drama. Moreover, the three-fold typology which has emerged, based as it is upon the value paradigm, is an artificial construct. These patterns of organization ambience, organization styles and forms-of-life do not ever exist in pure form; they are 'ideal types' abstracted for the purpose of analysis. What is to be found, felt and experienced in the empirical world is always a mix of types, perhaps with one clearly salient and distinctive, perhaps conflated to the point of blandness (as a mix of intense and vivid colours can produce merely a dirty grey). If analysis is to serve a useful purpose it must in the end be subordinated to synthesis. Or it must be in some way efficacious in dealing with the flux of events. It must lead to the generality of laws for the theorist, and to comprehension for the philosopher.

There is further synthetic critique which can be entered here. It is that contexts — however analysed — can have no sensible meaning unless considered in conjunction with the human actors who act upon and interact with those contexts. This is especially true if the aim is a synthetic comprehension of the whole picture. The whole will be more than the sum of its parts. Organizations are definable as human collectivities, the constituents of which are purposes, men and techniques. These three components will create both context and meaning. When an organization is born the world changes and so does its total complex of meaning. The experience of organizational context is phenomenological. It can only happen within a single, individual, human consciousness. The buck of 'meaning' stops within a human mind.

So far, by describing organizations and typing them in terms of meaning, that is, by analysing them in value terms, I have only established a backdrop to the complex whole of organizational action. It is an attempt to respond to Aristotle's plea for praxis as opposed to practice. An

Aristotelian exhortation which by and large has fallen upon deaf ears whilst his logic, on the other hand, has been whole-heartedly embraced. Indeed, over the millenia, logic and value have been progressively divorced and the discourse of organization theory has been scientifically sanitized. Nevertheless, value and fact are always inextricably intertwined. An organization always represents a context-of-meaning, a unique manifestation of philosophy-in-action.

The end-function of analysis should be enhancement of meaning, not its destruction, and just as the analytical distinction between administration and management permits us ultimately to fuse these concepts at a higher level of comprehension, so the value analysis of contexts should eventually permit their ultimate reunion with facts and cases at a higher level of sophistication.

For performance and action, actor and context must be compresent. The actor must be on stage. Analytically, then, we must now turn in the next chapter to that actor who is our central interest: the administrator, the executive, the *leader*. The same sort of analysis can be applied and if this takes into its account, directly or by implication, other members of the organization and the interrelations between them and the administrator, then the entire field will have been surveyed. That done, we shall have examined the whole of the administrative enterprise and should be in a position, at last, to seek in synthesis some redemptive wisdom.

6

Archetypes

Taxonomy is the beginning of science. We have no science of administration or leadership but we do have an overload of information and a surfeit of data. How can we make sense of it? Can the analysis of value provide an ordering principle?

To type is a very basic human instinct. It is a first attempt at imposing order upon a welter of experience so as to derive meaning; or, more accurately, so as to cope with excessive information first and then arrange its disorder into hypotheses and propositions which can provide schemes of meaning. The worth of this meaning depends upon the underlying logic of the typological schema and the ultimate use of that schema in practice or praxis. Typing permeates language. Indeed those languages are the greatest and the most powerful which encompass with the maximum precision the greatest multiplicity of names and forms, percepts and concepts (and this would include both dead languages like Sanskrit and the machine languages of computer technology). Thus science has a commanding prestige in our culture for its language games of, say, biochemistry and subatomic physics which exhibit an exquisite precision and a universal scope. Each language game (Wittgenstein, 1974:7) invents its own typing scheme. The ids and animas of depth psychology, the Platonic forms and the *gunas* of metaphysics, though they lack scientific precision and nicety, still persuade, are potent, and have practical effect.

In the study of administration the typing instinct has not been inactive. It has ranged from the trivial to the profound.

Some schemata have been based on empirical research such as Reddin's (1970) three-dimensional analysis of leadership and its classification of administrators into Compromisers, Developers, Missionaries, Autocrats and so on. Perhaps the most profoundly based and influential scheme has been Max Weber's formulation of charismatic, traditional and rational-legalistic administration; a set of types which is supported by exhaustive historical research and which is closely integrated into his general theory of bureaucracy. Weber's approach to typing is explained in the following passage:

> In the process of seeking insight and explanation, Weber made great use of classificatory schema and analytical models, and took for granted that it is necessary to formulate type constructs and generalized uniformities (Weber, 1947:109). He (Weber, 1947:89) recognized two forms of generalized schema: the typing which sought to represent the 'average or approximate' nature of phenomenon and that which represents 'the theoretically conceived *pure type*.' Pure types are of course ideal-types. These conceptually constructed and theoretically based models can clearly have no empirical form but remain as accentuated abstractions. Weber (1967:110) maintained that 'theoretical analysis in the field of sociology is possible only in terms of such pure types.' Hence he is constantly dealing with conceptual parameters, with limiting cases, rather than with empirically derived 'average' types such as those yielded through statistical research. (Allison, 1980: 161)

Thus Weber's ideal types are a sort of conceptual tool corresponding to the mathematical notion of the limiting case. They facilitate inquiry, research, philosophy and policy.

In addition to the Weberian ideal type and the statistical average type there is also the Platonic Form and the Jungian archetype. The Platonic Form can be construed as a special case of the ideal type, indeed the ultimate and absolute case. It is not abstracted from empirical reality; the latter is abstracted from it, what we experience as reality being but a dim approximation to that superstratum in which Absolute Reality is to be found. The Jungian archetype, on the other hand, emerges from the psychological substratum. The suggestion is that there are conceptually identifiable forms or types which persist across cultures and throughout history in the universal unconscious mind of the race and that these forms bear psychological potency. They reveal themselves to the clinician and they manifest themselves in dreams, art, religion and history. The conceptions of Plato and Jung share a metaphysical quality; they have a grandeur and abstruseness, however, which tend to place them very far from the administrative-managerial cycle. Moreover, Plato's ancient concern with human organization does not seem to have been matched by the modern Jung.

Finally, there is the stereotype. This tends to have negative connotations. It is the most weakly grounded of types and often tends to a cartoon sort of simplification. Nevertheless, it represents a basic kind of classificatory behaviour and undoubtedly has its utility as a coping device for dealing with complexity. Where the number of variables which impinge on the conceptual field is excessive, as it often is in interpersonal relations, the device may be unavoidable. At worst stereotypes seduce us into the avoidance of thought but at best they may be very practical and necessary affective coping mechanisms with a proto-science potential.

In titling this chapter, I have chosen to use the term archetype but wish it to be understood not in the strict Jungian sense but in a very general way so as to embrace some of the sense of all the typing forms which have been described above. The archetypes of this chapter result when the value paradigm is applied to organizational forms of life, especially to executives and administrators. In one sense they are vignettes, shorthand descriptions of leaders. In principle they could be derived from statistical investigation but they are also convenient stereotypes which would reveal in any fully explicated analysis ideal types in the Weberian and Platonic senses. And, to the extent that they underlie affective, cognitive and conative processes at the unconscious level, and have motivating force, they are archetypical in the Jungian sense. Their logical basis rests in the analysis of value, their utility in their philosophical application, their hermeneutic relevance to the study of administration and organizations, and perhaps in whatever truth is contained in the aphorism that Nature imitates Art.

In chapters 3 through 5 we have already examined the archetypes of organizational context. Now we can consider the actors in those contexts. Arbitrarily but naturally these fall into two sets: the administrators and the administered. More succinctly still, the leaders and the led. The former of these is the chief focus of our interest, although, of course, the two are inseparable in the final analysis. By definition, however, administrators are formal leaders and so the typology which follows can be interpreted as an extension of previous analyses of power, authority and leadership, in particular, the classical Weberian typology. But since leadership and followership are related as form is to substance, or sides of a coin to each other, some consideration of followership implications will be necessary in each pattern. And finally, let it be emphasized again that types make no one-to-one correspondence with empirical reality: there are no Dogs or Cats out there, only individual animals. To confuse member with class, or class with class of classes is to commit the homogenetic fallacy.

THE CAREERIST

The lowest archetype from the standpoint of moral or ethical approbation also happens to be that which is the most fundamental and the most basic in any clear-eyed analysis of human nature in its organizational forms-of-life. This is because the careerist archetype is characterized by Type III values, the values of the ego, of self-interest, of primary affect and motivation. Self-preservation and enhancement, self-centredness and self-concern, are the dominant value traits. At Level III we share our nature with the animal kingdom and indeed with all sentient protoplasm. Value calculus is pure and fundamentally simple. At the deepest level the maxim is, 'avoid pain — seek pleasure.' The motivation is hedonic; in Freudian terms it is essentially the libidinal impulse of the id. Frustration of that basic instinct generates stress, anger and rage. And this in turn, given social control of these impulses, can generate powerful needs for achievement, recognition and success.

This basal nature is ever-present in each of us. As advanced social animals we complexify this affective base by means of repression, sublimation, inhibitions and conditionings of various kinds (Freud's ego and ego-ideal). But deep down it is always there. Self-preservation is not only the first law of nature but the first metavalue and the first premiss in the study of value. Self as ego comes first, entering instantaneously and involuntarily into all our value calculations and all qualitative analysis.

The ego reveals itself in our preferences, the lowest level of the value paradigm. For the infantile, the adolescent, the immature, the search for gratification of Type III values is relatively uncomplicated. It tends to be an automatic and unreflective process that is not sicklied o'er by any pale cast of thought. Over time it is gradually conditioned by education and experience; the world intrudes upon the field of personality and becomes less and less a playground of sport and pastime, more and more a workplace of discipline and frustration. For the adult, for some adults at least, the upshot of this process can be a more sophisticated hedonism in which game rules, constraints, opportunities and prizes are dictated by culture and circumstance, but in which winning is still defined by and keyed to Level III gratifications. This is most clearly articulated in the playboy philosophy, which can be viewed as a sophisticated individualism in which the world problem — the problem of the competitive struggle for prizes — wealth, pleasure, leisure, power, status, fame and success — can be solved through adoption of the correct winning strategies and tactics. Such a technology of success is provided, for example, by the *arthasastra*. Pay-off tends to become the criterion of value judgement, the metavalue, and any moral reprehensibility which might result a matter of purely political concern.

The principle of selfishness can also be endowed with intellectual respectability through the doctrines of logical positivism in philosophy and deterministic behaviourism in psychology. Herbert A. Simon in administration and B. F. Skinner in psychology represent these respective standpoints. For each the apogee of value would be at most IIA and any noumenal or transcendental ethics would, in effect, disappear within the socially observable phenomena of morality. Indeed, positivism of one shade or another is entrenched in the orthodoxy of academe and in the conventional wisdom and mores of our scientific technocratic culture. Computerology and computer-cult reinforce this trend. The prize-winning study *Gödel, Escher, Bach* (Hofstadter, 1979) illustrates this in that in the end it arrives at a brilliantly disguised but undeniably logical positivist position.

If then man can be construed as an epiphenomenal ego adrift in a sea of universal flux where all things are relative and transient, where values ultimately resolve or dissolve into affective perturbations, where the sensory circuits are constantly under threat of overload from the multiplex information transmissions of the environment (Toffler, 1971:350-5), where the threats to the ego from that environment are many and the prizes limited to the few, where the evidences of self-seeking and malice, of ungodly prospering and righteous injustice are to be perceived all around — given all this it is at least understandable that some men may choose consciously (and even *conscientiously*) to walk the path of opportunism. Or they may do so unconsciously, reactively. Or their ordinary and natural pursuit of self-interest may simply be so reinforced by the contingency schedules of a materialistic econocentric culture that they evolve, discover or invent their own amorality in the course of their career search for success.

By one path or another the careerist is formed. In his pure archetypical form he is guided by the star of success and personal gratification. His thrust for ego-satisfaction and enhancement falls short, however, of translating his success-orientation into a Type I commitment. Instead he will constantly search and test the limits presented by circumstance, and in doing so practise the arts of opportunism unhibited by any absolute morality but using any available morality to his own inventive purposes and ends.

Other labels have been attached to this form of life: opportunist, hedonist, narcissist; but the common factor throughout is a self-concern and self-interest which is relatively pure, free from constraint and contemptuous of convention. This is not to say that mores, laws and proprieties go unrecognized. Far from it, they are sharply perceived but are understood as game rules. And since the objective of the game is winning and the concept of rules implies no ethic of self-restraint, it follows that the rules are there to be bent, broken and evaded if the end result can be unpenalized success. The old-fashioned liberal rule that one was free to pursue one's self-interest so long as doing so did not interfere with another's pursuit is reinterpreted as a licence to constantly press one's interests to the limits and beyond, if one can get away with it. This interpretation is an aspect of careerist ruthlessness. Scruples are for the tender-minded and the morally inhibited. The philosophies of hedonism, narcissism, opportunism and the *arthasastra* are all of a piece.Thrasymachus in Plato's *Republic* speaks for the careerist when he argues that might makes right and that the evidence is before one's eyes that the unjust reap the rewards of society. His successor Machiavelli reinforces the argument. The value of power is heightened to the point of veneration, for it is discerned that power not only determines the possibilities of enjoyment but even the definition of what ought and ought not to be. Power defines the game within which the prizes are to be distributed.

So the careerist is power-hungry and seeks power enhancement. This implies ambition, ambition which is either overtly displayed or renounced, depending upon social context and the approval or advantage to be gained by either public attitude. But this ambition is still at Level III; it has not yet been amplified to the point of ideological obsession with success so as to become the central focus and meaning of existence. The careerist is still capable of backing off, accepting defeat when frustrated, changing his strategies, bending before the wind. He does not yet see himself as the charismatic Superman. He is much more concerned with his private metavalues: role security, role advancement, power, authority, deference, status, the comforts and perquisites of office. He is achievement-oriented because the recognition, however fleeting, which attaches to achievement is reassurance of his status, public acknowledgement of his worth and, next to promotion and increase of power, the ideal ego-gratification. Defence of his *amour propre* is fundamental and, if necessary, all the weaponry of the *arthasastra* will be deployed in the maintenance of his organizational territory and the defence of his power base. Given the arts of modern dramaturgy this basic defensiveness can be carefully concealed behind outward façades of bonhomie, banality and even buffoonery. Yet perceived affronts to his ego will be remembered, malice nurtured and should safe occasions provide the opportunity then he will indulge the luxury of revenge.

In all of this a certain logic is discernible which is similar if not identical to that which ordains that the first duty of a government is to govern. So, too, the first duty of the leader is to maintain himself. And his second, to advance himself. The careerist administrator feels impelled to climb any hierarchical ladder that is accessible within his own organization and to move laterally to other organizations if that will permit hierarchical advance. In this progression others — colleagues, superiors and subordinates — may get hurt. So much the worse for them. The careerist attitude to others is essentially that of user. Of what use can this person be to me? Or conversely, what threat does he represent to my interests? Is he neutral, inimical, advantageous? Ruthlessness therefore becomes increasingly necessary, along with an avoidance of any affective entanglements which might prove detrimental or decelerative. Nor is this characteristic quality of ruthlessness to be disdained. Philosophers, theorists and practitioners of administration from Vedic times to the present day, from Hammurabi to Speer, have given persuasive arguments for its necessity. A certain detachment, even if it be from the wrong motives, and a certain force of will or decisiveness, again even if from the wrong motives, are essential to the effectiveness and efficiency of the administrative process.

This archetype gains added potency within a competitive society and culture. Modern technocultures, East or West, provide fertile soil for its cultivation. When, in addition, the culture is materialist, determinist and hedonist, multiple reinforcements obtain for the emergence of the careerist style of administration. The explicit and implicit reward systems of the culture make ever more ironclad the identifications of success with ascent of hierarchy, and of *meaning*, with success. As hedonic satisfaction becomes more and more attached to upward mobility so affective drives initially attached to self-indulgence in the ordinary or non-administrative sense become transformed into work patterns with perceived pay-off. Thus the frequent careerist commitment to hard work and long hours and, often enough, oversubscription to the classical work ethic. And this in turn is reinforcing, for it assists in assuaging any lingering moral qualms and may even permit the careerist to enjoy a sense of pseudo-moral righteousness and superiority.

The essence of the careerist character is, however, a kind of rugged amorality. Not beyond good and evil in the Nietzschean sense and not psychopathic either; recognizing and accepting the conventions of society which translate into moral codes but working around them without compunction whenever that is to his perceived advantage. The empirical workings of the archetype can be detected in the serendipitous data of the Watergate affair. Here one can observe how instantly and spontaneously public interest is reinterpreted as private career interest and how, in the event of failure or defeat, colleagues and subordinates are ruthlessly abandoned or betrayed. 'When the going gets tough, the tough gets going.' This ultimate collapse before *force majeure* is characteristic of the Type III, as opposed to Type I, commitment.

The archetypical behaviour is also evidenced in some notorious cases of functionaries: Lieutenant Calley and Adolf Eichmann, to cite famous examples. Both these men were on career tracks within large complex organizations. Organizational metavalues dominated their working ambience and their own personal imperatives, unconstrained by Type I ethics or Type II morality, determined their work performance. When, by the turning of events, they were asked to render an accounting it was natural at that point to disdain moral responsibilities and to attempt to fix blame on impersonal entities and forces.[1]

Notwithstanding these well-publicized instances it is difficult to draw more than suggestive illustrations from life. This is because the complexity of actual cases with their multitude of personality and field variables compounded by interaction and conflation obscures the vision of the underlying value archetypes. The value colours of real life are heavily mixed. Ongoing value complexes are synthetic not analytic. Yet for all that, the type emerges with recognizable clarity from time to time and a particularly horrific example is given by Drucker. When working on the Frankfurt newspaper *General-Anzeiger* in 1929 he made the acquaintance of fellow journalist, Reinhold Hensch. Hensch lacked social and academic credentials but aspired to a career. To that end he held early memberships in both the Communist and the Nazi parties. His attitude is revealed in this conversation:

'You never did [understand]. I'm not clever, I know that. I've been on the paper longer than you [Drucker] or Arne or Becker — you three are the senior editors and I still have the City Hall beat on which I started. I know I can't write. No one invites me to their homes. Even Elise's father — the dentist — thought his daughter too good for me. Don't you understand that I want power and money and to be somebody? That's why I joined the Nazis early on, four or five years ago when they first got rolling. And now I have a party membership card with a very low number and *I am going to be somebody*! The clever, well-born, well-connected people will be too fastidious, or not flexible enough, or not willing to do the dirty work. That's when I'll come into my own. Mark my word, you'll hear about me now.' (Drucker, 1978:164-5)

---

[1] The exceptional case of G. Gordon Liddy, the Watergate conspirator, is interesting. Here there would appear to be Type I values at work which remove Mr Liddy from the careerist category (Liddy, 1980).

He was heard about. Towards the end of the war the *New York Times* published the following:

> Reinhold Hensch, one of the most wanted Nazi war criminals, committed suicide when captured by American troops in the cellar of a bombed-out house in Frankfurt. Hensch, who was deputy head of the Nazi SS with the rank of Lieutenant-General, commanded the infamous annihilation troops and was in charge of the extermination campaign against Jews and other 'enemies of the Nazi state', of killing off the mentally and physically defective in Germany, and of stamping out resistance movements in occupied countries. He was so cruel, ferocious, and bloodthirsty that he was known as 'The Monster' (*Das Ungeheuer*) even to his own men. (Drucker, 1978:158)

Of course the affinity with evil is integral to this archetype and because both archtype and evil are integral to mankind it is not surprising that often enough the moral furies are invoked and storms of righteous disapprobation unleashed. Because of this the careerist student of the *arthasastra* seeks to maintain a façade of moralism sufficiently secure to disguise and conceal his private machinations. (Hensch was momentarily deficient in this.) It follows too that throughout the ages religious writing has concerned itself with this type and the passage quoted in full below from the *Bhagavad Gita* is of interest not simply because of its tone of calumny but because it also delineates the archetypal dimensions with some clarity and force.

> Men of demonic nature know neither what they ought to do, nor what they should refrain from doing. There is no truth in them, or purity, or right conduct. They maintain that the scriptures are a lie, and that the universe is not based upon a moral law, but godless, conceived in lust and created by copulation, without any other cause. Because they believe this in the darkness of their little minds, these degraded creatures do horrible deeds, attempting to destroy the world. They are enemies of mankind.
>
> Their lust can never be appeased. They are arrogant, and vain, and drunk with pride. They run blindly after what is evil. The ends they work for are unclean. They are sure that life has only one purpose: gratification of the senses. And so they are plagued

by innumerable cares, from which death alone can release them. Anxiety binds them with a hundred chains, delivering them over to lust and wrath. They are ceaselessly busy, piling up dishonest gains to satisfy their cravings.

'I wanted this and to-day I got it. I want that: I shall get it to-morrow. All these riches are now mine: soon I shall have more. I have killed this enemy. I will kill all the rest. I am a ruler of men. I enjoy the things of this world. I am successful, strong and happy. Who is my equal? I am so wealthy and so nobly born. I will sacrifice to the gods. I will give alms. I will make merry.' That is what they say to themselves, in the blindness of their ignorance.

They are addicts of sensual pleasure, made restless by their many desires, and caught in the net of delusion. They fall into the filthy hell of their own evil minds. Conceited, haughty, foolishly proud, and intoxicated by their wealth, they offer sacrifice to God in name only, for outward show, without following the sacred rituals. These malignant creatures are full of egoism, vanity, lust, wrath, and consciousness of power. They loathe me, and deny my presence both in themselves and in others. They are enemies of all men and of myself; cruel, despicable and vile. I cast them back, again and again, into the wombs of degraded parents, subjecting them to the wheel of birth and death. And so they are constantly reborn, in degradation and delusion. They do not reach me, but sink down to the lowest possible condition of the soul. (Prabhavananda and Isherwood, 1944:114-16)

But our careerist need not reek of brimstone, need not even be aware of any theological vilification. For all appearances he can be, indeed he usually is, a very pleasant fellow, master of the arts of bonhomie and swift to be congenial, especially if things are going well for him in his organization and in his pursuit of his interests. After all, the manipulation of others is essential to his success. And besides, the type exists in all of us to the extent that ambition and the needs for achievement and recognition go unconstrained by higher level archetypes. The careerist clearly can be of collective service. To the extent that he identifies with his organization he can make large personal sacrifices for its collective good and give unstintingly of his many administrative and managerial skills. This type is the most basic and primitive and therefore most easily associated with the organizational metavalues; organizations can come to revere their careerist leaders even when the façade is stripped away, for ruthlessness can be as necessary to the body politic as surgery to the body physical. The record of organizational history shows that the prince and the dictator, the tyrant and the man-on-horseback have always been welcomed and acclaimed for their common weal success.

FOLLOWERSHIP

The careerist can easily endear himself to the non-administrative ranks of his organization, he is easily perceived as a good leader. For the simple reason that when there is alignment between his own and the organizational interest the conjoint dynamism often ensures organizational growth and success. At the least he will appear as a good fighter for the sectional interests who seek his leadership. His image is endorsed and reinforced by his work habits, energy level, protestations of commitment, busyness, visibility and political skills. Even the quality of ruthlessness becomes admirable when it is interpreted through the stereotype of the strong leader who wins organizational advantage in a competitive arena, with consequent trickle-down benefits for the followers. Weakness and vacillation would be viewed as contemptible while the 'killer-instinct' would be something perhaps eminently to be desired. The world worships winners. The authority-dependent, the infantile, the followers who bear all the stigmata of Theory X; all these may welcome the empirical embodiment of the careerist.

Organizational context will therefore be an important factor in follower acceptance of the careerist leader. Political, *laisser-faire* settings with a maximum of line and a minimum of staff would logically be most advantageous. The professional, technical or ideological organization might prove less congenial, although, of course, the adept of image management can practice deceit as easily in church or party, in regiment or academy, as in more pragmatic organizational fields. By and large, however, obscurity of organizational purpose is advantageous to the careerist. Multiple and complex goals present opportunities for intraorganizational gamesmanship which would be denied where simple, measurable results provide a direct accounting of effectiveness.

The press to success is nevertheless binding upon the careerist-leader; failure is anathema. To retain his political support he must not only maintain his position, he must promise gains and rewards. So time is the enemy, for with the passage of time some of these promissory notes will be presented for payment. Better for him, then, if they cannot be cashed, that he has in the meantime moved onward, upward, out of the ambit of responsibility. So mobility is essential, vertically or laterally, between organizations as well as within them.

This enhances the short-term quality of careerist leadership. Since it implies a user mentality, the using of people as means or instruments to the leader's own ends, it follows that enemies are created as the recognition of this manipulation slowly dawns among the followers, and the possibilities of this recognition increases with the passage of time. The risks of exposure of duplicity, of trickery, of cunning, of fast dealing also increase with the passage of time, as too does the pressure generated from problems shelved and decisions delayed. For all these reasons time works against the careerist and therefore mobility coupled with short-term commitments proves to be his best defensive strategy. That resentment is created by the discovery of having been manipulated or used does not, of course, contradict the fact that in the largest sense everyone is instrumental to organizational goals. Everyone is a usee simply by virtue of organization membership. But the careerist breaches the zone of indifference. The very purpose of organization is to subordinate ego interest to collective interest (within the zone of indifference) but when it is eventually perceived that the subordination has been in part or in whole for the furtherance of another ego then resentment can be expected to mount exponentially. The user flourishes while the usee seethes. Morale fluctuates inversely with the rate of usage.

The problems of morale which a mobile careerist leaves in

his wake may be of great concern to his late followers but they are of little or no concern to himself for by then he has moved on to a new context, a new organization, and a new set of subordinates. A new field of predation. Nevertheless, it is in the immediate entourage, amongst the careerist's intimates and lieutenants, that the negative affect is most likely to be extreme. Psychological and social distancing can protect the leader image at other levels. The inner circle will be privy to some or many of the machinations of power, ambition and politics — may indeed identify, initiate and sponsor them themselves. They are also familiar enough with the leader's façade to observe its composition at close quarters and, on occasion, to see behind it. If it be true that familiarity breeds contempt then one of the explanations would be that it simply provides more opportunities for perceptive observation. So the careerist must be most on guard amongst those with whom, paradoxically, he should be most able to relax. Indeed he may have to chastise, bring down or humiliate his lieutenants and aides from time to time for this very reason. A climber himself, he must watch carefully the climbers around him; and so the executive suite is often the main site and source of executive stress. Certainly of sub-executive stress.

The larger followership may be ignorant and oblivious of all this. So long as the organizational metavalues are unthreatened, their own security and welfare maintained, the leader's façade may appear unblemished, his image fair to their perception. And when he goes they may speak highly of him, wishing indeed that he had not left. In sum, there is nothing within the careerist archetype to prohibit both the appearance and the reality of effective and efficient short-term leadership and organizational benefit.

PRAXIS

In the criticism of this archetype it is not enough to be simply moralistic, to heap opprobrium on narcissistic hedonism, plain self-seeking and careerist ambition. Unless grounded in logic, such a critique is itself merely emotive fulmination:

Type III affect at worst, Type IIB affect at best. To be effective the counter-arguments should strike at the philosophical infrastructure of logical positivism, for it is this, in the last analysis, that sustains the complex of attitudes, motives and value-behaviour which we have encapsulated in the careerist archetype. But it has already been shown (see p. 42) that this attack is not at all easy to mount. In fact, on their ground, the positivists would appear to be irrefutable. Their ground is, however, strictly with the perimeter of rationality — a rationality narrowly construed. Once a transrational element such as, say, moral intuition or Type I affective commitment is admitted into argument then the dialogue with positivism is superseded. This means then that the philosopher of administration who wishes to abjure careerism must rest his case upon foundations which are ultimately suprarational or transcendental. Or, to put it somewhat less stringently, the leader who would go beyond self-interest must establish his level of praxis in higher archetypes.

He may of course be content to cite folk-wisdom: That 'as one sows so shall one reap', that 'chickens come home to roost'. Or drawing upon the fund of his experience he may assert that self-centredness leads only to isolation and unhappiness; that self-absorption leads to self-consumption; that friends are more useful than rivals or enemies. All of this is at the level of received social doctrine, the common sense of the ethos, and none of it is likely to impress the adept of the *arthasastra*. The hard-headed practitioners of *Realpolitik* would be inclined to write such sentiments off as mere pathology, the pusillanimity of the weak.

The point for praxis is simple. The administrator who would reject careerism must have a countervailing commitment. This commitment must be sustained by certain minimal, unverifiable *beliefs*. These would include at one extreme a belief in a moral order in the universe — the Kantian proposition — and at the other extreme a belief in a moral order in society, a socio-moral foundation for codes, mores and laws — the Confucian proposition. Acceptance of this sort of commitment, to whatever degree, at once is inhibiting; it reduces individual freedom. The compensation for this constraint of value-orientation is to be found, one might speculate, in the proposition that thereby the value-structure of the individual becomes somehow more meaningful and profound.

Such assumption of moral responsibility does not, however, imply naivety. The praxis of higher archetypes never quite exorcizes the careerist; that archetype remains lodged within every breast, present certainly within the recesses of every administrative mind. It is the simplest truth of social wisdom that from time to time self-interest will be in the ascendancy, however and whatever the inhibitions of philosophy, law, religion, morality and group psychology. We are all of us careerists at some level of our consciousness. Hedonism and self-seeking only become corrupt when they become fixated. When they become binding elements in the psyche; blocks to the evolution of spirit. To seek pleasure is authentic and natural enough but not to seek refinement of pleasure, not to go beyond the pleasure principle, is to sell human nature short. Likewise, ambition for oneself is natural but if it fixates on the ego it becomes pathological; ambition too must reach beyond itself, must seek inhibition, refinement, transcendence — the greater commitment.

As for the *arthasastra* it can and should in praxis be rejected out of hand as ultimately anti-organizational, anti-social and dysfunctional. Yet this praxis admonition is only dogmatic; it can hardly deter the seeker after short-run gains and quick success. Praxis will always have to accommodate the lower levels of the value paradigm. Marcus Aurelius, whose own experience with the realities of administration must have been exceptional, illustrates the problem:

> How hollow and insincere it sounds when someone says 'I am determined to be perfectly straightforward with you.' Why, man, what is all this? The thing needs no prologue; it will declare itself. It should be written on your forehead, it should echo in the tones of your voice, it should shine out in a moment from your eyes, just as a single glance from the beloved tells all to the lover. Sincerity and goodness ought to have their own unmistakable

odour, so that one who encounters this become straightaway aware of it despite himself. A candour affected is a dagger concealed. The feigned friendship of the wolf is the most contemptible of all, and to be shunned beyond everything. A man who is truly good and sincere and well-meaning will show it by his looks, and no one can fail to see it. (Aurelius XI:15)

Such a classical commentary is modern enough in an era where dark glasses are often affected in the knowledge that the pupil dilation-contraction reflex is an involuntary signal of emotional response. Indeed, to a greater or a lesser extent, the careerist archetype is ever-present in practice and it is the onus of praxis to discern it within oneself as well as in others.

CREDO: *There is a moral order in the universe; adherence to it strengthens, departure from it weakens.*

As the credo implies, the intellectual case against positivism and selfishness is taken out of the strict confines of logical and rational argument. The precepts underlying the credo are non-scientific and can be summarized as, first, a belief that there is a moral order in the universe; second, that a pale reflection of this exists in the moral order apparent in societies and organizations; third, that individual men have, at least from time to time or *at times*, sufficient degrees of freedom to choose between these orders of morality and some other course of action or judgement. Also implicit in the credo is the notion that there are negative consequences to the individual if he suborns the larger principle of order — if he does not act *rightly*.

The first non-scientific precept establishes the distinction already entrenched in the value paradigm between the category of right and wrong and the category of good and bad. The discrimination between these categories is absolutely basic, for it would appear that *homo sapiens*, alone of all the animal life on the planet, is capable of making it. In Biblical myth it is the fruit of the tree of knowledge of good and evil. It is impervious to empirical verification; a matter for as much philosophical contention now as it was in the beginnings of human consciousness. Commitment to a careerist archetype would deny it and defy it.

The second non-scientific precept asserts that the moral order is to some degree manifest in the status quo of organizational society. Social pressures leading to conformity with the dominant culture, however attentuated by variant and deviant subcultures, assure the ongoing preservation of systems of law and quasi-morality.

The third precept is the doctrine of free will. Each administrator stands at the conjuncture of a determined past and an indeterminate future. The past is always a lost cause, the future always invincible with hope. The doctrine itself, however, is likewise unverifiable in any strictly positivist sense and is, indeed, denied by scientific determinists, along with, necessarily, the whole notion of moral order, thus leading to an entirely different concept of praxis. The position of this book is that there is limited free will, that there are some degrees of freedom, and that a man's moral stature does in fact depend upon his *will*. As to the number of degrees of freedom and the latitude of choice within a decision context, there can be endless contention. I suspect this depends upon a man's essence as well as upon his physical circumstances, it is a function of his moral development.

A commitment to a careerist archetype is as defensible under these precepts as commitment to any other value complex. If a deterrent to careerist commitment exists in praxis it is to be most persuasively found in the presumption of negative consequences. This quasi-hypothesis is testable in experience, in praxis. To be sure, the verification cannot be scientifically rigorous but it can be argued with some cogency that the consensus of experience in administration is that untempered careerism does result in dysfunctions and negative consequences both for the practitioner and for the organization. In sum, the private biographies of administrators can be elicited to support either the principle of moral retribution within the form of life of the individual careerist or the negative consequence of organizational pathologies at the collective level. To this extent the archetype can be abjured.

The careerist is the lowest of the archetypes, as Type III values are the lowest in the paradigm. But this also establishes its fundamental quality. All leadership incorporates, subsumes, this archetype and all men subscribe to the metavalues of their egos. There is no escape from the lower-case self. The counsel of wisdom is not to dismay over this but to accept it; to understand to the full the anti-collective forces within us, and to seek to refine or civilize them, harnessing the primitive energies of the archetype to higher-level purposes, values and goals. Praxis here implies raising our consciousness about this basal level of value logic. Present praxis is deficient. The ruthless have too easy access to the executive suite; and perhaps, under some obscure form of administrative Darwinism, the weak who fail to become wise deserve to go to the wall. To go beyond this is to require much greater moral sensitivity at all levels of organization and to demand scrutiny of the moral capacities of leaders and the moral component in leadership. Our tools for undertaking such scrutiny are perhaps not as sharp as we would wish.

The conceptual difficulty in the paradigm of discriminating accurately between Level III and Level I affect is also a critical difficulty of praxis. It carries forward into our discussion of the archetypes. In one sense the paradigm can be understood as a system of affect hierarchically organized upon ethical considerations, the meta-ethic of which is that larger interests are subsumed as the hierarchy is ascended. Within this sense the careerist archetype can be said to persist throughout the hierarchy of the value paradigm, but is overlaid, as it were, with ever-larger domains of value, and hence becomes, with the ascent, increasingly subordinated and sublimated as higher archetypes are achieved. In this sense too it can be noted that the lowest archetype foreshadows the highest; it falls short of that highest reach because the quality of commitment to higher and maximally refined 'selfishness' is lacking. The fault is perhaps one of vision rather than logic; ignorance rather than will.

In general the forces of order, social conditioning and prudential reason are strong enough to constrain the lower archetype and inhibit it, but when these forces weaken and conditions are right then the conversion to charismatic domination can occur, and what is good for one can become Right for all.

A final caution: the archetype is easier to conceive than perceive. Careerists avoid advertising themselves as such. Modern organizations provide adequate protective cover for their type of predatory inclination. It is a perpetual onus of praxis to penetrate all such camouflage, to perceive, to be aware, to discriminate, to act out of this awareness.

THE POLITICIAN

Politics is administration by another name. Its logic of value lies in the substantive reality of group preferences. The politician archetype is associated with the administrator whose interests have extended beyond those of self and the natural extensions of self to the point where they embrace a collectivity or group. This group, typically the organization for which he is responsible, is then allowed to have some degree of value hegemony and to affect his own value structure and behaviour. The politician archetype thus refers to a value complex which takes into its account the values of others, severally and jointly. It is especially affected by the *Gestalt* principle that the whole is greater than the sum of the parts. Whereas the term 'politician' often carries pejorative careerist connotations in popular usage, it is here used in its truer sense of seeking the will and welfare of a polity. In a neofeudal organizational society the politician archetype is clearly of major importance but the notion of psychological identification (by the administrator with his organization) should not be pushed to the point where it can be morally discounted as merely extended ego. The politician is a distinct type by virtue of his *authentic* concern with group preferences. The archetype is grounded in a principle of democracy which can be expressed as the belief that right action and right order find their ultimate legitimacy not in the individual but in the *group*.

This belief is at the heart of democratic ideology — East or West — and so widespread and oversubscribed is this ideology that, at its largest organizational level of manifestation, the State, it goes unquestioned. To be sure, the rhetoric of ideological justification varies from state to state or bloc to bloc, and the actual reference group varies from power elite to social class to national mass, but the root principle is identical whether the State structure be fascist, communistic, social-democratic or oligarchical. The metavalue is collective interest.

At a lesser level than the State the fields of administrative interest (and democratic metavaluation) are defined by the boundaries of the organizational constituents of society. The archetype is here reinforced by contemporary organization theory which from Barnard through to the Human Resources movement has stressed group morale, group cohesion and participatory democracy. Japanese neo-feudalism in industry and commerce provides a further illustration of the universality of this sort of democratic impress. In the West, administrative preparation programmes invariably include exposure to the rhetoric of human relations, motivation, job satisfaction and public relations generally, and this inevitably adds to this archetypal impress.

The politician is inclined to see himself as spokesman, articulator and leader of a group from which he draws energy and moral force. He has faith in the rectitude of the group he represents. One could say that his careerist narcissism has been sublimated or transcended through this identification with group values and group interest. This leads to a preoccupation with group harmony (Barnardian 'efficiency') and, hence, with the continuous maintenance of and search for consensus. The politician seeks to mitigate conflict by compromise, by the trading of values and the reconciliation of interests. His forte lies therefore in group dynamics and the minor arcanum of persuasion.

Nevertheless, between careerist and politician a quantum value shift has occurred. The nature of the politician's desires and the orientation of his values are such that his self-interest must be redefined or vindicated to align with his reference group. He feeds upon group approval. Group support is his meat and drink. He acknowledges to himself his own lively careerist interest but seeks to subsume and sublimate it under the legitimating cachet of his organization. The shift of level (from III to IIB) is, in short, the shift from self-interest pure and simple to self-interest 'impure' and complex; self-interest enlarged, refined and even upon occasion altruistic.

To identify group consensus, to identify *with* it and at times to negotiate it calls forth the full range of political skills. The task of the politician is simplified when consensus is clear, difficult when consensus is unclear, most difficult when latent or emergent consensus contradicts manifest value orientations. In his traffic with consensus, image is a matter of first importance for the politician. He must protect the group perceptions of his persona, for upon them depend his credibility and ultimately his power and legitimacy as a leader. Dramaturgy is essential. Roles must be played out; the management troupe must put on a good show. In meetings, formal and informal, any suggestion of hidden agendas will be denied with protestations of candour and the candour may indeed be authentic. Different images – the father, the uncle, the comrade, the fighter, the smoothie – will be presented as and where benefit is seen to be associated with their projection. After all, the politician must ingratiate himself everywhere but especially with the constituency of potency: those organization members who have power to make decisions or influence outcomes, a constituency which is very large indeed under conditions of participatory democracy. For this reason there is a tendency for the archetype to be associated with soft (liberal) decisions as opposed to hard (conservative) ones. Easy promotions, easy concession to work and wage demands, inflationary policies and bureaucratic growth – all may flow in some measure from the prevalence of the politician archetype.

Inevitably the politician must practise from time to time the arthasastric techniques of conciliation, Machiavellian courtiership and, in the modern euphemism, diplomacy. In the psychological jargon of contemporary leadership literature he will wish to score high on indices of consideration (Halpin, 1967:86, 197). Behaviourally, he does personal favours for group members; he explains his actions; he backs up members of the group; he does not act without consulting the group; he treats all members of the group as his equals; he is friendly and approachable; he does not demand more than followers can do; and he does not reject suggestions for change (Katz and Kahn, 1978:560-1; Fleishman and Peters, 1962).

The politician ideal type is both moral and rational. Moral because his circle of interest goes beyond that of self and extended self; it would be over-cynical to say that the organizational complex of interests makes up his extended ego, because in certain cases of conflict between collective interest and ego interest, he allows the former to override and modify the latter. Self-sacrifice and self-discipline are there, along with a commitment to truth as that finds expression in the honest value-calculus of group interaction. This is true morality, the basic claim to rationality being that group preferences, if actualized, will advance the potential for individual actualization of preference more than if *laisserfaire* pursuit of private desires were permitted, a logic which, it can be noted, runs contrary to that of classical economics (Smith, 1776) but which, nevertheless, establishes for the politician a claim to a rational logic of value. He sees himself therefore as the exponent of the moral collectivity of the group, and his lodestone is consensus. This is primitive democratic theory: the group knows best what it wants *and* what it ought to want; the function of the leader is to discover such values, formulate and represent them, then translate them into reality through the devices of organization and administrative process.

The politician is proto-charismatic at best, pseudo-charismatic at worst. He cannot be truly charismatic, for the man of charisma imposes his values upon the group rather than conversely, but there may be quasi-charisma to the extent that his interpretation of the group values and the collective will is accurate and to the extent that his popularity is bound up in perceptions of this kind of leadership. But group chemistry is mysterious, popular support is notoriously fickle and the signs can easily be misread. It follows that the politician is necessarily committed to a heavy schedule of personal interactions with his constituents. He cannot neglect the informal organization nor can he afford to be aloof. He must be busily engaged in a continuous series of personal contacts, his calendar full, his time fragmented, his possibilities for in-depth study of organizational problems limited. At times he must skim the surface like a water-spider. But always jocular, congenial, willing to listen and play to the full the dramaturgy of sympathetic sentiment. His worship at the altar of consensus means eating, drinking and talking with a lot of people; rarely can he indulge the luxuries of solitude or deep reflection. The world of his organization presses too much upon him. He must be about his political business, persuading, soothing eliciting support.

To all this there is a relatively short-term orientation. It is the immediate problem which is pressing; it is the short-run that counts. Pragmatically (and *ceteris paribus*), the long run can be left to take care of itself. Psychological compartmentalization helps; it is, after all, business-like and systematic. What matter if the militaristic and excisionistic fallacies are committed so long as the ship stays on course, fires are put out, egos stroked and an overall atmosphere of co-operative efficiency and well-being is maintained. It is the great forte of the politician-leader that he is capable of just such maintenance. It is the even greater forte of the archetype that this is to be done without cynicism, in authentic commitment.

Such achievement necessitates the arts of suasion. The politician watches carefully his reciprocity index, trades judiciously in favours, accumulates intelligence through all the information circuitry of the organization. He is at the centre of a communications network, and values this position of command. He values discretion and confidentiality but also knows the value of discreet indiscretion.

Within the taxonomy of process (see pp. 26-28) the politician is centrally located at the critical politics-mobilizing juncture. The value logic of this location entails a certain flexibility of commitment but also imposes empathetic demands and a requirement for those qualities and value attributes summed up in the terms 'humanistic' and 'diplomatic'. The greatest strength of the archetype lies in its resonance with the democratic ethos and ethic. To the extent that the exponent of this archetype is authentic he tends to achieve strong group cohesion and high morale, a Theory Z type praxis, and commendable quality of work life.

It ought not to be forgotten, however, that Type IIB values are but Type III affect elevated one degree. The latter are non-moral, the former a first form of morality. But this first form or first level of morality can be fragile and treacherous. It can be merely hedonistic narcissism writ large; the clamourings of the dark urges of the mass. 'There go the mob,' says the Comte de Mirabeau, 'and I must follow them for I am their leader.'

> Both Goebbels and Hitler understood how to unleash mass instincts at their meetings, how to play on the passions that underlay the veneer of ordinary respectable life. Practised demagogues, they succeeded in fusing the assembled workers, petits bourgeois, and students into a homogeneous mob whose opinions they could mould as they pleased...But as I see it today, these politicians in particular were *in fact moulded by the mob itself*, guided by its yearnings and its daydreams. Of course Goebbels and Hitler knew how to penetrate through to the instincts of their audience; but in the deeper sense they derived their whole existence from this audience. Certainly the masses roared to the beat set by Hitler's and Goebbels' baton; yet they were not the true conductors. *The mob determined the theme* (Speer, 1970: 19-20, my italics)

The slide of the politician into one sort or another of moral-ethical corruption is always easy, for the skids are well greased, the slope very slippery. The line between seeking and manipulating consensus is often difficult to draw. Nor in matters of value any more than in matters of fact is there any proof or guarantee of truth or rectitude through group aggregation of values. Groups are often notoriously wrong and notoriously oppressive. By slight process of degeneration the ideal type rapidly results in such familiar organizational forms of life as the confidence man, the trickster, the gamesman skilled in dramaturgical artifice, and the peerocratic spokesman for group-think. From group suasion to group tyranny is but a step, and within each politician is a careerist.

A further weakness of the politician archetype is the short-term orientation. Group membership fluctuates and group values form short-lasting consensus. Like his careerist forerunner, the politician may be inclined to take the cash and let the credit go, to avoid long-run considerations, for in the long run the group and their leader will both be otherwise or other-where. This accords with the pragmatic philosophy of taking one day at a time and with its possibly inherent wisdom of not trying hypothetical cases drawn from scenarios set too far in the future. Still, short-run actualizations of value can be merely hedonic and not necessarily consistent with long-term benefit.

FOLLOWERSHIP

The politician provides the form of leadership which, by and large, is most congenial to followers. This derives directly from man's social nature, and the general democratic intent of this leadership style, and indirectly from the praxis aspect of idiographic consideration. Upon similar value logic, it can be argued that the patrimonial or familial type of organization described by Weber is the one most congenial to human membership. Followers achieve ego-satisfaction to the extent that their values are perceived by them to be taken into the organizational account. Thompson (1976) has argued persuasively upon this theme and has described the devices and attempts made to reconcile the form of rational-legal bureaucracy with the demands of the idiographic dimension. He has called this the problem of administrative compassion and it is a problem which, despite the patchwork of pragmatic panaceas from ombudsmen to encounter sessions, remains largely unsolved. Of all the archetypes, however, it is that of the politician which would seem closest to its resolution, the pejorative popular usage of the term notwithstanding.

For all men the first experience of organization is the family. The leaders of this organization, father and mother or their surrogates, tend naturally to incorporate the politician archetype, often at its best. As the family extends, with maturity, to include larger abstractions, the corresponding value logic of *communitas* and democracy is unconsciously assimilated by the individual. The norm that majority preferences should therefore be given priority in the value calculus is easily, though at times painfully, accepted as a righteous discipline. Thus the politician-leader is rewarded with votes, endorsement and power. Follower approval is reinforced by ethos (V_5; see p. 24) and further reinforced by the subculture (V_4) of the human relations movement. The fact that followers are susceptible to manipulation through corrupt forms of this archetype, or that they themselves may individually be of the careerist persuasion, does not detract from the general appeal of this leadership form of life. The universality of its appeal is evidenced by the fact that, with few exceptions and regardless of the political classification of the state within which they are comprised, organizations everywhere employ some form of participatory democracy in their leadership praxis, whether it be by way of soviet, collegium, praesidium or simply old-fashioned committee.

PRAXIS

The exponent of this archetype must have some sensible, though possibly unexamined, faith in the wisdom of the mass. This need not have been subjected to intellectual scrutiny, it may simply be there as a component of personality. Perhaps, subliminally, he believes in the self-correcting cybernetic qualities of large human systems. The ideal of praxis would be that he examines the values implicit in these assumptions, raises them to the level of conscious reflection, and reaffirms his authentic commitment to them. The rewards for this exercise would be a private moral reinforcement and an enhancement of his own psychological and philosophical security, rewards impressive enough for anyone bearing the stresses of the leadership role. The politician archetype does, after all, represent the first form of administrative morality; it is an authentically moral, though elementary, form of life.

The quality of this morality, and its derivative praxis, will be a function of the authenticity of the leader's identification with the preferences and values of his group. Note that this commitment is to a sort of collective will, Rousseau's *volonté générale*, and *not* necessarily to the nomothetic or formal goals of the organization. In the extreme case this might mean that the politician will assist his men in mutiny. Indeed, if the paradigm stopped at level IIB this might be the rule rather than the exception. The point, however, is that to some sensible degree the politician type of leader seeks to embody the will, the values, of the followership, and is willing himself to be led where they lead. And this praxis implies the practice inherent in the Barnardian commandment: know the informal organization; be idiographically alert; be value-conscious!

As with all the higher archetypes there is entropy as well as negentropy, a potential for degeneration, a tendency for the running down of moral energy and erosion of value, which can lead eventually to pathological formations in organizational life. The politician archetype is associated most directly with such corruptions as the tyranny of the majority and excessive pressures to group conformity. Whyte's *Organization Man* (1956) remains the classic exposition of this syndrome. Oversocialization can only lead to the ethics of the herd, the swarm, the insect hive (Orwell, 1949). To counter this the true politician must cherish variant value orientations, perhaps even cultivate them. Modern theories of bioethics and sociobiology notwithstanding (Mackie, 1977) there is no reason to suppose, under our

paradigm, that the group is invariably right. Higher archetypes exist. Groups are notoriously wrong. Progress is often
made against the will of and in spite of the group. So the
administrator whose value persuasion would reach beyond
this archetype must to some extent take the side of Plato
against Aristotle. Plato distrusted the masses while his pupil
thought their values and motives provided the best long-run
guide to action. This classical division is incorporated in the
value paradigm: Type IIB consensual values representing the
Aristotelian, and Type IIA the more Platonic, emphasis.

Praxis at the present level of paradigm is prone to other
well-known pathologies: the manipulative administrator,
the political gamesman and operator, the trader in favours,
wheeling and dealing, the demagogue and rabble-rouser.
Democracy has its mobocratic face. The slope inclines towards the lowest level of archetype and is slippery. The line
between manipulating consensus and allowing its authentic
emergence is easily traversed and any skilled organizational
gamesman knows the techniques. So, too, is the negentropic
tendency to take the line of least resistance, to adopt the
superficial overview of preference, to avoid hard decisions
and slide through on soft, to *succumb* to the group. Authentic democratic leadership is often stressful and difficult and
the onus can be strenuous for those practitioners who most
fully embody this archetype. This would be reason enough
for their deserving of honour. They resist the Type III slide.

True politicians practising the true art of the possible make
the organizational world work. We must salute them. Without
this archetype there is nothing. But one can go beyond it.

THE TECHNICIAN

The second level of the value paradigm is the modal level for
administration. Most administrators tend either to the politician (IIB) or technician (IIA) archetype. Both types can
be classified as rational, humanistic and pragmatic but it is
possible to discriminate between them. The former grounds
its value logic in the politics of consensus and the latter in

the rational analysis of the consequences of value judgements in action. The latter is pre-eminently rational-cognitive and rational-legal; it gives us the archetype of Technician. Such an archetype seems almost metavaluational, beyond question, in a culture which is itself technological, science-based, complex in its organizations and institutional framework, deeply invested with the ideology of reason. I have chosen the term 'technician' but it is clear that, used properly and in its correct sense, the term 'bureaucrat' would have done just as well. However, the pejorative semantic connotations of popular usage attaching to the word series 'bureaucrat', 'bureaucracy' and 'bureaucratic' run against the positive value which should properly be applied to this archetype. Ideal-type bureaucracy *pace* Weber and its approximations in the real world constitute a technology of organization which can be said to constitute one of mankind's highest accomplishments, popular affect notwithstanding.

The values of Weberian bureaucracy accord with the archetype. So do those of science and the academic institution. They are the values of the intellect and of logic. They include dispassion, impartiality, logical analysis and problem solving, efficiency, effectiveness, goal accomplishment, planning, the utilitarian maximization of the good. Justice is equated with fairness (Rawls, 1972:60) and economic distribution finds its righteousness in equality of opportunity. Implicit is a belief in the ultimate virtue of rationality, a faith that if human problems can be stated they can ultimately, in principle, be resolved, and that the chief instrument of resolution is knowledge, pure and applied. Implicit, too, is a tendency to partial-out affect, a preference for the quantitative and the conceptual over the qualitative and factual, the nomothetic over the idiographic. God is not only a mathematician but also a systems theorist and his evolution unfolds according to an architecture the earthly analogues of which are MARS, PPBS, and PERT.[2] The state of that evolution can be assessed by the degree of negentropy

[2]   Model Adaptation and Redesign System; Planning, Programming, Budget Systems; Program Evaluation Review Technique.

present in the social structure of organizations at any given time.

Our own time is a good one because it is one in which, despite ecological limits, it seems that organization subserved by science can accomplish almost anything, from the penetration of intergalactic space to the perpetration of life itself. The morality of the technician therefore takes on large dimensions and it subsumes that of politician and careerist both. It is funded by a variety of analytical tools: systems theory, operations research, quantitative methods, cost-benefit and cost-efficiency analyses, computerology, all the apparatus of rational, comprehensive planning; all of which tend to convince of justification and rightness when once attached to an organizational goal paradigm. Nor is this fund of rationality so simplistic that it cannot be adapted to the realities through the techniques of mixed scanning or even disjointed incrementalism and muddling through (Lindblom, 1959, 1979; Etzioni, 1968). Whether the rationality be complex, simple or super-sophisticated the lodestone of the technician's values entails the commitment to reason, to the best calculable determination of the rational consequences of action.

None of this means that the technician need be a-valuational or amoral. It is a mistake to treat the technician-leader, as Katz, Kahn and Simon have done, as being value neutral or value-neutered, the agents and factotums of other-directed imperatives. The moral commitment of the archetype extends beyond organizational directives to larger fields of interest and to the value clarification of such larger interests. In his mode as Weberian bureaucrat the technician is the self-effacing and self-sacrificing civil servant rightly directed by a sense of duty, committed to the public interest and the even better determination of that interest.

All archetypes subsume their lower ranks so the technician transcends and subsumes the values of careerist and politician. It is elitist and aristocratic and reflects the conception that administration, government and leadership are the more desirable the more they manifest rule by the *best* (as opposed to rule by the most or merely rule by the powerful). While the technician acknowledges the realities of power and politics he has an end-faith in the ultimate merits of expertise and professionalism. This flows from the fact that the body of knowledge must of necessity be continually compartmentalized and refined through the subdivision of disciplines. As the unity of science is co-operative and interdependent but increasingly molecular and articulated, so too must be social structure and organizational life. So, too, administration creates its own expertise and becomes a matter for professionals rather than amateurs.

In the public sector this type of technician sometimes acquires the tag of mandarin. This popular but pejorative usage may overlook, as has happened with the word 'bureaucrat', the possibility of a form of life often dedicated to public service. Depictions of this kind of life are to be found in both popular and technical literature (Snow; Dale) and at its best the type approximates the ethos of Platonic guardianship. Nevertheless, the true technician remains within the rubric of Type II values. His ethics are rational and utilitarian, however much they are reinforced by elitism of training and professional sense of responsibility. Technician and politician are both pragmatic, though the former has a more long-term orientation which is backed up by the technologies of planning and general systems. Within the taxonomy of process (see p. 26) the technician can be most easily associated with the phases of planning and managing; but also he must cope with some of the components of philosophy and monitoring. This relative detachment from the hurly burly of interactive reality (R_{II}, p. 77) concurs with a general proclivity for self-effacement and impartiality. The technician would be dispassionate in the best sense of that word.

In contrast with the politician the technician would tend to stress the nomothetic over the idiographic. He subscribes to the goal paradigm: that the chief end of administration and organization is to accomplish ethically legitimate goals, as effectively and efficiently as possible. In behavioural terms he would schedule work, maintain definite standards, emphasize deadlines, encourage uniformity, clarify expectations, and co-ordinate problem solving (Katz and Kahn,

1978:51; Fleishman and Peters, 1962). He initiates order within the untidy affairs of men.

The archetype can also take the phenomenal form of the *éminence grise*; the clever staff officer behind the titular commander, the Deputy Minister who forms the ministerial mind.

The basic philosophical ground of the technician is to be found in the doctrines of utilitarianism. He is as much at home in communist as in capitalist or socialist societies. He would maximize the good by the most efficient means. It is not unreasonable to lump together Frederick W. Taylor, Robert McNamara, and Albert Speer as illustrations of the class. *Zweckrationalität*, Weber's rationality of purpose, is characteristic. Give the administrator a goal, an aim, a purpose; then let him achieve it. Of course, philosophically, this is not good enough, although it supports the highest value type so far. It is open to all those criticisms levelled against utilitarianism, and especially to the criticism that rationality itself is insufficient (though necessary) for the advance of quality of human life through organizational means. One might say that the technician runs the risk of committing the fallacy of pursuing the good instead of the Good.

While the technician archetype subsumes all lower archetypes and, as it were, corrects for them in the value or ethical sense, it is itself, like all of the value archetypes, susceptible to corruption and to the general postulate of degeneracy (Hodgkinson, 1978:115). When it comes to manifestations of this in the empirical world, examples are plentiful. F. W. Taylor's IIA scientific management led, in our times, to a regression to the IIB political: worker resistance and the human relations movement. Weber's ultra-rationalism bred the grand assortment of the bureaupathologies. McNamara's technocratic leadership of the US military in the Viet Nam war incurred heavy criticisms (Gabriel and Savage, 1978) while the unification of the Canadian armed forces, touted as the essence of rationalism, has been blamed for a disaffection of morale and the destruction of commitment (Cotton,

1979).[3] Professor Speer's brilliant technical-political leadership in wartime Germany committed the militaristic fallacy on a gigantic scale and ended with twenty years' imprisonment for the leader, although it must be confessed that had the war ended otherwise our texts on the philosophy of administration might have been printed up somewhat differently.

The list could be extended indefinitely and the profusion of examples merely points to the fact that this archetype is characteristic of our times. This is the age of the technician and ours is a bureaucratic, scientific-technological, rational-legal, complex, but withal neo-feudalistic society.

Those administrators who consciously or unconsciously espouse this archetype can lay claim to the best of intentions; not theirs is any defect of motive nor any deliberateness of malice. They wish merely to better achieve organizational aims. And even to achieve better organizational aims! In the latter case the technician does not commit the militaristic fallacy but looks beyond that circle of interest which ends at the boundaries of his organization. At worst, of course, the technicians *are* guilty of philosophical myopia: a failure to understand and comprehend the complexity of human nature, the richness of its intuitive and affective side, its *trans*rationality. Paradoxically and ironically for this archetype this could be called the fault of ignorance. Nevertheless, this is a highly honourable ideal type despite its easy degeneration into the modes of faceless bureaucrat, apparatchik and disengaged organizational man. Together with the politician this type most represents the component of reason in the logic of administrative value. The technician approaches the limits of that aspect of the logic.

FOLLOWERSHIP

It has already been stated that the most congenial form of

---

[3]   In both of these military examples the argument centres about the substitution of an 'econometric' or 'civilian' model for the traditional or classical model of soldiering. In the latter case there has also been a demolition of the irrational infrastructure, the symbol system, by clothing all members of the organization in the same uniform.

leadership is that represented by the lower archetype of politician. Nevertheless, as organizational life becomes increasingly bureaucratic and technological so too does the technician archetype move into the ascendant. This means that, now and in the future, the modal form of life for followers is likely to be one determined by technocratic leadership imbued with the values of this archetype. If anomie and the dysfunctions of bureaupathology are to be avoided there is a strong implication here that the follower, too, must somehow come to be imbued with the goal paradigm and the technocratic ethos. There must somehow be some voluntary self-abnegation to the nomothetic impress, some willing or programmed subscription to it which would afford the follower an authentic sense of personal worth. Here, perhaps, is the very nub of the problem of leadership in the twentieth century.

Examples of attempted solution of this problem are to be found in communist ideology where the evolution of a new Soviet Man is from time to time proclaimed. Such a follower would be a moral paragon without the defects of nature attributable to bourgeois economic history, willing and glad to endorse the technician's lead. Or there is the sometime Japanese practice of training their workers in the discipline of Zen, the general idea being that follower fulfilment can then be found in self-transcendence through focusing upon task (an idea of pure praxis, uniting simultaneously the supremely metaphysical with the ultimately practical). But these ideas, and even those of Ouchi's Theory Z, are quasi-Utopian. The practical reality is very likely to contain intractable problems of conflict between nomothetic and idiographic dimensions; between personality and role. Some followers are infantile and authority-dependent; others will bring to their roles psycho-biologies unamenable to organizational education. Some will be evil plain and simple, some born to rebel. Since the value paradigm applies to followers as well as to leaders no simple solutions seem likely.

One aspect of technician-followership that is worthy of note, however, is the increasing number of organization members with professional or quasi-professional commitments. In Gouldner's terms some of these will be locals and some cosmopolitans. Their fields of value interest will extend, along with their expertise, beyond the organizational embrace. Whether or not this trend might mitigate or aggravate line and staff tension is a matter for empirical as well as philosophical exploration. Thompson (1961) perceived it as a major source of organizational conflict but it must also be conceded that professional and technical norms generally are those which resonate with the technician archetype. Moreover, the archetype suggests that line officers, administrators and leaders, will be themselves the embodiment of expertise and professionalism. On the other hand, it may be allowed that the values of impartial justice and detached objectivity, though implicit within the emergent culture, have never been particularly noticeable at the individual level. In the end it may be that the individual will simply have to succumb; the age of the specialist endorses the metavalue of expertise. For the future the central problem of followership will be whether the possibilities for self-transcendence can come to outweigh the probabilities of alienation.

PRAXIS

The first problem of praxis under this archetype is not that of determining the primary maxim. What that is is already perfectly plain. It is the apparently straightforward rule of utilitarianism: act so as to maximize the greatest good of the greatest number. For the technician such a metaethical maxim is internalized to the point where it is almost metavaluational.

The problem of praxis is other, and twofold: internal and external. Externally the problem is to be continually aware of the organizational purposes and to keep them under adequate scrutiny with an eye to the organization's environment and its value milieux. It is so easy, so sweetly seductive in its irresponsibility, to cease to critically examine the organization's *raison d'être*. What is good for General Motors is surely good for the country — whatever the General Motors, whatever the country. Weber's *Zweckrationalität*, rationality of purpose, has to come up for periodic audit. The utilitarian aim of the technician should be to achieve the best reconciliation of organizational interest and the largest possible compass of humane responsibility. The Socratic dictum that the unexamined life is not worth living has to be raised to the organizational level so that only the examined purpose becomes worthy of individual commitment. Such a praxis might have saved Albert Speer. Such a praxis did indeed dignify the work of Frederick W. Taylor for, rightly or wrongly in the judgement of history, he himself had no doubt that his *Zweckrationalität* was also *Wertrationalität*. A logic of worth as well as of purpose. So, too, Bismarck writing letters to himself in his several offices as Chancellor and Minister of War. So too perhaps, with some of the more committed adherents of Management by Objectives.

The second praxis problem is even more difficult. It is internal to the organization. Let us call it, along with Thompson, the problem of administrative compassion. How are we to reconcile the general and the particular, the nomothetic and the idiographic? Often, in praxis, this comes down to making exceptions, bending rules, putting the telescope to the blind eye, being, in short, morally, ethically and valuationally 'flexible' or, in Barnard's circumlocution, *complex*. No maxim or set of maxims can be laid down here. It is an intensely human art and, like all art, in the end idiographic, a function of personality, character, moral structure. From the standpoint of value theory the principle of subsummation must be remembered; the technician archetype subsumes that of the politician. The technician-practitioner must look to the politician within himself in seeking the praxis solution of this problem. Good praxis can be rewarding: it pays off with richness in the quality of work life on the one hand and with authentic administrative fulfilment on the other.

Nevertheless, this and every archetype is vulnerable to philosophical attack. All of the criticisms of utilitarianism, for example, apply with force to the technician, with direct implications for praxis, most specifically, the assertion that the utilitarian maxim is vain, for no hedonic calculus is possible. Subjective qualities are non-comparable and, indeed, from the standpoint of inter-subjective truth the *quality* of work life, the *quality* of any human and social life, can never be determined or assessed quantitatively, not even in principle.[4]

So the technician, knowingly but dangerously, pursues what may be a chimera and ever runs the risk of mistaking the good for the Good. This may explain a certain malpraxis tendency with this archetype which manifests as a desire for quantification in decision processes and the assumption of a posture of value neutrality. The spurious gloss and illusion of rationality so easily presented by economists, stasticians and accountants is preferred to the point where administrative and phenomenological realities become increasingly lost to praxis. Leadership responsibility is abdicated in favour of crisis management (when the chickens of pseudo-rationality come home to roost).

The error of positivism in praxis can also be compounded by the fallacy of agency. The leader says, not I but the corporate body do this to you. The victim says, not you but They have done this to me.

This archetype is by its very character prone to lead to the praxis errors of compartmentalization, psychological distancing and the militaristic and excisionistic fallacies. I once asked a true exponent of the type, a long-time high-ranking bureaucrat, about the religion of a Prime Minister whom he had long and intimately served. He was indignant. What difference did his religion make? What one did at the sacred level was personal and private and not be be confused or contaminated by what one did at the secular level which was public and official. The doctrine of the Two Swords expounded by Gelasius of Constantinople in the fifth century was apparently still alive in this technician's mind with, one cannot help but wonder, whatever negative implications for praxis.

---

[4]   Cf. Arrow's General Impossibility Theorem (1963:59) and paradox where group preferences ordered $A > B > C$ lead to the decision outcome $C > A$.

Errors of philosophy and praxis such as these can have a multiplier effect in their practice ramifications. This is because the technician leader is often to be found at the head of large and powerful organizations, capable of massive dehumanization and positive harm. We reject with force, therefore, Simon's notion that the administrator or leader is a factotum or agent. This notion is not dead. Thayer (1980) has noted that some scholars may have to apologize with embarrassment for arguing anew that 'no serious student would today accept the separation of "politics" and "administration"' but also feels obliged to comment on that selfsame separation as being a prevalent ideology amongst bureaucrats (Rohr, 1978:26).

At the end of the day, when all the risks of praxis have been accounted, we must, however, honour the technician, for he represents the highest of the archetypes that it is ordinarily possible for the administrator to aspire to and attain. This sets the safe limit to the moral ambitions and aspirations of administration. Schools of leadership can with confidence set their sights no higher. Bureaucracy and the technician together represent mankind's greatest administrative accomplishments and the technician-leader is the standard bearer of rational virtue.

But suppose this is not enough? A philosophy of leadership cannot rest even here; it must go beyond rationality, science, technology, even mathematics. Bewitchment of the intellect by intelligence is still bewitchment.

THE POET

> Stood you confessed of those exceptional
> And privileged great natures that dwarf mine —
> A zealot with a mad ideal in reach,
> A poet just about to print his ode,
> A statesman with a scheme to stop this war,
> An artist whose religion is his art,
> I should have nothing to object! Such men
> Carry the fire, all things grow warm to them
>
> (Robert Browning, 'Bishop Blougram's Apology')

The speaker in the quotation is a successful administrator, a bishop, who fully enjoys the material rewards of his office but is placed in the position of defending his form of life to an impoverished and younger friend. The bishop is both astute enough to detect the lack of authenticity in his friend's critique and wise enough to accept that there are other and higher forms of life than his own. Although he advocates at best a kind of Type II technicianship — which would at least carry with it the comfortable rewards of material prosperity — he realizes that there are other values in the value hierarchy. Enough, we would say, to constitute another archetype. It is this last which I have called the Poet.

The poet 'carries the fire', makes things and men grow warm, extends the reach of language (and hence thought, concept and rationality), steals fire from the gods, even — in the limit — reconciles for the instant God and Man. Heidegger has identified the crisis of our age as the conflict between technician and poet (Barrett, 1979:247). Poetry in this sense refers to the higher and deeper intuitions, to some sort of transrational grasp which can only partially, if not at all, be expressed in the linear logic of ordinary language. It is also the voice of the Will. The ultimate symbolic and actual expression of freedom. It is the *Götterdämmerung* of Nazi ideology in the rubble of Berlin and the stoic glory of the Roman Republic. Athens *and* Sparta; Pericles *and* Caesar. It is not mythos *opposed* to logos but mythos subsuming and transcending logos.

In administration this Type I quality led Plato to formulate the concept of the Guardian whose moral bases are more profound than those discussed so far in that they extend into the transrational domain of faith-activated will, perhaps into strata of unconscious mind inaccessible by ordinary means. In contrast to the technician the poet is guided by the Good rather than the good. And in the Platonic Republic it would have been this very quality of moral insight which would serve as the credential of the philosopher-king. Although Type I value commitments tend to be absolute and unassailable for the value-holder in the ideal type these coexist with the moral codes previously outlined, subsuming and transcending them. The poet-administrator is not naive. His sophistication embraces the lower forms.

Other names have been assigned to manifestations of the archetype throughout history and across cultures: mandarin, samurai, brahmin, hero, prince, aristocrat. In politics he may articulate the unspoken dreams of the masses and be charged with charisma, the mythic leader of historical moment and greatness.

Whether stemming from dream or myth or religion, whether sacred or secular, the poet's *will* is the justification of right and the determinant of good. In his mode of saint, whatever is right is good for him, and in his mode of super-man whatever is good for him is right. But throughout, and at much lesser levels of organizational complexity than empire or State, the poet exhibits those properties of moral complexity and responsibility discussed by Barnard. Across seas of preferential turbulence and through storms of rational and political opposition he negotiates those principles which he cannot compromise. All the instruments to this end which the political and social sciences can provide, together with all the skills of the *arthasastra*, are ready to his hand. With these he engages in the greatest of all art forms — the making of history, the unfolding and actualization of purpose.

Type I values, and their poetic manifestation, create awesome difficulties in a variety of milieux — in theory, in philosophy, in the social sciences, because of the homo-genetic fallacy and the problem of differentiating between Type III and Type I affect — in the untidy world of adminis-trative reality because they do violence to pragmatic requirednesses and the spirit of compromise. They are threatening because they invoke the will in its highest regis-ters of motivating force, because they represent the ultimate commitment of which man is capable. Although they might be suspect to the technician as rational man and uncom-fortable for the politician as pragmatic man, one can also hypothesize that these values lie at the core of the phenome-non of charisma. True charisma then becomes a function of Type I commitment.

The attitude of the rational administrator towards the

charismatic phenomenon is necessarily cautious. The record of history and experience is mixed and ambivalent. On the one hand the course of collective evolution is accelerated by the poet-leaders, on the other hand we collectively bear the scars of quantum excitations and great leaps forward that have failed. One approaches even discussion of this archetype with an attitude of awe and a sense of deep inadequacy, for the very language of analytical discourse has here to reach beyond its grasp. The *Lebensform* of the archetype is partially inaccessible and where it is accessible is so only through its interpretations in the behaviours and understandings of organizational interactions. It is philosophy-in-action extraordinary.

The magic of the Platonic ideal has nevertheless continued throughout the ages to fascinate, motivate and enthrall. From the Communist Party as the 'elite vanguard of the proletariat' to the Society of Jesus to the cloisters of Oxbridge and Ivy League, the poetry of the Academy persists. Why is this? It may be true because true religion is the highest experience that life has to offer and of which man is capable. In Plato this 'religion' is expressed through an acquaintanceship, however fleeting, with the Form of the Good. The Guardian, the Poet, the Prophet then becomes the *moral* leader, calling men beyond their circumscribed fields of interest, their petty rationality, their prudential insecurities. He has the quality of charisma. He knows men do not live by bread alone. He knows and voices for them their deeper, hidden yearnings. He knows too that men are led by baubles.

In one way or another then the poet comes to be an embodiment and personification of transrational desire. Such desire can from time to time call men in their collective activity to heroic convulsions of effort and sacrifice. It is as if the charismatic leader provided a leaven of mutation in the evolution of *collective* activity. Without the poet history would unfold arithmetically, with him, geometrically.

According to the theory of archetypes, the true poet would subsume the lower categories. He would therefore be acting on the highest ethical plane and thereby seeking higher states of welfare for his organization, states not necessarily perceptible to all subordinates since their clear perception would be a function of the leader's greater value consciousness. The poet would transcend the value forms of life associated with the lower archetypes. He has a sense of the unconditioned and the unconditional; an authority intensified by moral force. He may appear as the 'man of principle' or the 'man of conscience' or the 'man of intuition' whose Type I value commitments are such that they cannot be compromised, even if they fly in the face of the sweetest arguments of prudence and calculation. Martin Luther, Gandhi, Sir Thomas More display historical manifestations of the form.

The poet archetype in its purest form is antithetical to that which would be associated with the practice of *arthasastra* and *Realpolitik*, the careerist is at one extreme of the paradigm and the poet at the other, but this is not to say that the poet would not avail himself of these techniques, without scruple, if his ends necessitated those means (nor that, as discussed below, extremes cannot meet). The type has often been portrayed with adulation and yields cross-cultural and cross-historical instances of mythic stature: Joan of Arc, Moses, Arjuna in the *Bhagavad Gita*, the legendary King Arthur — all linked by some special Vision of the Good. To the extent that the poet's special achievement is to impress his will upon the unfolding of events through his art of administration the aphorism may indeed be true that history is the biography of great men. Of course history is continuously in process through collective action anyway. The special role and influence of the poet is reserved for the mutative leaps in the unfolding of human affairs.

Closely associated with this archetype are the phenomena of charisma, phenomena not understood by science and perhaps impervious to rigorous or formal investigation. It is, however, most certainly real and is an attribute of personality which manifests itself in social interaction. Whatever his private qualities of morality and ethics — and the theory calls for deep commitments and superior if not superhuman engagement of the *will* — the poet has an ability to communicate, influence, inspire others through his interaction with them. He must be seen and heard for maximum effect although, once he is entrenched in the leader's role, the power of myth and image alone can be sufficient to perpetuate the organizational momentum. Often the poet is precisely that, a master of language. Lenin, Churchill, Mao Tse-tung exhibited this quality. The poet has the gift of playing language games in such a way that desire-ideas, values, affective yearnings which would die in the light of Level II reason and pragmatics instead become invested with a transrational and transcendental motivating force, alive with fire and inspiration, compelling men to Type I commitments.

Poetry, ideology and religion run together hand in hand. They cannot be entirely eliminated from organizational life though they can of course be perverted and degraded through the power of the planner and the philistine, through the best intentions of the technician and the politician, and the worst intentions of the bourgeoisie and the masses. The fact that our higher and deeper yearnings remain and are in some sense ineradicable renders the poet archetype so dangerous. The moreso when the type appears to us in the form of the Good Man, the hero of virtues, the administrator who impresses us with his integrity at close quarters, who changes our life — or even the imaged leader, never met, who nevertheless strikes the chord which reverberates in the depths of our being, resonating with dreams of honour, glory, self-sacrifice and fulfilment; dangerous in the extreme; brinking, like genius, on madness. The poets represent the ultimate in leadership but they command by will, not reason. Their persuasiveness lies not in mere positive affect modulated by some rational calculus of incentives, but in the triumph of the Will.

When this archetype is translated into fact through the working out of events in the world, that is, when R_I clashes with R_{III} through R_{II} (see p. 77), then its constituent values, whatever they may be at the time, are submitted to empirical testing. This is the test of history. Those values which pass the test become established parts of a culture ($V_{5, 4, 3}$). Those which fail are expunged from the official record. If they are held at all it must be covertly and with the threat of persecution to the deviant value actors. With the lower archetypes, on the other hand, this endless process, the continuous differentiating out from and assimilating into the value fabric and ethos of a society, is relatively innocuous. It may even go unnoticed. It is at Level II, in any event, *pragmatic*. But at the level of the highest archetype the value commitments are of a different logical order[5] and of radically different affective intensity. The poet lives by and is prepared to die for the values to which he is committed. These (Type I) values form his depth-personality infrastructure and engage the whole force of his will. 'What am I but what *I stand for*?' To be sure, in administration the poet may resort to technical and political modes of negotiation but in the end he will not compromise. 'Here I stand,' says Martin Luther and, afterwards, 'I could do no other.' It is the administrative equivalent of 'Let justice be done though the heavens fall,' where justice is equivalent to the will of the poet.

If this offends, and it usually does, the more rational and detached of administrative philosophers, then it must be allowed that there are compensating aspects in reality. The intense personal commitment of the leader may have galvanic effect. Through his personal magnetism and charisma, the organization itself can be invested with a synergetic sense of purpose. In the ordinary sense this can be accomplished at best by the technician-as-Guardian but with the poet there is no *ordinary* sense. This archetype takes us beyond the confines of normality; it exhausts normality. It gives birth to a new order.

A difficult problem now arises. Can we admit to the ranks of leaders governed by this archetype those past charismatic administrators upon whom history has handed down a negative, or at least equivocal, judgement? Hitler, Napoleon, Genghis Khan? How is megalomania to be reconciled with the archetype? Were Christ and Buddha poets?

---

[5] Kant's 'reverence for the moral law' appears to be of this order, which Kant would distinguish from ordinary affect because it is *self-produced* by a rational concept (cf. Williams, 1971:69).

This problem refers us back to the difficulty, already discussed, of discriminating between Type III and Type I affect. One can conceive, for example, of a careerist become so committed to his personal success that this has become the dominant element in his form of life. His will committed to this value and engaged at Level I, he seeks to impose, poetically, the impress of his commitment upon the world via his organization. Such megalomania is not unknown in administrative life. The quantum shift between the extreme levels of the paradigm has occurred. Putting it somewhat differently, in this instance the force of the leader's will concerning the values of his personal career has become sufficient to enlist the subscription of *other* men to these values and this end. A threshold has been crossed.

While this scenario is conceivable in principle, it would, however, be unusual or exceptional, for this reason: unless deceived or constrained by circumstance or coerced by force or misguided by miscalculation, men do not normally enlist themselves and *their* careers in the service of another. Mere *careerism* is insufficient. The success-hungry will not achieve that necessary quality of charisma which typifies the poet unless he can also offer something more. That something more is an appeal to the inchoate and latent values of *others*. If the careerist can do this he is no longer a careerist but is translated to the poet rank. The poet articulates for the masses.

Nevertheless, we are forced to the conclusion, distasteful though it may be, that megalomania and poetry can merge in the archetype, that the charismatic administrator can lead to hell on a promise of heaven, and that such types can so transmute their own career and self-interest so as to tap a domain of powerful and dangerous value which can bewitch and bemuse beyond mere reason. Adolf Hitler was certainly a poet — perhaps the greatest of our times — the contrast with technician Speer is illuminating — and, in the verdict of history, a poet whose values failed.

What of Christ and Buddha? The distinction here is that, charismatic though they certainly were, these men were not *organizational*. They were not administrator-leaders but teacher-leaders. Indeed both were often expressly *anti*-organizational. Their claim to poetic rank must be at one remove through the lieutenants and disciples who established organizations after their demise. In that sense the power of their charisma and of the archetype persists to the present day. The special kind of leadership represented here will be discussed again in the next chapter. One ought not to be surprised, however, at the intimate relationship between religion and the poet archetype; Type I values by definition go directly to the heart and the soul. They establish the upper and lower limits of human phenomenology.

FOLLOWERSHIP

While the most congenial form of leadership is that of the politician and the most beneficial that of the technician, the most committing, demanding and in its own way fulfilling is that of poet. As I have already said, he calls his followers beyond themselves, he taps inchoate motives and values within the followership, he permits them to participate in a vision. For all of these reasons, and because of the essentially religious quality of the archtype, the followers themselves tend to become as dangerous, to themselves and others, as their leader. They become invested with a quality of fanaticism or zealotry which can lead within their own ranks to inter-necine rivalries and, outside these ranks, to violence against the infidel. Perhaps, in both directions, to persecution mania. This judgement is made, of course, from the standpoint of the lower archetypes. For the poet and his followers there is no such equivocation or diffidence or caution. Leader and followers are *committed*.

Why all this seems dangerous from the purely rational standpoint is because of the ability of the poet to create the true believer, the fanatic. He has a magic gift, he can endow his followers with a sense of value elitism. The cadre becomes an elect. Inspired by the poet-leader they may undergo that form of psychological experience which James (1902) has described as conversion. The follower finds in such leader-ship his own calling, vocation, mission, life-meaning. He gets religion. All this, of course, is dependent upon historical and organizational context but, if the contingencies are right, the master will find his disciples and the ranks of the faithful will begin to form. From the seed of the initial cadre can spring ever more expansive and complex ideological structures: the Holy Roman Empire, the Fascisti, the SS, Boy Scouts and Young Pioneers. And of course some followers will be more faithful than others, even unto the end — Christian martyrs, Napoleon's grenadiers — heroes or saints, lemmings or lunatics — the followership born of this archetype is capable of ultimate dedication. Whether this dedication is to be lauded or lamented depends upon the values of the observer, where he stands in the paradigm, and the verdict of historical process. Opinions differ and appraisals shift: the Irish terrorist hunger strikers may be in current disrepute while kamikaze pilots of the second war may be restored to their laurels. *O tempora! O mores!*

The followership of this archetype also risks the trauma of disenchantment, the crisis of loss of faith, the despair of deconversion. This is compounded by the fact that the prime pathology of the poet-leader is megalomania. When and if he should lose his vision, or be frustrated in his superimposition of it upon the world, the form corrupts and madness can ensue. The vision lost, he may be left only with the power of his office against the frustration and implacability of the realities. The followership may sense this and falter. The scenarios begin to assume tragic, even cataclysmic proportions: the Holocaust and the Gulags of modern times; value sickness in extremis, infectious and deadly aberrations of desire and will which can lead to the immolation of followers and havoc in the organizational environment. So it would seem from the *outside*.

PRAXIS

To the ancient question *Quis custodiet ipsos custodes?* the answer must be, no one. No one guards the Guardians. No reasons can be given for their morality (Beehler, 1978: 145-64). The poet answers only to his intuition (*in*-tuition), his inner guide and voice. One could say that he walks the razor's edge which divides the dark side of Irrationality from the Light. And the cynic could reply that on the showing of history he would seem to have balanced abysmally, plunging more often than not himself and his followers into night and fog. There is much in common between poets, saints, supermen and psychopaths. Genius, when it appears in administration, is marvellous to behold but often difficult and sometimes appalling in its consequences. The praxis distinction has to do with the break between Type II and Type I values. The former refers to morals and the ordinary pragmatics of administration whilst the latter takes us into the region of the *ethical*. The region in which Wittgenstein would have us become silent (1922:6.421, 6.423, 7). The region which in administration is associated with charisma.

Generally, then, for this archetype there can be but one maxim of praxis: Beware charisma! The charismatic leader may wish to lead where others cannot or ought not to follow. To beware does not necessarily mean or entail 'Avoid!': there can be greatness and glory here as well as danger — superlative rewards for superlative risks — but it does enjoin consciousness. Be *aware*! Then choose.

If praxis is taken in its fullest Aristotelian sense to mean the conscious union of politics and ethics, that is, the deliberate welding of the moral and the administrative forms of life, then it is precisely when the poet archetype appears that we might expect praxis to be at its most powerful. *Fiat justitia ruat coelum*, let the leader's will be done, let the world be changed, let the heavens fall. When the intrusion and pervasion of value from R_I through R_{III} carries this supercharge of commitment and psychological investment what counsel can be given other than for pause, for hesitation, for extroverted and introspected caution and only then, if at all, allow the die to be cast. And for the true manifestations of the type such advice might be simply vain, anyway.

I have attempted to construe, with instances, the benevolent aspects of the poet; yet I must confess to a personal uneasiness at the empirical possibilities of this value form of life. The appearance of the poet, albeit in impurely manifested form, suggests the strong likelihood of ultimately negative consequences in the world of fact. Can we really give with assurance instances from the history of administration where charismatic leadership proved in the long view to be of organizational benefit? Perhaps the question is impossible to answer for, as with any utilitarian analysis, the hedonic calculus does not exist which would allow us to conduct the true analysis of costs and benefits. And even if we could, upon what basis other than arbitrary choice could we establish the point in the seamless web of history at which the balance sheet were to be drawn up? Nevertheless, such leadership can break organizational moulds, release energies and revitalize jaded practices. Even the staidest of bureaucracies might be catapulted into new projects. Deadlocks, political and technical, can be broken and a heady sense of new beginnings may be imparted to an enthused followership. But some if not all of this is within the scope and competence of the technician-guardian and the politician, the technocrat and the democrat. And the end results of such leadership performance may be evil. As the novelist Saul Bellow asks, 'With everyone sold on the good how does all the evil get done?'

The important point for praxis which must be noted is this: our discussion is perforce from the standpoint of the non-poet and therefore from the standpoint not of the leader, as hitherto, but of the follower. For the poet himself there is no point to discussion of praxis;[6] he simply *is* praxis, his own Type I values embodied and invested in the field of executive action. He is the keeper of his own flame. Armoured in his rightness, righteously beyond the reach of any praxis exhortations.

The lieutenant, on the other hand, may retain, for a time at least, and if he is not overwhelmed by charisma or charismatic organizational programming, an option of choice, a suspension of commitment. If such a window of opportunity should open, if such a degree of freedom should obtain, then the praxis advice would be no different from what we have already dispensed.

---

[6]   Marcus Aurelius might prove the exception to this rule.

Administration at this level, and by 'administration' I mean the whole taxonomy of process subsuming the leader and the led, can be construed as the ultimate art-form: the deliberate, meaningful, praxis-laden making of history. There is an analogue of sorts in the case of the cinema where the *auteur*-director seeks through complex organization to realize aesthetic values, but in the real-life case of administration the values would have to do with an *ethic*. This ethic may be peculiarly representative of and personal to the poet but it can never be solely that, because it must also have tremendous appeal for at least some other men, especially those who become the cadre of lieutenants, the executives of the art, the disciples. So again the maxim must be the same: be aware. Be value conscious. To come into contact with this archetype through its poetic embodiment is to risk first seduction and then conversion as the lesser will becomes suborned by the greater. That the poet commands such access to the well-springs of motivation is indicated in the following passage which shows once more how extremes can meet in the working out of the value paradigm:

> Speer nominated as Hitler's greatest strength his ability as a *Menschenkenner*. 'He knew men's secret vices and desires, he knew what they thought to be their virtues, he knew their hidden ambitions and the motives which lay behind their loves and their hates, he knew where they could be flattered, where they were gullible, where they were strong and where they were weak; he knew all this...by instinct and feeling, an intuition which in such matters never led him astray.' This gave him an extraordinary power over others (including Speer himself). As a strategist he showed the same unerring eye for his enemy's inner weaknesses. This knowledge, far from engendering sympathy, left in him a supreme contempt for his fellow creatures. (Davies, 1980:69 n.)

This leaves us with a philosophical perplexity. Perhaps the largest question raised by this aspect of the paradigm, is how good is Good? I want to say that neither the poet himself, nor his Type I values, nor the commitments they entail can be placed beyond the reach of critique. Each represents just this, a limiting form within the conceptual value hierarchy.

Yet, between careerist and poet, the beginning and end points of our analysis, there seems to be an axiological discontinuity which corresponds to the ontological discontinuity between animal and man. In values and in value manifestation we find hierarchy, just as we do in biology, in organization and in logic. The administrative forms of life occupy depths as well as heights. The poet breathes the more rarefied air. He reaches beyond the ordinary grasp.

CAVEAT

Having discriminated at some length these four analytical 'pure types' which theoretically exhaust the value possibilities, it is now necessary to repeat that they are immanent, inchoate, teleological or potential and unlikely to be manifested in any but an impure version in the world of fact. This empirical impurity is further compounded by the principles of subsummation and conflation. These state that any value actor is the bearer at any given time of a complex of values which are hierarchically distinct but which coexist contemporaneously, the higher value types subsuming the lower.[7] What is more, actors need not even be aware of any affective dissonance in this state of affairs (Rokeach, 1973:215-35, 286-313). Not all values need be within the scope of everyday consciousness. And others may be sublimated or repressed. We are forced then to acknowledge the extreme complexity and subtlety of value phenomenology — the desire nature of the human condition — while at the same time having a practical faith in the possibility and utility of its ultimate and proximate analysis. The next chapter will return to this topic, together with its implications for administration. For now it must be admitted that, no matter how great the

---

[7] The empirically-minded might be attracted to the possibility of combining Likert-type scaling with Sheldon-type coding to produce a 4-digit typification of any given leader — a 7777 being the ultimate and a 1111 the nadir — and while it would be simple to type administrators in this way it should be noted that this would entail the risk of committing both the homogenetic fallacy described above and what Professor Georgescu-Roegen (1971: 60-83) calls the arithmomorphic fallacy.

complexity may be, leadership can never be understood unless the problem of value is incorporated into its study. For now, too, it is enough to appreciate the analytical status of the archetypes, their consonance with the value paradigm, and their general relation to other schemes which purport to typify leaders.

MAPPING

Many typologies for the description of leadership are to be found in the literature. I cannot examine them all and have limited consideration to two which have superior claims to theoretical justification (Weber and Zaleznik) and one (de Bono) which does not set out to present a specific leadership theory but which is certainly replete with administrative implications. Together these will serve to illustrate authoritative thinking on the topic and relate it to the general theme of this book.

Max Weber's categorization is classic and consists of the triad of charismatic, traditional (patrimonial) and rational-legal modes of administration. It is substantiated by historical research and carries in its train a whole theory of historical evolution and organizational dynamics. Zaleznik's (1966: ch. 9) categories consist essentially of three leadership *styles*: proactive, mediative and reactive, which refer respectively to (1) 'actively seeking out environmental possibilities, enlarging scope for organisation's creative potential', (2) 'procuring internal changes in response to environmental pressure', and (3) 'maintaining (homeostatically) the internal stability, "steady state" of the organization'. This scheme, too, is heavily substantiated by research and case study. Lastly, there is the suggestive and provocative work of de Bono which derives from his research into cognitive functions (1967, 1969, 1971, 1976). It has yielded the constellation of administrative-managerial traits given below.

> *Organizers.* Those whose talent lies in organizing things — in a practical rather than a theoretical way. This must include the talent for running organizations, not just for designing them.

Information compilers. Those who are good at collecting and collating information. They know where to find information and they know how to keep it alive and accessible.

Detectives. Those who are good at following a trail and at finding things out. Those who can be set a general direction and will then find their own way from there.

Researchers. Those who are good at putting together information to expand upon an idea or to support it. Those who are good at doing experiments in the real world or in the world of already accumulated information.

Idea generators. Those who pride themselves on their ability to generate new ideas, new concepts and new hypotheses. Those who are interested in creativity and new ideas. This must be a general ability — not the intention to pursue one single new idea that may have arisen at some time in the past.

Synthesizers. Those who are good at putting together a mass of data and then boiling it down to what is important. Those who are good at bringing different things together and from the synthesis creating something new.

Reactors. Those who are good at reviewing and reacting to existing situations or to the ideas of others. This is indeed a critical role, but it involves the genuine appraisal role of criticism and not the destructive approach.

Explainers. Those who are good at taking a complicated situation and explaining it in a direct and simple way. This is not unlike the role of a science journalist. This task of clarification and simplification must not assume special intelligence on the part of the receiver.

Communicators. Those who are good at communicating with others, either in a direct way (face to face) or through some other medium (for example, writing). There is an overlap here with the explainers but also a distinct ability to communicate something as distinct from explaining it. A good teacher is a good communicator.

Salesmen. Those who are good at the very important process of creating interest in others. This is the ability to help other people see something in a new way. In its proper sense it is a way of enrolling the emotions of others through a change in their perceptions.

Group organizers. Those who are good at the type of organization required for handling a local or regional group. This must take into account the realities of human nature and fluctuating enthusiasm. It must include the determination to keep things going in addition to a sensitivity to the way things are going.

Diplomats. Those who are especially good at getting on with people. Those who have a facility for dealing with people on a one-to-one basis. Those who can put across a point of view without offence.

Leaders. Those who like taking responsibility and making decisions. Those who find leadership a natural role rather than an opportunity to exert a power they feel they need. This should be based on past experience of leadership qualities rather than the desire to suppose that one is a leader.

Effectors. Those who are good at making things happen. This is the most important role of all. It includes activity, direction and determination and also the skill to overcome obstacles. It is a personality skill more than an intellectual one. (1979:254-5)

	Hodgkinson	Weber	Zaleznik	de Bono
philosophy	technician*	rational-legal*	proactive	{ idea generators / synthesizers
planning	technician	rational-legal	proactive	{ researchers / information compilers
politics	politician	traditional-patrimonial	mediative	{ explainers / salesmen } diplomats
mobilizing	politician	traditional-patrimonial	mediative	{ communicators / organizers } leaders
managing	technician	rational-legal	reactive	{ group organizers / effectors
monitoring	technician	rational-legal	reactive	{ detectives / reactors

* The careerist archetype is pervasive and can appear within any aspect of process. The poet archetype, when it appears, can also exert itself at each level of process. The same qualifications apply to the charismatic leader type.

FIGURE 9   Leadership patterns and administrative processes

Taken all together these several interpretations, ranging between the extremes of the cognitive-behavioural and the affective-experiential can be mapped onto our taxonomy as shown in figure 9. The correspondences and imputations of this figure reveal that despite an incompleteness of the conceptual map and notwithstanding inevitable frontier disputes, *terrae incognitae*, and unclaimed territories there is still a broad general agreement about the principal boundaries and a consistency of pattern which suggests that the field of executive action is both comprehensible and structured with an inherent logic. It is the task of administrative philosophy to advance and refine this geography by continuous conceptual exploration.

The conceptual leader-types derived in this chapter can be summarized in shorthand as follows. The careerist archetype takes the lower or basal form of *predator* and the higher form of *opportunist*. The politician at worst is *demagogue* and at best *democrat*. The technician can degenerate to disengaged *bureaucrat* but can aspire to *guardian-technocrat*. The poet has the respective forms of *guardian* and *megalomaniac*. With respect to charisma it may be said that it applies specially to all variants of poet. The technician type is generally a-charismatic but may be quasi-charismatic in its higher form. The politician is pseudo-charismatic at worst, proto-charismatic at best. Careerist variants often appear to be pseudo-charismatic but are essentially, because of their egoistic focus of concern, a-charismatic.

We are now in a position to consider the philosophy of administration *qua* leadership.

7

The Philosophy of Leadership

Möge Gott dem Philosophen Einsicht geben in das, was vor
allen Augen liegt. (Ludwig Wittgenstein)

ADMINISTRATION AND LEADERSHIP

It is now time to make explicit what has been implicit all
along. Administration *is* leadership. Leadership *is* administration. These identities need surprise no reader who has
come this far but still there is a certain strangeness to these
expressions which is a carry-over from common usage.
There is a tendency in the ordinary language to conceive
of leadership, loosely understood, and it is nearly always
very loosely understood, as if it were a sort of increment
to the administrative-management process which might or
might not be present. An epiphenomenon. As if one could
administer without leadership or lead without administration. The flaw in this understanding can be seen once
evaluative epithets are attached. Then it somehow does not
make good sense to talk of having at one and the same
time good leadership and bad administration, or conversely.
In short, good leadership is simply good administration and
bad administration is simply bad leadership.

A *Führerprinzip* follows from this. Leadership extends

from apex to base of organizational hierarchy.[1] It pervades the organization. No one can escape leadership acts and leadership responsibilities any more than they can evade the administrative-managerial processes. If the basic axiom of this book holds, that administration is philosophy-in-action then, similarly, leadership can be understood as the effecting of policy, values, philosophy through collective organizational action. An understanding which, among the plethora of leadership definitions seems only to have been fully appreciated by Etzioni (1961:116) and Barnard (1972). To phrase it differently, either leadership or administration is the moving of men towards goals through a system of organization. It can be done well or it can be done badly, or it can be done indifferently, but it cannot not be done at all.

Of course, the administrative-leadership *emphasis* will differ and fluctuate in accordance with the taxonomy of process, the personalities of actors, and the contingencies of circumstance. *Prima facie* arguments can be made for some roles being more technical and managerial and staff, and less general and administrative and line than others, and so less leadership-sensitive. This can be acknowledged as another way of saying that the mix of value and fact varies with process, contingency and role, but however routinized and homeostatic an organizational role may be it is still integral to its organization. In time of crisis or special contingency it would become supersensitive to leadership action and capability. The NCO isolated with his men on the battlefield, the petty bureaucrat suddenly in a 'whistle-blowing' crisis, the disgruntled worker with an opportunity to sabotage — all may have to make crucial organizational decisions, exquisitely difficult value judgements. If then in the realities of the world anyone can administer, so too it can be said that anyone can lead. And so they do. The point of dissension is not about leadership itself but about leadership *effectiveness*.

---

[1] It is of some interest that the Nazi SS organization ensconced this principle in its system of ranks and titles (*Scharführer, Standartenführer, Gruppenführer*, etc.) so that even the lowliest member was semantically sensitized to his leadership responsibility.

In the ordinary language it is positive effectiveness which has come to be equated with leadership and which is understood as a kind of gloss which may or may not be superimposed upon the organizational workings, but for our more technical purposes the terms 'administration' and 'leadership' merge and become synonymous.

An important qualification must now be entered. The central concern of this book is the administrator-leader, the man who practises his leadership within and on behalf of an organization. But in addition to the organization men, the exponents of praxis, there are also solitaries: extra-organizational independents such as artists, inventors, writers and scholars, teachers and innovators who, by virtue of their private genius and creativity come to alter indirectly, at one or several removes, the world of context within which organizational life transpires. These too are leaders. Theirs too is leadership, but of a different sort. The distinction is, of course, they operate individually as opposed to corporately (in the interstices, as it were, of the neo-feudal web): Marx, Freud, Buddha, Christ, Blake, Turner, Matisse — alone in library, cell, study, studio or desert. They are, of course, never alone, merely relatively free of organizational commitments and responsibilities.

CREDO: *Since everyone has an inalienable birthright to philosophy anyone can lead.*

LEADERSHIP THEORY

Leadership, variously and however defined, has not gone unresearched. On the contrary it has, especially since the end of the last world war, become the object of intensive and extensive scrutiny. But a curious thing has happened along the way. There has developed a tendency to concentrate study under the rubric of psychology so that there has come about a certain specialization and monopolization; what we might call the psychologizing of leadership. Leadership thought is now a subdivision of psychology rather than of philosophy. What began in antiquity as a profoundly philosophical concern — how to find the Guardian — has become demythologized, secularized, empiricized, democratized and psychologized, and now flourishes as a thickly tangled web wherein notions of values, ethics and morality have been leached away, ignored, or deprecated as irrelevant.

The sequence of exploratory research has been, in the general line of its logic, from maxims or rules of thumb through trait theory, to factor analytic trait theory (yielding the classical two dimensions of task orientation and person orientation), to situational qualifications, to interactive considerations (task plus leader plus followers plus interactions), to the latter-day refined maxims of path-goal analysis and to the current complexities of Professor Fiedler's work (1967, 1978; House and Baetz, 1979). In all of this it is difficult to discern the explication of values, ethics, morals, much less the psychologically embarrassing factors of consciousness and will. By a progressively more positivistic research strategy the problem of such compounding and confounding elements has been elided. What then, at the end of the day, do we know of the psychology, if not the philosophy, of leadership?

By way of response to this question, I should like to examine philosophically what is perhaps the most sophisticated, advanced and substantiated theory of leadership extant, the Fiedler contingency model.[2] This work is prototypical in its underlying logic and an examination of it will serve to provide a general critique of psychological and empirical studies to date.

The logical infrastructure is simple enough: the leadership concept is conceived globally as consisting of a set of variables which constitutes a universe of observation. In Fiedler's studies this set would probably be less than (subsumed under) the set of variables corresponding to administration (certain routine managerial activities being excluded, for example). Nevertheless it would be potentially infinite (v_∞). For practical purposes a finite subset of variables (v_α) is

---

[2] For contemporary critique by psychologists see Graen *et al*, 1971 (a), (b); Ashour (1973); Schriessheim and Kerr (1977).

drawn and these are operationalized for measurement and study. Illustrative in the contingency model are such variables as position, power, task structure, leader-member relations and, more recently, intelligence, stress, experience, task complexity and others. Among all these quantitative reductions, two variables deserve special note because of their logical status. These are (1) leader personality, the input variable, v_1 and (2) leader effectiveness, the output variable, v_0. The former Fiedler measures by a short paper-and-pencil test, the Least Preferred Co-worker scale (LPC). The measurement of the latter varies with organizational context but is ostensibly 'objective'. Input v_1 as mediated by v_α is then explored for relationships with v_0. The result of this ongoing research is the contingency model with its current and emergent qualifications; a highly sophisticated statistical model which on average, it is claimed, can account for some 25 per cent of the variance among the empirical correlates of the leadership concept.

Such research is not to be deprecated. It represents the meritorious technical effort of quotidian social science. It should be encouraged, emulated, replicated and pursued. But one should also be able to place it within a philosophical perspective and have some understanding of its philosophical critique. The latter can be summarized in the following way.

First, the central variable v_1 engenders a certain philosophical queasiness. Is the essential truth about personality, even if our solitary focus of interest is something called leadership behaviour, to be derived in five minutes from a uni-dimensional scale? Perhaps it is. Yet there is evidence aplenty of the multi-dimensionality of man, and a growing literature in the psycho-biography of leaders presents us with overwhelming data of qualitative *complexity*, however much simplicity is ardently to be desired and scientifically to be sought.

Second, it is the rare case where we can say with any philosophical assurance what v_0 is. Organizational life is a continuous seamless web and v_0 measures have to be taken at a point in time. They are subject to the same strictures as apply to balance sheets when these are used as measures of

:conomic effectiveness. A rowing coach may have his leadership effect evaluated in terms of wins and losses but even in this apparently simple case the measure may be crude since some may row for the intrinsic value of it, which might include the leadership performance of the coach himself. In more complex cases the value judgement of effectiveness may have to be made by expert testimony, e.g. juries, which testimony is itself contaminated since it is a logically dependent function of the *philosophy* of the evaluators themselves.

Of course, as Campbell (1977:18) has pointed out, to ask global questions about organizational effectiveness is virtually useless, and Fiedler is certainly endeavouring to avoid precisely this pitfall; but the price exacted for operational precision may be an excessive loss of meaning and, if so, the psychological theory is again in philosophical trouble.

Third, this sort of research has tended studiously to avoid the value-ethical domain. The positivistic tendency to reduce value to affect and to subsume the latter in behavioural observations has already been discussed and there is extant a considerable literature of methodological critique (Greenfield 1978(a), (b), 1980: Gronn, 1982 *inter alia*). The fact that man-as-leader and man-as-follower is always and above all else a value-actor has become obscured and even forgotten. So too with the phenomena and phenomenology of commitment (Lang, 1982). The aspect of will is ignored. It is, one senses, a psychological and behavioural embarrassment. And, *a fortiori*, the value fallacies discussed in this book tend to be perpetrated on all points of the compass.

The final critique has to do with comprehensibility. Notwithstanding the misgivings outlined above I am prepared to acknowledge that the general productive effort of this type of research, particularly as it is embodied in Professor Fiedler's work, yields us the best theory that we have to date in the domain of psychological discourse. I would suspect, however, a paradox. The closer such theory approaches the *truth* the more incomprehensible it will become. Present theory is already unwieldy and confusing, perplexing even to the authorities. In astronomy the Ptolemaic theory yielded to the Copernican when the paradigm of the former broke under the weight of its own complexity, and perhaps we can look for a parallel development in this field. But there is no real sign of it yet. Available theory does have some pedagogical merit in so far as it sensitizes its students to the existence and interconnection of critical variables in the complex field of executive action but philosophically it falls short. The grasp for comprehension exceeds the reach.

It is almost as if science were a subdivision of nescience, always expanding the frontiers of ignorance. The philosophy of leadership must take leadership theory into account and must do so continuously and voraciously but it demands more than has ever yet been forthcoming. Most expressly, it demands for its adherents some comprehensible grasp of the logic and technology of organizational behaviour and, even more importantly, a corresponding grasp of the logic of value as the basis for praxis and administrative philosophy. Not just, how *does* the leader get through the day, how *does* he cope, but how *ought* he to cope? What does it *mean* to be a leader, a man of action, in our times, and what *can* it mean? What *ought* it to mean? These questions go beyond theory.

THE PRIMACY OF VALUE

Since leadership covers the gamut of administrative-managerial process and since, as has been shown, this process is partly logical but massively valuational, and since the distinctive administrative act is decision making, it follows that a philosophy of leadership, to be viable, must deal with values. In other words, the prepotency and pervasiveness of affect in human behaviour suggests that the philosopher give precedence to this branch over the other branch of administrative philosophy. The task of the latter is important and continuous, of course. It is to discriminate the concepts (themselves valuational) used in the discourse of administrative and organization theory, if possible to elucidate and order them in such a way that they can be articulated into models yielding testable and predictive

/potheses. In this way philosophy would subserve theory but in the praxis of leadership it is even more important to have a logic of value or an analysis of affect which can fill the void at present left by positivistic science and jejune theory.

Affect, motives, attitudes, beliefs, values, ethics, morals, will, commitment, preferences, norms, expectations, responsibilities — such are the concerns of leadership philosophy proper. Their study is paramount because the very nature of leadership is that of practical philosophy, philosophy-in-action. Leadership is intrinsically valuational. Logic may set limits for and parameters within the field of value action but value phenomena determine what occurs within the field. They are indeed the essential constituents of the field of executive action, all of which is to say that the leader's task is essentially affective. If this were not true then leadership behaviour could be routinized and, ultimately, computerized. How then are we to deal with this affective domain? How can the value paradigm be applied? Is it indeed applicable?

Dye (1978:39) in his treatise on policy analysis has suggested six criteria for evaluating the usefulness of concepts and models. They are, in brief, an ability to *order and simplify*; an ability to *identify* really significant problem aspects; a *congruence with reality*; an ability to *communicate* something meaningful; a potential for *directing inquiry and research*; and a capacity for *suggesting and explanation* of complex behaviour. It would seem to me that these criteria hold for the value paradigm, and in that faith I shall now attempt to expound it as an integral part of leadership philosophy.

THE ANALYSIS OF AFFECT

It is of interest to compare value and language. Both are mysterious and abstruse phenomena. Both are internalized through conditioning and programming as humans are born into the various value and language cultures. Both are externalized through participatory action as we speak, are spoken to, make our wishes felt or have the wishes of others imposed upon us. But value is purely subjective first and intersubjective second (we are not born value-*tabula rasa*) while language is intersubjective first (it is already in place when we arrive) and purely subjective second. As we master a language it becomes instrumental to expression of our individual form of life. Our values ultimately are couched in language and we seek more or less continuously to change the values of others through such language games as rhetoric, politics and diplomacy. Conflict is implicit and, in the last Clausewitzian analysis, war becomes the logical continuation of the value language game. So in this sense the very terrain of leadership is linguistic. The battles fought on that terrain are affective and valuational and the unending work of leadership is not only to mediate and resolve conflict but from time to time to initiate it. Even to inspire it. In all of this paradigmatic analysis can be applied.

The first thing to note is that value conflict must be either *inter*hierarchical within the paradigm, or *intra*hierarchical.

Interhierarchical conflict refers to values being in contention at different levels as when, say, one has the problem whether to stay in bed or get up (III versus IIA) or to report an incompetent professional colleague (IIB versus IIA) or to decide whether to desert in battle because of fear (III) or else go over the top into the enemy fire with one's comrades (IIB or IIA or I).

Two general principles can be applied to the resolution of interhierarchical conflict: (1) the principle of hierarchy (or the principle of *principle*), and (2) the principle of least principle. The first suggests the second-order valuation I>IIA>IIB>III. So in the illustrations of the previous paragraph one *should* get out of bed, report the incompetent and go into battle. Or, in general, the leader should be prepared if principles are at stake (I) to override prudential considerations (IIA) or a group feeling and political factors (IIB) and certainly his own private affect (III). And, *mutatis mutandis*, so down the hierarchy of the value paradigm.

Quite *per contra* the second maxim: the principle of least principle would state that the administrator should seek to resolve value conflicts at the lowest level possible. This for pragmatic reasons and simply because the affective wear and tear upon the leader, the sheer emotional involvement, would be exhausting and destructive if all organizational arguments were driven upwards in the value hierarchy. If, in other words, the *moral* issue or the question of principle were constantly to be raised in organizational affairs little would get done and leader-led relationships would ultimately break down and be destroyed. Therefore, the maxim dictates, the leader should seek by means devious or otherwise, by artfulness and skill, to avoid conflict, reduce value tensions, put out fires, strive by negotiation, conciliation and linguistic or diplomatic skill to scale the level of argument downwards.[3]

The coexistence of these two logically contradictory maxims and the dialectical tension which is entailed explains, I think, Barnard's vague but profound observations on the moral *complexity* which he associated with leadership and executive functions. It is clearly a part of the great art to know when to raise and when to suppress or avoid the question of principle. Any philosophy which tries to dispose of this dialectic, in one direction or the other, is oversimplistic and unrealistic.

Intrahierarchical conflict refers to values being in contention when these values are of the same logical status and hierarchical level. Thus, the choice between two wallpapers is a contest at Level III. Or a choice between family and ideology, as say when a spy is contemplating whether to defect, may be a Level I conflict. Value conflicts of this sort must ultimately be resolved by some sort of force even if the violence brought on is merely the internal movement of the will against the subjective integrity of the psyche. The resolution maxim is therefore: look to the will! What *is* the will? Here and now!

The quality of will varies with the level of value. At Level III it has the quality of affective preference and that value *should* emerge as dominant which has attached to it the

---

[3] Simply contriving sufficient passage of *time* may often be enough to dissipate certain affective tensions.

greatest force of affect. At IIB it is a matter of collective affect and group persuasion, group will; at IIA of reason and logic, and the force of rational argument should here prevail. And at the highest level (I) we again enter the region of imponderability, intransigence and intractability where the will at last stands most nakedly revealed and where value conflicts may be the most calamitous, to psyche and to collectivity alike.

Value analysis and conflict management are integral parts of decision making and leadership skills. They share a common logical structure: a phase of problem awareness is followed by analysis and then by action after which the problem situation ramifies, diminishes, or achieves an equilibrium state. Awareness, analysis and action could also be more aggressively translated into military metaphor as advance, analyse and attack. It is the central analysis phase which we have been discussing here and its logical structure in turn comprises the essential elements of praxis: (1) information gathering and intelligence collection; (2) study and reflection, including the interpolation and discrimination of values and facts; (3) engagement of the will prior to action in the world (commitment). It is this general phase of pre-active pause which can make the very largest of demands upon the leader's consciousness, and which, ultimately, distinguishes good from bad praxis; strong from weak leadership.

It is most important to note that value conflict *need not be resolved.* One can simply live with the affective tension. This has been the case between the world's superpowers now for over a quarter of a century. In Ireland and the Middle East it may be the case for generation after generation. In the more microcosmic worlds of intraorganizational dispute one is reminded of this negative principle as it was expressed by Barnard:

> The fine art of executive decision consists in not deciding questions that are not now pertinent, in not deciding prematurely, in not making decisions that cannot be made effective, and in not making decisions that others should make.(1972:194)

The fact that much of administration involves just this, the everyday living with unresolved affective tensions, surely goes far to explain much of the phenomena of executive stress and, latterly, as organizational life becomes increasingly complex, of the terminal version known as executive 'burn-out'. Value analysis neither implies nor entails any demands for logical 'closure' where values are in contention. Conflict is an inevitable part of both organizational and individual life. There is no escape from it and much must be endured. Always much must be endured!

Next, it follows from the analysis of value that true value conflict is always *intra*personal. This is a subtle but important point. The essential subjectivity of value dictates that any conflict *between values* must occur within the individual consciousness; it must be part of the affective life of the individual and private to that phenomenology. One cannot have value conflict while one is asleep or in coma, nor can one have value conflict *outside* a field of consciousness. It is a perturbation of the will. What is usually thought of as *inter*personal value conflict is apparent rather than real. It is a conflict of *interests*. Ultimately it is in fact a power struggle; a conflict between value *actors*. An interest is a value cathected on a fact. Conflicts of interest are conflicts of values at one or more removes. Such conflicts are resolved in various ways: by force, power, persuasion, juridical verdict, warfare, negotiation, legal process, diplomacy, politics and so on, but the point to be noted is that the overt actions of value actors *in the world* tell us nothing about the resolution of value conflict within the individual actors. Does the loser of a war or a civil suit thereby change his conception of the desirable? Do *I* determine *my* guilt or innocence by the actions of the court? Is my *will* reshaped by the actions of *others*?

THE VALUE AUDIT

For the leader in the praxis situation there is an obligation, a philosophical obligation, to conduct where necessary a value audit. This is an analysis of the value aspects of the problem he is facing. Such an analysis should be as sophisticated an appreciation as is possible within the factual constraints. It should at least be more than a back-of-the-envelope calculus of pros and cons followed by lightning closure and impulsive action. It should include at least the following questions: What *are* the values in conflict in the case and can they be named? What *fields* of value (V_1 through V_5) are most affected? Most salient? *Who* are the value actors? How is the conflict distributed interpersonally and intrapersonally? Is it interhierarchical on the paradigm? Or intrahierarchical? Are any of the major fallacies operative: homogenetic, naturalistic, militaristic, excisionistic? What principles or strategies for conflict resolution are most fitted to the case? What are the *metavalues*? What metaethic, if any, is invoked? Is there a principle (Type I value) to be raised? Or to be avoided? Can the tension of non-resolution be accommodated? What rational and pragmatic consequences attach to the possible and probable scenarios? What bodies of value consensus and political interest, if relevant, are affected within and without the organization? To what extent does the leader have control over the informative and affective media in the case (press, radio, television, lines of communication, informal organization, etc.)? What is the analysis of affect control amongst parties in the case? What is the analysis of commitment?

It is the careful reflection upon such questions (and the audit can never be either fully exhaustive or fully conducted), prior to administrative action, which is the hallmark and warrant of leadership responsibility. And, perversely, it is also within the very nature of affect itself to conduce to an avoidance of such responsibility. In this lies the heart of the problem of administrative morality. Avoidance of audit entails bad praxis and irresponsibility.

Illustrations from organizational life are plentiful enough. Prototypical decisions of hiring, firing and promotion may be at best Type IIA for the leader but for the affected party they may be Type I. This interhierarchical conflict may easily be overlooked. That a middle-aged employee is about to lose all career prospects through some highly rational realignment of organizational structure may go inadequately assessed or not assessed at all. At the very least the decision maker should not commit the homogenetic fallacy nor be unaware of the interhierarchical value conflict before him. And by which maxim is it to be decided? Is the integrity of the affected individual sufficiently at stake to justify the subversion of the apparently larger interest of the nomothetic collectivity? Is it, *pace* Kant, that the individual ceases to be a means to an end and has become an end in himself? Or is it a case for straight-out toughmindedness and moral 'ruthlessness' with the leader as the moral equivalent of surgeon? The value audit does not lead easily to the answers to value questions but at least it provides a safeguard for the ultimate protection of humane values in an organizational context and the maxims proposed above sensitize the pragmatic leader to the importance of principle, and the ideological leader to the corresponding importance of pragmatics.

The final phase of the value audit is action. This includes the possibility of inaction since, logically, the latter is merely negative action. Action necessitates the employment of power, authority and influence and, for the leader especially, the commitment of will. Implicit also in this is the employment where necessary of the whole armamentarium of the *arthasastra* when action is directed to the resolution of value disputes. If Type I values are not engaged then one can hope for value change to follow upon value action, however grudgingly and slow. One may also expect realignments of interest patterns in the fields of value action and predictable shifts in the continuous flux of political consensus. The leader is sensitive to and monitors all this. On the other hand, no such comfortable evolution of value change is to be expected if Type I values come into conflict. It must be remembered that power (in the last analysis *force*) can alter relationships and events without altering values. The international arena (Ireland, Poland, the Middle East) is replete with examples of this intractability. Of value problems at this level of systematics it can be said that they are never solved, however they are forcibly resolved. They are insoluble though resolvable.

Such problems erupt from time to time within the lesser systems of organizational life. It then becomes the onus of leadership to subject them to analysis, monitoring and audit. The analysis of any problem does not entail its solution but its methodical application does enhance the prospects for its resolution in praxis.

THE CONTROL OF AFFECT

The analysis of affect is but one of the leader's obligations; to be able to control his own affect is another. The latter may be much more difficult than the former. The potential for harm greater. A sudden impulse, acted upon, can consign the finest analysis to oblivion, and untold organizational actors to uncalculated calamities. Even the simple and ever-present desire for closure can lead in a weak moment to a policy gamble which is self-destructive. Argentinian military adventurism in the Falklands might provide an instance. Analysis in itself is merely academic if it not be complemented by right action which, in turn, means adequate emotional control on the part of the leadership. Praxis is always a function of the leader's affective state. What can be said about this?

Philosophically speaking, the formal leader has a specialist function in that he is expected to gain a position of value perspective which affords him a degree of detachment, non-attachment and affective disinterest different from and greater than that to be expected in other organizational roles. He is expected to perceive the total organizational situation in a clear-eyed and cool-headed way. There is an onus of perspective and affect control which is quite apart from the leader's personal complex of interests. Value analysis itself presupposes this. But there are obstacles to this desideratum. The administrator is human and shares in the normal human endowment of imperfection, including the ebb and flow of affective impulse. This range of crude affective reaction to situational stimuli runs all the way from panic to insensitivity. Primal motivations are continually being triggered or inhibited, occasionally indulged. Such emotive response is free-floating and uncathected. It is crude and primal, directly related to ancestral instincts to fight, freeze or flee. This generalized and prepotent complex of affect can be logically subsumed under the principle of self-preservation if that principle is taken to include the impulse to sexual gratification encompassed in the Freudian notion of the id. Affect of this kind has not yet attached itself to implicit or explicit values as *concepts* of the desirable. It does not yet invest particular values. But it has motivating force none the less and can be a powerful behavioural determinant even through the simple dynamism of forcing the actor to seek relief from the anxiety or tension which it generates.

It is a large part of the leader's canon of self-knowledge to be aware of his private potential for this type of response to stimuli. He is always obliged to seek to have it under control, an onus neither easy nor simple, for '... It is doing that is subordinate here to being, our actions to the consciousness that can irradiate them and give them meaning' (Barrett, 1979:86). That consciousness runs the risk of being swamped by the tides of affect that can surge in the psyche.

Administration, or leadership, poses its own hierarchy of interest through the levels described above as V_1 to V_5. This in turn implies a corresponding and parallel hierarchy of disinterest or detachment. Simply, at the lower levels, this means that the leader must place the interests of *others* above his own, of groups over individuals, and of his organization over component parts of that organization. This is the affective equivalent of the principle of conflict resolution discussed in the previous section. Less simply, at higher levels, he might be placed in the difficult position of considering the interests of other organizations with better claims than his own, or even of the environmental or macrocosmic interest over lesser hierarchical elements. All of this necessitates affect control and ego control on the leader's part. Such control leads us to knowledge imperatives or knowledge obligations which can be stated as maxims and expressed as follows:

1 *Know the task*. What is the mission of the organization? What are the subfactorings of this mission? How are they articulated and co-ordinated?
2 *Know the situation*. What are the *significant* and salient features of context which interpose themselves between organization and task? Which need special attention? Which can be ignored?
3 *Know the group*. A knowledge-value to which there is in principle no upper desirable limit save that imposed by the other three maxims and the ordering constraints of time and space.
4 *Know oneself*. An unending obligation, limited only by individual capacity. Above all, what are my weaknesses?

It is this last maxim which raises the question of affective management. Short of some sort of mystical illumination, one cannot, of course, ever know oneself fully. Always it must be in part, always through a glass darkly, never exactly as others see us, each of us a Ulysses on a separate odyssey. In the end no one can have more intimate access to one's form of life than one's self. Since our private phenomenologies are publicly inaccessible and since affect or emotion is at least as much of a psychological mystery as leadership itself, it may seem presumptuous to say anything at all upon this subject. I shall, therefore, confine my remarks with diffidence to the problem of *negative* affect, affect which can be administratively dysfunctional or dangerous. This upon the principle that the good can take care of itself. It is in the coping with adverse emotion — rage, anger, frustration, fear, hatred, envy, resentment, avarice — that controls are most eminently to be desired.

First let us note the importance of attention, consciousness and compartmentalization. The administrator cannot attend properly to more than one thing at a time, and, having decided what that one thing is to be, he ought not then, despite the importunings and pressures of affect, to allow the intrusion into his field of attention of irrelevant problem material. Success in this is called the ability to compartmentalize. Leader legend is replete with folklore about it: how Napoleon could take a refreshing nap in the midst of a raging battle; how Hitler could break off a storming tirade when the gong went for lunch, and resume again at the exact point where he had left off once lunch was over. And it is true that every efficient administrator must to some extent be master of this psychological art-form. The philosopher will be quick to note, however, that there is more than psychology here. There is praxis. Simone Weil has said that 'true morality lies not in judgement but in attention' (1962:10). We are responsible for what is within the contents of consciousness, and what is without — a terrible freedom if one truly reflects upon it!

Attention is equivalent to an awareness. A general attitude which may be partly a function of our will, of our innate form of life, and partly a function of philosophy, our acquired aggregation of values. One can imagine a continuum from concentration with its sharply focused attention-to-task at one end and an open-ended awareness with a widely focused receptivity of consciousness at the other. The latter end of this continuum would accord with a remark of the Buddha who, when asked whether he was a god or a man replied, 'I am neither, I am *awake*.'

Between these extremes there would be intermediate degrees of awakedness, awareness or concentration. To the extent that the leader really knows himself, he has some sense of where he stands in this progression of consciousness. His success in compartmentalization may be a function of this self-knowledge. Certainly it will depend on the structure of his field of attention. And it may well be that a certain mental toughness or ruthlessness is necessary if the shifting of attention from one sector of the executive field to another is to be conducted efficiently and effectively, with appropriate control of affect. The leader who cannot perform these psychological manoeuvres has, the philosopher of administration would claim, a moral obligation to withdraw from the executive role.

CREDO: *Self-observation precedes self-control.*

What is at the heart of emotive control is an ability to concentrate and focus attention and then to shift that focus at the behest of will. The ability to build and maintain compartments within the field of consciousness and to sustain them against affective flooding. For the leader to be overwhelmed by emotion would be dangerous in the extreme. Neither, such is the dilemmic nature of administration, would it be organizationally advantageous if he were impervious to emotion and totally phlegmatic. Again a golden mean or middle path is to be sought. This is shown rather vividly in a British recruiting advertisement for officer cadets at Sandhurst. It depicts marble columns filled with long lists of names of war dead who were graduates of the college together with the caption, 'A hard act to follow'. The text then goes on to explain that candidates are unsuitable who are either overly or underly affected by this elegiac aspect of the military profession.

It is my belief and contention that right control of affect directly implies two things. First, a general *mindfulness*; a quality of alertness to the situation in which one *is*; an awakeness and command of the powers of consciousness and a sensibility of the will. Second, a continuous monitoring of the ego, and its overriding wherever necessary. This last is a life's work but it can be aided by three inhibitions:

1 Not identifying emotionally to the point of loss of control with the ongoing flux of events, the ups and downs of vagaries of circumstance and chance. This somewhat resembles the sangfroid of the accomplished gambler. It is quite apart from and something other than the organizational commitment of the administrator which we shall be discussing below.

2 A determination not to consider one's own ego, much less one's id, if the impulsions of that consideration contradict one's organizational commitments in any way.

3 A general inhibition against *expressing* negative emotion, unless it be for deliberately calculated political purposes. This is not to say that the leader will not feel negative affect, only that he will not normally express it. Nor is this

to be confused with the popular psychology of 'positive thinking'. The leader may well be profoundly pessimistic about the turn of events but he has a dramaturgical duty to express and inspire confidence and maintain commitment — so long as he can do this without trenching on the unauthentic or undermining his credibility.

To list desirabilities is academic. To translate them into action is leader-praxis. Over time and with effort the inhibitions necessary for affective control can be instilled. Over time and with experience the art can be learned of when and where to flout the rules.

COMMITMENT

This difficult concept, subsuming as it does the whole topic of motivation, is central to the problems of leadership and followership alike. But of especial interest to the former. Like the leadership concept itself it is elusive and protean, its empirical investigation only a matter of recent decades, its theory jejune. Buchanan (1974:533) draws attention to the component elements of identification, involvement and loyalty (each one of which is philosophically obscure) and defines its organizational form as 'partisan, affective attachment to the goals and values of the organization, to one's role in relation to goals and values, and to the organization for its own sake apart from instrumental worth'. This definition is generally concordant with that of empirical researchers such as Mowday, Porter and Steers (1982). In its emphasis upon values, however, it does seem to open doors to philosophy, the draft from which might tend to slam shut those they are struggling to keep open for positivistic behavioural science. Vickers (1980:55) on the other hand, seizes upon the moral aspect of commitment and treats it as a sort of internalized set of self-expectations which can be acquired either through cultural and social programming or else by 'an act of conscious artistry on the part of the ego, desiring him to emulate some human possibility which experience has revealed to him and which claims his commitment'. Whatever the definition, it seems clear that philosophy and psychology meet in this concept and that their academic divorce must somehow be set aside.

Commitment can be at any level of system. The identification, loyalty and involvement which are its referents can attach to systems into which the actor is born: family, tribe, nation. Often these set up the strongest and most immutable of behavioural expectation patterns and affective reactions. But the actor can also choose or is thought to be able to choose his other commitments: to organization, to task, to person, to idea, to play, to symbol, to myth. All these are laden with significance for the praxis of leadership and their effect upon organizational life has been discussed in previous chapters. To the extent that the leader monitors values to that extent he is also engaged in monitoring commitment.

My understanding of commitment is that it is an attachment of the will to a project. Projects include human relationships, institutions, specific tasks, ideas, sentiment complexes and symbol systems as well as organizations. Once this attachment is made a pattern of self-expectations is established in the psyche which functions as a self-regulating standard. These normative controls constitute, in Freudian terms, ego-ideals. Since all of this can also be understood as a value phenomenon, the internalization of a matrix of concepts of the desirable, the paradigm applies. Commitment can be at any of the three levels. It is not homogenetic. A child's commitment to play is affective and transitory, Type III. Work, by contrast, introduces higher levels of value: obligations to and expectations from the group (IIB), a rational flow of benefits and costs in consequence of the commitment (IIA), service to an ideal or ideology or myth (I). In general one can say that work commitments and organizational commitment comprise a moral component (II) or an ethical component (I) in addition to whatever affective predispositions may be operative. These moral-ethical components will always be programmed or conditioned by socio-cultural impress to some extent. They are never pure. But also it must be said that some degree of free agency, however minimal, must obtain. The sentiment (or is it commitment?) of nationalism (or is it patriotism?) is illuminating. To what extent are our feelings involuntary? To what extent free? What are the bounds of the behavioural expectations imposed upon us by a commitment to the country of our birth? What is the logical and valuational type?

Our commitments are often thrust upon us. By birth, accident, chance or, more insidiously, by the persuasive forces of culture: advertisement, media, propaganda, parental suasion, peer group pressures. Choice may be much less than we think. Artistry, in Vickers' sense, may be rarer than we might care to admit. Some intermediate degree of struggle, and middling commitment, the norm.

The leader is interested in the commitment of his followers because he seeks their loyalty, identification and involvement. He must monitor their commitment and he must study his own. His greatest accomplishment is to motivate; to invest the organization with meaning and value above and beyond any prudential calculation; to captivate the will of the follower. The moral climate or ethos or morale of an organization is an expression of the general level of commitment to that organization. And as goes commitment so goes the level of expectations of performance.

It follows that much of the leader's art has to do with a sort of cultivation or education of the will, his own first, then that of others. One wishes almost to say that leadership is moral education. But 'will', as we have seen, is a psychologically embarrassing term. It has been described by Barrett (1979:253) as '"deliberative desire", the place in our psychic landscape where reason and appetite meet; where wishes and emotions submit to reason; and reason in turn is activated by desire; hence the central pivot of the human being as a practical agent.' A beautiful statement and true, even if it fails to discriminate between level III and level I desire. It has also been said, again I believe with truth, that '...At the root of our being, we are *will*, that is, the "real" self is a moral being, an acting being, a being capable of making moral judgements and performing moral acts. All other things in the world, including our own empirical selves, are conditioned, ordered, but at the same time limited by the forms of space, time, and causality....' (Brennan, 1973:85.) In short, it would seem that with the concept of will we have come at last to the ultimate frontier in philosophical psychology. Is it this which is the determinant of the form of life? This which was born and this which might not die? This that regulates that degree of right tension in the nervous system, right awareness in the consciousness, right mindfulness in the mind?

The mystery of this is such that it leaves the reader free to construct his own philosophy of the will. One can, however, presuppose that commitment, the investment of the will, follows a logical sequence of stages: incommitment, commitment, and decommitment. In the first stage the new organization member is exposed to a group (V_2). His initial enthusiasms or misgivings are quickly tempered by these earliest experiences and his commitment is either stillborn or established and fixed at one of the paradigmatic levels. He adopts the symbol system and language games of the organization and incorporates within himself its set of sociopsychological expectations. This is followed by a plateau of commitment, the surface of which may be very uneven,[4] but which represents the mean level at which the member has internalized the organizational culture. Finally, the member can become decommitted. Infinite are the avenues to disenchantment: disaffection with peers, superordinates, subordinates, clients; routine and alienation, understimulation, overstimulation, stress and distress, failure to rise and overrapidity of rising – the will erodes and the attachment breaks. Decommitment in itself constitutes a whole area for empirical investigation which has hardly yet begun to be explored.

If commitment is cyclical in this way then an administrative task is to study its nature and nurture. But the leader

---

[4] This unevenness would be due to temporal fluctuations in many factors. Task interest, energy level, personal circumstances, perceived behaviour of other organization members, ambivalence or confusion of expectations, perceived alignment of personal and organizational values are all examples of mediating variables. Carried to excess any such fluctuation can contribute to, or directly cause, permanent loss of commitment.

has to look inward first. The question he must ask himself is, what is the character of his own commitment? Is it Type I or prudential, or lower yet on the hierarchy? It has a beginning, a middle, and an end. It is a function of will. Where am I then? Where is he? Where are they? By virtue of his office the leader must be a constant student of human values and a constant practitioner of persuasion. He has to formulate his own philosophy of the will and personally seek out, sense and embody the organizational will. His art is to manufacture ethos, to give life through commitment to the spirit of the organization, *la volonté générale*.

ETHICAL OPTIONS

To this point we have been rather more concerned with the desired than with the desirable; that is, with values rather than ethics. We have tended to describe rather than prescribe. Ethics prescribe. They tell us what we ought to do. Yet they speak with many and conflicting tongues. The range of ethics is considerable. When applied to administration it yields a set of ethical possibilities, differing discretionary bases for administrative action, which are themselves subject to paradigmatic analysis. Let us explore some of these options, but first an assertion.

CREDO: *Consciousness and ethics are correlative.*

In searching his ethical bases the administrator may first consult the archetypes. He will find there ideal types. These function, however, as more than an analytical device; they operate as psychological archetypes and thus translate into empirical reality as components in the complex ego-ideal structure of the administrative psyche. For the philosopher of administration they also reveal, first, that each is capable of rejection on transvaluational grounds (i.e. metaethical critique) and, second, that each tends to be compounded or complexified in any empirical case, all of which simply underscores the moral complexity of administration. The archetypes imply ethics, they do not prescribe ethics; they are essentially psychological. Where else can the leader seek ethical foundations? Let us apply the paradigm.

The lowest ethic which has been well formulated is that of the *arthasastra*. I shall not dwell upon it. Pure careerism of this sort is a logical construct and one suspects that some degree of psycho-pathology is necessary to pursue this particular logic to its conclusion. The ethicist cannot condone it but the realist must recognize it. This is Level III.

Next the leader might adopt an ethic of group-careerism or sectional interest (IIB). The leader should seek the group interest *over* that of competing groups of individuals. Underlying this ethic is a sort of *laisser-faire* belief in the rational ecology of games. The idea that, after the manner of Adam Smith's economics, the workings of the macro-system or market-place ensure in the end that collective good is maximized through individual self-seeking. Therefore the righteousness of competitive struggle. Therefore compete! Thus the naval chief of staff who pushes his demands for an aircraft carrier against the claims of social welfare or the trade union leader class-blind to the common good.

At Level IIA ethical bases can be derived from professionalism. Many professions proclaim written codes of ethics and, whatever the cynic may think of them and their impotence in restraining guild greed, the fact remains that they are there as options for the free agent to act upon. The ethical ideal underlying professional ethics is one of service; the placing of the expertise of a specialist group at the service of some larger interest. In some utilitarian logic this is thought to be conducive to a general maximizing of the good. Where the specialist or elite knowledge is that of administration itself it may lead, as in classical bureaucratic theory, to the posture of unswerving loyalty to the hierarchy. In the public service, this ultimately means the Minister who in turn is representative of the people and supposedly the *vox populi*. Where disagreements or value conflict occur between professional administrator and his amateur superior they are argued in private and never in public. At the end of the day the will of the polity is supposed to have prevailed. Indeed this could be called a polity ethic. It overlaps and sometimes conflicts with the ordinary rationality-based professional ethic.

At the highest level (I) there is a wide range of bases for administrative discretionary philosophy, an assortment of ethical possibilities which can only be selectively illustrated here. Perhaps, indeed, it is the presence of this plethora which deters and overawes the would-be writer on administrative philosophy. At least he does not wish to rush where truly angels fear to tread. Nevertheless any one of the established ethical systems can profoundly inform the discretionary behaviour of the leader; that is, his praxis.

CREDO: *Praxis is the reciprocation of the mind and the will.*

The following illustrations indicate the wide range of ethical positions to which a free agent could commit himself.

Guardianship. The administrator sees himself as a self-effacing and dedicated agent and servant of the largest good, maybe even of the Good. As a public servant he may see himself as representing the *true* State and the true ideals of the State as against the competing interests of which the state is democratically (or fascistically or oligarchically) composed. Variants are the leader as keeper of the national flame, the soul or spirit of the Nation or the Race.

Confucianism. The leader cherishes an ethic of tradition, culture or order. He seeks to perpetuate through organizational means an ethic of civilized behaviour and a reverence for historical and social continuity. Extremes are anathema, haste is dangerous, bad manners are to be deplored. There is the Oriental concept of 'face'. There is also an implicit natural continuity under heaven which organizational life should properly sustain.

Social equity. The leader subscribes to what has been called the 'new public administration' (Frederickson, 1974:1-51).

He uses his office and organizational power to advance the interests of some particular group which he perceives as underprivileged (e.g. Negroes, the working class, the handicapped). He is deliberately prejudicial on their behalf to the end of a supposed improvement in social equity or justice. Such an ethic would allow concealment and deceit in the service of its ideology.

Neo-stoicism. The leader adopts a strong ethic of duty and commitment to a set of classical ethical values in combination with an attitude of disinterest to outcomes and of non-attachment to rewards. The ethic is perhaps best expressed in the *Bhagavad Gita* and in Aurelius's *Meditations*. It will be further discussed below.

Hyper-professionalism. The leader sees his primary role, the primary element in his form of life, as consisting of a commitment to intensified professional values. He regards himself above all else as soldier or professor or scientist or artist. His vocation is his passion. It is his life-meaning and the values which attach to that calling dominate his ethical system.[5]

Human relations. The leader adopts as his pre-emptive ethic the psychological and material welfare of those with whom he has to deal within his organizational field. The theme can extend to clients and customers of the organization. It is rooted in humanism and altruism in its basic conceptions. Sometimes it may take on egalitarian overtones (Thayer, 1973); sometimes religious themes may predominate, as where an ideology of Christian brotherhood and love is espoused.

Religionism. All religions, sacred or secular, provide ethical systems to which the administrator can subscribe. Each or any of these may, of course, conflict with other discretionary

---

[5] The writer Tom Wolfe gives vivid portrayals of this ethic at work among American military aviators and astronauts.

bases for action and sources of value decision rules. As always the critical factor is the stage and degree of commitment which can be ascribed to the value actor.

Any of these positions, any system, can provide a set of imperatives and decision rules for application to problems of administrative discretion. The leader might not wish to commit himself to any; he might wish existentially to invent (or reinvent) his own; or he might strive to be stubbornly eclectic, or more accurately to cherish the illusion that he is eclectic. One cannot, unfortunately, to the confusion of science, predict what any individual, be he leader or follower, will do with his ethical nature. That is a function of his form of life, and the eye sees only surfaces or, to be more precise, reacts to light reflected from surfaces. It cannot see what forms and informs the surfaces. It cannot see, that is, the form of life. Another kind of eye is needed for that. But, where there is form at all, there will be some degree of ethical consistency, some degree of commitment and choice. It is the shape of the will which is the form of life.

THE POSSIBILITY OF HONOUR

Philosophy is not science, however much it might worship at that shrine. It has its own inner duty which goes beyond science; it has to work its way delicately from the descriptive to the prescriptive. It cannot therefore be entirely divorced from its practitioners, its professors and its spokesmen. And so at last I am led to the expression of values and ideals which are idiosyncratic and personal even though I would strive to have them logically connected to some systematic philosophical whole. Another perhaps frustrating feature of philosophy is that it can say nothing new. In ethics there is no new thing, no discovery to be made. What will be has been and there is no new thing under the sun. Eternal verities merely lend themselves to restatement and infinite individual reinterpretation. What follows then need have binding force on no one.

The world of action, the executive's world, is a world of change and dynamics. In a world of change the only permanence is that provided by patterns, by the forms of life. Marcus Aurelius put it this way, 'One thing hastens into being, another hastens out of it. Even while a thing is in the act of coming into existence, some part of it has already ceased to be. Flux and change are forever renewing the fabric of the universe, just as the ceaseless sweep of time is forever renewing the face of eternity...' (VI:15.) What is persistent is the form of life, and among the multiplicity of forms of life what is of concern for us is the organization and its associated role of leader. What persists also, fuelling the flux, is action and work. And certain great and grand ideas such as honour, duty enlightenment, humaneness, fulfilment... ends which cannot be specified or detailed but ends to which work, which can be specified and detailed, is the means. I would like to propound a philosophy of honourable work or, what is the same thing, leadership honour. More reasonably, I would like to suggest the *possibility* of such a philosophy.

The term 'honour', now degenerate and in desuetude (except perhaps in the debased rhetoric of international politics) is a term which deserves to be restored. By it I mean an ethic of work, of duty and of sense.

First of work, because work and action are primal. There is no escape from either, no disentanglement from the endless intermeshing chains of cause and effect, the web of action, reaction, contingency and consequence. The honourable attitude here is this: work must be performed for the work's sake only. The actor must not affectively attach himself to the outcome but to the process. Means must be translated into valuational ends. A divorce, psychological and philosophical, must be made between work and the extrinsic rewards of work. The commitment is to the work itself; to the race and not the prize, to the battle and not the victory. Work in this sense becomes intrinsically honourable and satisfying through a process of moral commitment and understanding. Such a process is possible.

Second of duty, because this is defined by the nomothetic

dimension of the administrative commitment. The honourable leader is engaged continuously in the searching of his duty. Because he is practising the most powerful and most dangerous of the arts affecting, however humbly, the quality of life and the human search for meaning, he ought to have — if honourable, he has to have — an obsession with duty. What are his responsibilities? What is it that is right? Honour demands this praxis, this constant philosophical search. Such searching is possible.

Third, of sense, in two ways: common sense and uncommon sense. *Common* sense because this philosophy argues for a humanistic grounding of value at the Type II level and because organizational life must always be subject to the pragmatic test. There is much more to this than is made explicit by the literature of human relations. There is a moral component which social science elides. The leader has to take Buber's counsel and fight against the law of moral inertia by which 'every Thou tends to slip back into the condition of mere object in our eyes. Only by continual moral effort of a concentrated order can we keep the "Other" (the being to whom we stand in the I-Thou relation) from diminishing in our thoughts and prospective actions to the old status of "thing".' (Brennan, 1973:102.) Difficult indeed is this but this too is possible.

And, finally, honour must include *uncommon* sense for common sense is not enough. Man does not live by bread alone. The bases of his duty and vocation extend into transrational and metaphysical space. To establish and develop these bases is also possible.

Administration is a basic but imperfect activity of man which has through evolution become partially sophisticated and partially humanized. It remains for it to become truly philosophical, an affair of the intellect and the spirit, an affair of honour. But it is possible.

This leadership ethic of private and personal honour, one could even say *secret* honour, which I am seeking to explicate in these final words has its psychological as well as its philosophical side. Both aim at an ideal of non-attachment, of self-transcendence through work: 'Work for the work's sake only', 'Work without hope of reward', 'Do one's duty and let the chips fall where they may', 'Let the means be the ends.' These are the canons of guardianship in general and of the ideal type of the Technician-Guardian in particular. To advocate them is easy but what seems to be required to tie them into praxis is a special sort of self-education, a self-training which includes as an integral element the cultivation of an *art of indifference.*

THE ART OF INDIFFERENCE

Indifference here, of course, is to be understood in a special sense. It does not mean that the leader does not care. The leader is and has to be concerned about outcomes, especially those human and organizational outcomes in which he has full or partial responsibility. What, for the sake of honour, he must be indifferent to are the results of actions as they accrue to him personally. Given that his course of action is right, his duty discovered and performed, what is then a matter of indifference, of no concern, is his *own* success or failure. This is the ideal. His own ego has to cease to count, it has to be eliminated from the equation of organizational variables. It has to be transcended. Outrageously idealistic as this might seem, this praxis too is possible.

How can it be accomplished? By approximation. In the same way in which we all learn to walk. By constant failure and constant effort.

Let me be more psychologically specific. The following phases occur and recur and overlap in the affective conduct of leadership. Since leadership and administration is a progression from problem to problem, decision to decision, a first requirement is a general attitude of mindfulness, of sensitivity to the flux of events and the possibilities of action. Awareness or awakeness is the first affective condition. Into this field of attention flow consecutively and sometimes concurrently the matters to be dealt with, the problems to be solved, resolved, shelved; one question after another, each with its affective demands.

The first step towards non-attachment or indifference is paradoxically what might seem to be its very opposite, concentration. The leader concentrates his attention upon the problem and should do so throughout all the standard phases of decision making as these have been described in the orthodox texts. Intellect, affect and will are all brought into play. This is essentially a phase of analysis, observation and deliberation where the ego participates through the imputation of its values to the contingent facts.

The next step in this art is discrimination. The leader has to discriminate between fact and value, as well as between fact and fancy, fact and probability. And more: he must discriminate between himself as subject and the objectives to be sought by the organization, or by the specific project or plan. He must, if he can, and to the extent that he can, discriminate between himself as role incumbent, as formal leader, and himself as ego, himself-as-himself. Discrimination breaks identification; it frees the actor from the impending act. The consciousness of this duality is most desirable in the pause, the fateful pause, before commitment. Thereafter at once ensues the flood of action with all its ramifying possibilities and probabilities of consequence.

Discrimination, however, is not detachment. It is its prelude and prerequisite. Many leaders can analyse and discriminate without being able to achieve that degree of affective control which would enable them to be liberated from distracting and distorting egoistic involvement. The art of indifference calls for the cultivation of an ability to disengage the ego and *its* always-present interests from the flux of organizational events and organizational responsibilities, and, ideally, for something more. This something more broaches upon the inexpressible if not the ineffable. It means a transcendence of the ego in favour of a will beyond that of the self, the alignment of personal existence with the moral order of the universe. If this can be done, in whole or in part, if this idiographic aspect of the leader can be temporarily suspended, then he has achieved detachment, he is free and clear to deal righteously with problem solving, decision making and the searching of his duty.

The last phase of indifference is again compartmentalization; here, affective compartmentalization. Problems dealt with are problems disposed of, until they properly re-emerge within the cycling process of executive activity. The leader is indifferent to them. He sleeps at night. He plays bowls on Plymouth Hoe. He does one thing at a time.

I have dwelt on the praxis of indifference and affective control because it would seem to me to be a prerequisite, if the possibility of an ethic of leader honour is to be at all real as well as ideal. Ethics are values writ large and while it is true that everyone is a value actor, the leader is a value actor writ large. Because of his nomothetic function he can make values for others. Ethically this implies more than either passion on the leader's part, or impartiality. It really calls for a kind of impassioned impartiality: an artistry of indifference.

The leader should be especially aware of the three value-actor roles which he shares with his followers: carrier, educator and judge. As carrier he is the bearer and propagator of values, his own and those of the organization; as educator he is both teacher and learner of values, again with special relevance to the organizational field; and as judge he is critic and decider − the executive who visibly resolves value disputes and moves values into and out of dispute.

This book has dwelt heavily upon values. Nothing is more important than values for they are the source of all meaning. It may be as Wittgenstein has declared that the meaning of the world lies outside the world (1922:6.41) but the administrator as leader acts within the world and his value roles are amplified by the cycle of administrative process. Great then is his responsibility.

The philosophy we have discussed throughout this book would seek to redeem administration as a value activity. Indeed, as the highest of callings. It would seek to help leaders serve man through Meaning. It is intended to be neither rhetorical nor hortatory but practical.

It is possible. This book is its cartography.

ENDWORD

The quintessence of this philosophy of leadership can be expressed succinctly. Philosophy is nothing but marks on paper or vibrations in the air unless and until it roots itself in the values of a man and changes his life. It is the singular wonder of leadership that such a change in one man's life has the potential for changing other lives. Such power is awesome.

PROPOSITIONS[6]

6   'Power' is the first term in the administrative lexicon.

6.1   Administrative power is a function of the will.

6.11   The metavalue of Machiavellianism is success.

6.12   If one has power be of a mind to wield it.

6.2   Authority is legitimized power.

6.22   The legitimacy of authority rests on its connection with the organizational purpose.

6.3   Authority transcends logic.

6.4   The term 'leadership' is an incantation for the bewitchment of the led.

6.41   Leadership is an event, not an attribute of a personality. It is a description given to a dynamic complex of action.

6.42   Leadership is the conjunction of technical competence and moral complexity.

6.43   Charisma plays upon our lust for purpose.

6.431 There is no aspect of administration more dangerous than that which forges the link between power, charisma and men.

---

[6] These are extracted from the author's previous work (1978:217-20) while the maxims and credos which follow are taken from the foregoing pages.

CREDOS

1   I believe in the potentiality of individual free will, in partial determinism and degrees of freedom, and in the possibility of enhancing human autonomy, for ourselves and others.

2   The frustration of the ego, and its discipline under a collective and hierarchical regimen, is an essential part of organizational life. It can refine the ego; it can be a means of spiritual growth.

3   No one is indispensable. Everyone is irreplaceable.

4   Wisdom is a particular ability to look at the world and to look at one's looking (de Bono).

5   Pay-off is the ultimate test of any organization. This is more than a belief, it is a tautology.

6   Common sense is a necessary but not sufficient condition for right administration, for praxis.

7   There is a moral order in the universe; adherence to it strengthens, departure from it weakens [the leader].

8   Since everyone has an inalienable birthright to philosophy anyone can lead.

9   Self-observation precedes self-control.

10 Consciousness and ethics are correlative.

11 Praxis is the reciprocation of the mind and the will.

MAXIMS

The leader has four responsibilities. He should:

       1 Know the task.
       2 Know the situation.
       3 Know his followership.
       4 Know himself.

CANON

Work for the work's sake only.

References

Allison, Derek (1980) 'Weberian Bureaucracy and the Public School System', unpub. dissertation, University of Alberta

Argyris, Chris (1957) *Personality and Organization*, New York: Harper
(1964) *Integrating the Individual and the Organization*, New York: Wiley
(1973) 'Personality and Organization Theory Revisited', *Administrative Science Quarterly* Oct.

Arrow, K. J. (1963) *Social Choice and Individual Values*, New York: Wiley

Ashour, A. S. (1973) 'The Contingency Model of Leadership Effectiveness', *Behaviour and Human Performance* 9:339

Aurelius, Marcus (1964) *Meditations*, Staniforth, Maxwell (tr.) Harmondsworth: Penguin Classics

Ayer, Alfred J. (1948) *Language, Truth and Logic*, London: Gollancz

Barker, J. (1969) *The Legacy of Logical Positivism: Studies in the Philosophy of Science*, P. Adenstein and S. Barker (eds.), Baltimore: Johns Hopkins Press

Barnard, Chester I. (1958, 1966) 'Elementary Conditions of Business Morals', Barbara Weinstock Lectures, Berkeley: Univ. of Calif.
(1972) *The Functions of the Executive*, Cambridge, Mass.: Harvard

Barrett, William (1979) *The Illusion of Technique*, New York: Doubleday

Bateson, Gregory (1979) *Mind and Nature*, New York: Dutton

Beehler, Rodger (1978) *Moral Life*, Oxford: Basil Blackwell
and Drengson Alan R. (1978) *The Philosophy of Society*, London: Methuen

Beer, S. (1959) *Cybernetics and Management*, New York: Science Edns

Bendix, R. (1962) *Max Weber: An Intellectual Portrait*, New York: Doubleday

Berger, Peter L. and Luckmann, Thomas (1972) *The Social Construction of Reality*, Harmondsworth: Penguin

Blau, P. M. (1955) *The Dynamics of Bureaucracy*, Chicago: Univ. of Chicago Press

and Scott, W. Richard (1962) *Formal Organizations*, San Francisco: Chandler

Brennan, J. G. (1973) *Ethics and Morals*, New York: Harper & Row

Buchanan, B. (1974) 'Building Organizational Commitment: The Socialization of Managers in Work Organizations', *Administrative Science Quarterly* 19:533

Buckley, W. (1968) *Modern Systems Research for the Behavioral Scientist: A Source Book*, Chicago: Aldine

Burnham, James (1941) *The Managerial Revolution*, Bloomington: Indiana UP

(1943) *The Machiavellians, Defenders of Freedom*, New York: Day

Campbell, J. P. (1977) 'On the Nature of Organizational Effectiveness', in P. S. Goodman and J. M. Pennings (eds.) *New Perspectives in Organizational Effectiveness*, San Francisco: Jossey-Bass

Cohen, S. and L. Taylor (1978) *Escape Attempts: The Theory and Practice of Resistance to Everyday Life*, Harmondsworth: Pelican

Cotton, C. A. V. (1979) 'Military Attitudes and Values of the Army in Canada', Toronto: Canadian Forces Applied Research Unit, Report 5

Crozier, Michel (1964) *The Bureaucratic Phenomenon*, Chicago: Univ. of Chicago Press

Culbertson, J. *et al.* (1981) 'Symposium on the Theory of Practice', *American Educational Research Association* Los Angeles

Cutt, James (1980) 'Accountability, Efficiency, and the "Bottom Line" in Non-Profit Organizations' (mimeo), School of Public Administration, Univ. of Victoria

Dale, H. E. (1941) *The Higher Civil Service of Great Britain*, Oxford: Clarendon

Davies, A. F. (1980) *Skills, Outlooks and Passions*, Cambridge: Cambridge

de Bono, Edward (1967) *The Use of Lateral Thinking*, Harmondsworth: Penguin

(1969) *The Mechanism of Mind*, Harmondsworth: Penguin

(1971) *Lateral Thinking for Management*, Harmondsworth: Penguin

(1976) *Teaching Thinking*, Harmondsworth: Penguin

(1979) *The Happiness Purpose*, Harmondsworth: Penguin

Dimock, M. (1958) *A Philosophy of Administration*, New York: Harper

Dostoevsky, F. (1951) *Notes from the Underground*, Harmondsworth: Penguin

Downs, Anthony (1967) *Inside Bureaucracy*, Boston
Drucker, P. (1942) *The Future of Industrial Man*, New York: John Day
    (1967) *The Effective Executive*, London: Heinemann
    (1978) *Adventures of a Bystander*, New York: Harper
    (1981) 'Behind Japan's Success', *Harvard Business Review* Jan.-Feb. p. 83.
Durkheim, E. (1957) *Professional Ethics and Civic Morals*, C. Brookfield (tr.), London
Dye, Thomas R. (1978) *Understanding Public Policy*, 3rd edn, Englewood Cliffs, NJ: Prentice-Hall
Ellul, Jacques (1954) *The Technological Society*, J. Wilkinson (tr.), New York:
Enns, Frederick (1981) 'Some Ethical-moral Concerns in Administration', *Canadian Administrator* vol. xx May
Etzioni, Amitai (1961) *A Comparative Analysis of Complex Organizations*, New York: Free Press
    (1964) *Modern Organizations*, Englewood Cliffs, NJ: Prentice-Hall
    (1968) *The Active Society: A Theory of Societal and Political Processes*, New York
Eysenck, H. (1958, 1960) *Sense and Nonsense in Psychology*, Harmondsworth: Penguin
Feyerabend, Paul (1975) *Against Method: Outline of an Anarchistic Theory of Knowledge*, London: New Left books
Fiedler, Fred (1967) *A Theory of Leadership Effectiveness*, New York: McGraw-Hill
    (1978) 'The Contingency Model and the Dynamics of the Leadership Process', in L. Berkowitz (ed.) *Advances in Experimental Social Psychology*, vol. ii, New York: Academic Press
Fleishmann, E. A. and Peters, D. R. (1962) Interpersonal Values, Leadership Attitudes and Managerial Success', *Personnel Psychology* 15:127-43
Frederickson, H. G. (1974) 'Symposium on Social Equity and Public Administration', *Public Administration Review* 34 Jan.-Feb.
Gabriel, Richard A. and Paul L. Savage (1978) *Crisis in Command*, New York: Hill and Wang
Georgescu-Roegen, Nicholas (1971) *The Entropy Law and the Economic Process*, Cambridge, Mass.: Harvard UP
Georgiu, P. (1973) 'The Goal Paradigm and Notes towards a Counter Paradigm', *Administrative Science Quarterly* 18:291
Getzels, Jacob W. and Egon Guba (1957) 'Social Behavior and the Administrative Process', *School Review* Winter, 423

and H. A. Thelen (1960) 'The Classroom Group as a Unique Social System', in *The Dynamics of Instructional Groups*, 59th Yearbook of the National Society for the Study of Education, Chicago: Univ. of Chicago

Giddens, A. (1977) *Studies in Social and Political Theory*, London: Hutchinson

Gödel, Kurt (1931) 'Über formal unentscheidbare Sätze der *Principia Mathematica* und verwandter Systeme', I *Monatshefte für Mathematik und Physik* 38:173-98

Gouldner, Alvin (1957) 'Cosmopolitans and Locals: Toward an Analysis of Latent Social Roles', *Administrative Science Quarterly* 2:281-306

Gowen, Herbert H. (1931) *A History of Indian Literature*, New York: Appleton

Graen, G. B., Orris, J. B. and Alvares, K. M. (1971a) 'Leadership Effectiveness: Some Experimental Results', *Journal of Applied Psychology* 55:196

——— (1971b) 'Contingency Model of Leadership Effectiveness: Some Methodological Issues', *Journal of Applied Psychology* 55:3,205

Greenfield, Thomas B. (1973) 'Organizations as Social Intentions: Rethinking Assumptions about Change', *Journal of Applied Behavioral Science* 9(5):551-74

——— (1978a) 'Organizations as Talk, Chance, Action, and Experience', in A. Heigl-Evers and V. Streeck (eds.) *Die Psychologie des 20 Jahrhunderts*, Band VIII, Zürich: Kindler Verlag

——— (1978b) 'Reflections on Organization Theory and the Truths of Irreconcilable Realities', *Educational Administration Quarterly* 14:2 Spring 1-23

——— (1979) 'Ideas versus Data, or, How Can the Data speak for Themselves?', in G. Immegart and W. L. Boyd (eds.) *Problem Finding in Educational Administration: Trends in Research and Theory* Lexington, Mass.: D. C. Heath

——— (1980) 'The Man who Comes Back through the Door in the Wall: Discovering Truth, Discovering Self, Discovering Organizations', *Educational Administration Quarterly* 16(3):26-59

Gronn, P. C. (1982) 'Neo-Taylorism in Educational Administration', *Educational Administration Quarterly* 18(4).

Gulick, L. and Urwick, L. (eds.) (1937) *Papers in the Science of Administration*, New York: Institute of Public Administration.

Habermas, J. (1971) *Knowledge and Human Interests*, Boston: Beacon

Halpin, A. W. (1967) *Theory and Research in Administration*, New York: MacMillan

Handy, Charles B. (1976) *Understanding Organizations*, Harmondsworth: Penguin

Herzberg, F. (1966) *Work and the Nature of Man*, Cleveland: World Publishing

Mausner, B. and Snyderman, B. (1959) *The Motivation to Work*, New York: Wiley

Hodgkinson, Christopher (1978) *Towards a Philosophy of Administration*, Oxford: Basil Blackwell

Hofstadter, Douglas R. (1979) *Gödel, Escher, Bach*, New York: Basic Books

House, Robert J. and Baetz, Mary L. (1979) 'Leadership: Some Empirical Generalizations and New Research Directions', *Research in Organizational Behavior* I:341

James, William (1902) *The Varieties of Religious Experience*, Boston
(1907) 'The Moral Philosopher and the Moral Life', in *The Will to Believe and Other Essays*, New York: McKay

Kaplan, Abraham (1966) *The Conduct of Inquiry*, San Francisco: Chandler

Katz, Daniel and Robert L. Kahn (1978) *The Social Psychology of Organizations*, 2nd edn, New York: Wiley

Kluckhohn, F. R. and Strodtbeck, F. L. (1961) *Variations in Value Orientations*, Evanston, Ill.: Row, Peterson

Korzybski, J. (1933) *Science and Sanity: An Introduction to Non-Aristotelian Systems and General Semantics*, Lakeville, Conn.: International Non-Aristotelian Library

Ladd, John (1970) 'Morality and the Ideal of Rationalization in Formal Organizations', *Monist* 54:488

Lang, (1982) D. 'The Nature of Organizational Commitment in the Military', unpub. MA thesis, Univ. of Victoria

Lasch, Christopher (1979) *The Culture of Narcissism*, New York: W. W. Norton

Laslett, P. and Runciman, W. G. (eds.) (1967) *Philosophy, Politics and Society*, 3rd series, Oxford: Blackwell

Laszlo, Ervin (1972) *Introduction to Systems Philosophy: Toward a New Paradigm of Contemporary Thought*, New York: Gordon and Breach

Liddy, G. Gordon (1980) *Will*, New York: St. Martin's Press

Likert, R. (1967) *The Human Organization*, New York: McGraw-Hill

Lindblom, Charles E. (1959) 'The Science of Muddling Through', *Public Administration Review* Spring 155-69
(1979) 'Still Muddling: Not Yet Through', *Public Administration Review* 39:517-26

Litchfield, G. H. (1956) 'Notes on a General Theory of Administration', *Administrative Science Quarterly* vol. 1 no. 1

Low, Albert (1976) *Zen and Creative Management*, New York: Doubleday

McGregor, D. (1960) *The Human Side of Enterprise*, New York: McGraw-Hill

Machiavelli, N. (1886) *The Prince*, London: Routledge

Mackenzie, R. A. (1969) 'The Management Process in 3-D', *Harvard Business Review* Nov.-Dec.

Mackie, J. L. (1977) *Ethics*, Harmondsworth: Penguin

March, James G. (1974) 'Analytical Skills and the University Training of Educational Administrators', *Journal of Educational Administration* XII no. 1 May

and Simon, H. A. (1958) *Organizations*, New York: Wiley

Marquis, L. and Goldhammer, K. (1961) 'American Values' in D. S. Wengert *et al.* (eds.) *The Study of Administration*, Eugene: Univ. of Oregon Press

Marx, Karl (1927) *Das Kapital*, London: Dent

Mascaró, Juan (tr.) (1962) *Bhagavad Gita*, Harmondsworth: Penguin

Maslow, Abraham (1954) *Motivation and Personality*, New York: Harper

(1968) *Toward a Psychology of Being*, 2nd edn, New York: van Nostrand

Matsushita Corp. (1980) *Introduction to the Matsushita School of Government and Management*, Kanagawa, Japan

Mayo, Elton (1933) *The Human Problems of an Industrial Civilization*, New York: MacMillan

(1947) *The Political Problems of an Industrial Civilization*, Boston: Harvard

(1949) *The Social Problems of an Industrial Civilization*, London: Routledge & Kegan Paul

Merton, R. K. *et al.* (1952) *Reader in Bureaucracy*, New York: Free Press

Miles, Raymond E. (1975) *Theories of Management*, New York: McGraw-Hill

Milgram, S. (1963) 'Behavioral Study of Obedience', *Journal of Abnormal and Social Psychology* 67:371

(1965) 'Some Conditions of Obedience and Disobedience to Authority', *Human Relations* 18:57-76

(1974) *Obedience to Authority*, New York: Harper & Row

Mintzberg, H. (1973) *The Nature of Managerial Work*, New York: Harper & Row

Monsen, R. Joseph (1971) 'Social Responsibility and the Corporation:

Alternatives for the Future of Capitalism', Seattle: Univ. of Washington report series.

Moore, G. E. (1903) *Principia Ethica*, London: Cambridge UP

Mowday, R. T., Porter, L. W. and Steers, R. M. (1982) *Employee-Organization Linkages: The Psychology of Commitment, Absenteeism and Turnover*, New York: Academic Press

Naipul, V. S. (1981) *The Return of Eva Peron*, Harmondsworth: Penguin

Nietzsche, Friedrich (1956) *The Birth of Tragedy and the Genealogy of Morals*, F. Golffing New York: Doubleday

Orwell, George (1949) *1984* Harmondsworth: Penguin

Ouchi, Wm. G. (1980) 'Markets, Bureaucracies, and Class', *Administrative Science Quarterly* Mar.

and Price, R. L. (1978) 'Hierarchies, Class and Theory Z: A New Perspective on Organization Development', *Organizational Dynamics* Aug.:3-23

Parsons, T. (1951) *The Social System*, New York: Free Press

Peters, R. S. (1960) *The Concept of Motivation*, London: Routledge & Kegan Paul

Pitkin, Hanna (1972) *Wittgenstein and Justice: On the Significance of Ludwig Wittgenstein for Social and Political Thought*, Berkeley: Univ. of Calif.

Plato (1974) *The Republic*, Desmond (tr.), Harmondsworth: Penguin

Popper, Sir Karl (1948) 'What can Logic do for Philosophy?', *Proceedings of the Aristotelian Society* 154

(1966) *The Open Society and its Enemies*, London: Routledge & Kegan Paul

Prabhavananda, Swami and Isherwood, Christopher (trs.) (1949) *Bhagavadgita*, New York: New American Library

Rawls, John (1972) *A Theory of Justice*, Cambridge, Mass.: Harvard

Reddin, W. J. (1970) *Managerial Effectiveness*, New York: McGraw Hill

Roethlisberger, F. J. and Dickson, W. J. (1939) *Management and the Worker*, Cambridge, Mass.: Harvard UP

Rohr, John A. (1978) *Ethics for Bureaucrats: An Essay on Law and Values*, New York: Dekker

Rokeach, M. (1973) *The Nature of Human Values*, New York: Free Press

Sahlins, Marshall (1972) *Stone Age Economics*, Chicago: Aldine

Schriessheim, C. A. and Kerr, S. (1977) 'R.I.P. LPC: A Response to Fiedler', in J. G. Hunt and L. L. Larson (eds) *Leadership: The Cutting Edge*, Carbondale, Ill.: Southern Illinois

Schumacher, E. F. (1977) *A Guide for the Perplexed*, New York: Harper & Row

Scott, William G. and Hart, David K. (1979) *Organizational America*, Boston: Houghton Miflin

Self, Peter (1972) *Administrative Theories and Politics*, London: Allen & Unwin

Silver, M. and D. Geller (1978) 'On the Irrelevance of Evil: The Organization and the Individual Action', *Journal of Social Issues* 34 (4):25-136

Simon, Herbert A. (1965) *Administrative Behavior*, New York: Free Press

Singer, Ethan A. and Wooton, Leland M. (1974) 'The Triumph and Failure of Albert Speer's Administrative Genius: Implications for Current Management Theory and Practice', *Journal of Applied Behavioral Science* 12 no. 1:79-193

Skinner, B. F. (1971) *Beyond Freedom and Dignity*, New York: Knopf

Smith, Adam (1776) *The Wealth of Nations*, London

Snow, C. P. (1961) *Science and Government*, Cambridge, Mass.: Harvard UP

Solzhenitsyn, Alexander (1974) *August 1914*, Harmondsworth: Penguin

Speer, A. (1970) *Inside the Third Reich: Memoirs*, New York: MacMillan

Steers, Richard M. and Porter, Lyman W. (1975) *Motivation and Work Behavior*, New York: McGraw-Hill

Stufflebeam, D. L. *et al.* (1971) *Educational Evaluation and Decision Making*, Itasca, Ill.: Peacock

Taylor, Frederick W. (1915) *The Principles of Scientific Management*, New York: Harper
(1964) *Scientific Management*, London: Harper (New York, 1947)

Thayer, Frederick C. (1973) *An End to Hierarchy! An End to Competition*, Pittsburgh: Franklin-Watts
(1980) 'Values, Truth, and Administration: God or Mammon?', *Public Administration Review* Jan/Feb.:91

Thomas, Rosamund M. (1978) *The British Philosophy of Administration: A Comparison of British and American Ideas*, London: Longmans

Thompson, J. D. (1967) *Organizations in Action*, New York: McGraw-Hill

Thompson, Victor A. (1961) *Modern Organization*, New York: Knopf
(1976) *Bureaucracy and the Modern World*, Morristown, NJ: General Learning Press

Toffler, Alvin (1971) *Future Shock*, New York: Bantam
Tönnies, Ferdinand (1955) *Community and Association*, London: Routledge & Kegan Paul
Tribe, Lawrence H. (1972) 'Policy Science: Analysis or Ideology', *Philosophy and Public Affairs* Fall:66-110
von Bertalanffy, L. (1968) *General Systems Theory: Foundations, Development, Applications*, New York: Braziller
Vickers, Sir Geoffrey (1965) *The Art of Judgement*, London, New York: Basic Books
   (1972) *Freedom in a Rocking Boat*, Harmondsworth: Penguin
   (1980) *Responsibility — Its Sources and Limits*, Seaside, Calif.: Intersystems Pub.
Waldo, Dwight (1977) *Democracy, Bureaucracy, and Hypocrisy*, Berkeley: Inst. of Governmental Studies, Univ. of Calif.
   (1980) *The Enterprise of Public Administration*, Novato, Calif.: Chandler & Sharp
Weber, Max (1947) *The Theory of Social and Economic Organization*, A. M. Henderson and Talcott, Parsons, (trs.), London: OUP
   (1956) *Staatssoziologie*, Berlin: Duncker und Humblot
Weil, Simone (1962) 'Human Personality', in *Selected Essays*, R. Rees, (tr.), New York:
   (1965) *Oppression and Liberty*, London: Routledge & Kegan Paul; Amherst, Mass.: Univ. of Massachusetts Press
Whyte, William H. Jr. (1956) *The Organization Man*, New York: Simon and Schuster
Williams, B. (1971) 'Morality and the Emotions', in J. Casey (ed.) *Morality and Moral Reasoning*, London: Methuen
Wise, Arthur E. (1977) 'Why Educational Policies Often Fail: The Hyperrationalization Hypothesis', *Curriculum Studies* 9(1): 43-57
Wittgenstein, Ludwig (1922, 1961) *Tractatus Logico-Philosophicus*, Pears, D. F. and B. F. McGuinness, (trs.), London: Routledge & Kegan Paul
   (1974) *Philosophical Investigations*, G. E. M. Anscombe (tr.), Basil Blackwell
   (1980) *Culture and Value*, Peter Winch (tr.), Oxford: Basil Blackwell
Wolfe, Tom (1979) *The Right Stuff*, New York: Farrer, Strauss, and Giroux
   (1980) *Mauve Gloves and Madmen, Clutter and Vine*, New York: Bantam

Zaleznik, A. (1966) *Human Dilemmas of Leadership*, New York: Harper & Row

Zimmer, Heinrich (1956) *Philosophies of India*, New York: Bollingen Foundation

Index